PRAISE for T

Positively Main Street

"A first-rate novelistic account of Thompson's own psyche as he uncovers the Dylan few people know. A new look at young Dylan, done with kindness, enthusiasm, and superb language."

William Kennedy
Look magazine

"Essential reading. Thompson, unprecedentedly, managed to interview not only Echo Helstrom, almost certainly the 'Girl of the North Country,' but Dylan's mother and brother, his uncle, his friends."

Michael Gray
Bob Dylan Encyclopedia

"Toby Thompson was there first."

Greil Marcus

Saloon

"I had a wonderful time with this book, reading it in two sittings. I found the writing strong, clear, occasionally electric. In some odd way it seems a sociological masterpiece. For the first time the American drinker has his Michelin, and for myself it would be unthinkable to start another journey without it."

Jim Harrison

"Toby Thompson found the place to study the country, and he got it down."

Thomas McGuane

"This book is a good place to get a drink."

Richard Brautigan

The '60s Report

"A stunning book. Insightful, lovingly crafted."

Tim O'Brien

"Toby Thompson's writing represents the best of 'The New Journalism.'"

Terence Winch

Riding the Rough String

"Toby Thompson is a writer and journalist of the old school, a standup guy who knows music and literature and walks the walk and understands the human heart...."

James Lee Burke

"Toby Thompson knows Montana's bars, books, bridges, and backcountry. I'll read anything he writes."

Tim Cahill

"...Toby Thompson played it smart and went west. His sharp eye and interviewer's ear caught every nuance. *Riding the Rough String* sets it all down with verve and assurance."

William Hjortsberg

Metroliner

"*Metroliner* is a first-rate collection, impressively diverse and vastly enjoyable. Toby Thompson is blessed with that rare journalistic talent for painting epic pictures with small, unforgettable details."

Carl Hiaasen

"'Ratfishing in Manhattan' is fabulous. It's suspenseful, funny, wonderfully written—a piece of poetry that stands as a conceit of New York itself. Thompson obviously is an intrepid adventurer of Central Park...an intrepid tripper in the Merry Prankster sense, and an Urban Thoreau."

Tom Wolfe

METROLINER
Passages: Washington to New York

TOBY THOMPSON

Bangtail Press

Montana
2013

METROLINER

The author and publisher would like to thank the publications in which versions of these pieces originally appeared. *Washingtonian*: "The Long Goodbye," "A Walk on the Wild Side," "The Beltway," "Forgive them Jody," and "Night Watch." *The Washington Post Magazine*: "The Throne of the Third Heaven of the Nations' Millennium General Assembly." *The Washington Post*: "Postcard of a Hanging." *Vanity Fair*: "Dandy Tom," "The Long Goodbye," "Mailer's Ghosts," and "Loyalties." *Outside*: "Gunkholing the Chesapeake," "The Bassmaster," and "Seasons through the Park." *Esquire*: "Prince of the City." *The Village Voice*: "Sessions at the Gate." *American Film*: "How Sweet it Was." *Rolling Stone*: "Making it Nightly." *Flatiron News*: "Ratfishing Manhattan." And *St. Albans School: The First Hundred Years*: "The Long Goodbye."

Published in the United States by

Bangtail Press
P. O. Box 11262
Bozeman, MT 59719
www.bangtailpress.com

Cover photo, "Passengers Waiting for an Amtrak Metroliner Train," is a public domain image provided by the National Archives and Records Administration.

*To the memory of Zack Sanders, Clarence Riner,
and Georgia Riner—and to the
little house in Cabin John.*

"For reasons which many persons thought ridiculous, Mrs. Lightfoot Lee decided to pass the winter in Washington."

Henry Adams
Democracy

"So I went to New York City to be born again."

Kurt Vonnegut
Bluebeard

TABLE OF CONTENTS

Author's Note

This compilation of East Coast pieces is meant as a companion volume to my 2012 collection, *Riding the Rough String: Reflections on the American West*. Its preface and selections were written over a thirty-six-year period. Thirty-three years old when I scribbled the first, I was sixty-eight when I typed the last. If their style and voice have changed, so have their author's. The juxtaposition of who I was, versus who I have become, is startling. John Updike wrote, in the foreword to *Hugging the Shore*, a collection of his nonfiction, that "An artist mediates between the world and minds...[he] therefore must even at the price of uncouthness and alienation...maintain allegiance to the world and a fervent relation with it." *Metroliner* has as its goal that relation to the world. Its selections are not inclusive—I composed many other pieces and six books during this time—but I have chosen what I feel to be the most representative of my writings about Washington and New York. If variances in style and voice surprise, be assured they surprise the author. The pieces' arrangement is meant to suggest a history or a memoir.

Washington and New York, since 1977, have changed markedly. And the writer encountered that year was a different person than that met in 2013. So one hopes.

Toby Thompson
October, 2013

Preface: Locomotion

On January 8, 1977, a Georgetown hair cutter named Ray Urgo, during an act of love, slipped the barrel of a .357 magnum between the lips of his girlfriend, Dana Kisacky, and fired. "What I remember is the smoke coming from her mouth," Urgo later told me. He dropped his pistol, called police and cried, "There's been a shooting... it was an accident...life is ruined, life is ruined. Oh, Dana, Dana, Dana."

It had been a slow Saturday in the nation's capital. Urgo and Kisacky, plus two female friends, had kicked back with wine, Quaaludes, and a little marijuana, and were in Urgo's bed. According to news accounts, the erotic use of handcuffs, chains, and the .357 were in play. One woman drew a bath and immersed herself. Kisacky slipped into the tub beside her. A third woman rang Urgo's bell and, naked, he answered the door. She had stopped by for a Quaalude. Soon she was in Urgo's bed. The women turned their attention to each other, and Urgo—from frustration or to impress—removed his .357 from a drawer, loaded five of its six chambers, cocked

3

its hammer and approached Kisacky. They had fantasized this scenario "from *Hustler* or one of those raunchy magazines," a participant recalled, and "Dana was smiling." She leaned toward the gun. Its barrel was placed in her mouth. Urgo pulled the trigger on what he believed to be an empty chamber. There was "a muffled pop," the woman testified, and "[Dana] had blood coming out of her mouth. She was white and her eyes were all bluish. Urgo told police, "All the blood that came spurting out of her mouth. It came dripping out of the sides…the fact that she was shot with a .357 magnum."

I was in New York, researching a book, and did not immediately learn of the incident. It was covered widely, however, and a profile of Kisacky appeared in the Washington *Star*. I would not read of the case until an editor from G.P. Putnam's contacted me to ask if I'd write about it. She forwarded various pieces, and when I read them it was as if the top of my head had been blown off.

The Putnam's editor knew of the book I then was preparing. It concerned the white middle class's exile from city to suburbs during the 1950s, its rebelliousness during the 1960s, and its trickling back to urban neighborhoods during the 1970s. *The '60s Report*'s overriding theme would be my generation's fixation upon hip and its return to drugged-out, dangerous quarters of American cities. She proposed that I contact Urgo to see if he would agree to be interviewed for a book. I was interested, as Kisacky's death crystalized my darkest fears about urban resettlement.

An attitude of hostility had permeated Georgetown since the late 1960s, when hippy shops lining its main drags succumbed to top-dollar emporiums, garden trattorias, and salons like Bogart, where Urgo cut hair. He was thirty-two, darkly handsome, and alluring to women like Kisacky. She was twenty-five, a blonde divorcée from the Washington suburbs, wild, lovely, hip and fashionable. She wished to become a model, perhaps a stewardess. He had migrated to Georgetown from New

York where, as the son of working parents in an Italian neighborhood, a lower-middle-class future was ordained. He had artistic ambitions; later he would study classical guitar at Mannes conservatory. But his cousins cut hair and that was body art—he began there.

Hair cutters by the mid-1970s had become trend setters, their craft and cuts metaphors for change in every free-flowing style of the 1960s. Snip it, shag it, shape those freedom locks into a look that spelled success. Their scene was beguiling; perhaps they'd let you into it— one of expensive drugs, boutique clothing, champagne evenings, and orgiastic sex. It was a scene that proved fatal to Kisacky.

"Do you believe a hairstyle can change someone's personality?" her ex-husband told the *Star*. "[Dana] used to have really long hair. Then she got into a gypsy shag."

By the time I met Ray Urgo, he'd been convicted of involuntary manslaughter and was serving a mere five-year sentence at the Rappahannock Regional Jail in Stafford, Virginia. What I recall most vividly of that chat is the setting in which it took place. It was visiting hour, and as we talked all around us girlfriends or wives wrapped themselves about prisoners in sexual displays so grotesque as to parody the acts in which Urgo had participated.

He wore prison denims, was well-groomed, fit. His curly hair was shorter than in news photos, and his Mediterranean features were chiseled. He had been working as a hair cutter at the jail. He spoke engagingly; he had charm, one could see that. But he was agitated, nervous. "Prison is the closest thing to death for a conscious man," he said. Looking around, I believed him.

How different it was from the Georgetown salon he'd left. His cousin, Robert Novel, who in partnership with another cousin owned Bogart, the shop where Urgo had worked, would describe for me life at its predecessor, Hair Inc., which Novel founded in 1969 and is credited with starting the Georgetown salon craze of the 1970s.

"A typical day there was insanity," Novel said. "People were taking a lot of drugs, at that time, there was a great deal of drinking going on, every day, and it was not unusual...every day we would order up seven or eight bottles of champagne at about three or four o'clock in the afternoon. The day would end with a party, which would continue on into the evening. And our whole entourage would go with us. I mean day after day after day would become pretty strenuous. But when you're having so much fun, you're young and making a lot of money, you don't have to worry about it. We drank Veuve Cliquot champagne in the shop. We also served wine in the salon, in those days, for the customers. I've seen customers come in for a haircut and hang out for four hours getting [high] just on the wine we'd serve them. We'd go out and there would be customers with us. At the end of the night they'd come with us to restaurants or wherever we'd go to party afterwards. None of us had any attachments, in the way of family—wives, children, etc.—so we had no real responsibility. Sex during the day was rare, but it occurred from time to time in the shop. After closing there [were] parties and such that included sex and drugs. We smoked hash, opium, [took] cocaine, Quaaludes, uppers, downers. The most popular was actually smoking hashish. Or opium. Cocaine wasn't as readily available in those days. Although you could get it and it was much cheaper. Most everyone was into smoking marijuana. And taking pills like speed. If anybody did drugs they would start later in the afternoon. Some people would take stuff in the morning to get started. Like take a hit of speed. It was a social thing."

This life both appalled and fascinated me. It was locomotion, a dance that even as late as 1977 Urgo and Kisacky were caught up in. Its finale touched upon themes I'd been exploring, and upon leaving Urgo at Rappahannock that afternoon, I thought we might strike a deal. But his lawyer wished for more quid pro quos than I could provide, and I demurred. Urgo eventually lost interest in the project. I did not.

I tried the story as fiction, and wrote most of a novel that took its protagonist to a block near Fourteenth Street, where he purchased a barber shop in a black quarter that was cohesive in its sense of neighborhood, but shaken by the drug trade at its perimeter. My protagonist, Chris Cortland, was artistic and like Urgo a New Yorker. He was married to Vivian Darby, a girl from the suburbs like Kisacky, and had lured her downtown. Their relationship was much like my marriage, which had ended in divorce. The novel had been abandoned, as I could not bear to imagine, let alone write, its climactic scene. The nearest I came to it was one of Cortland, in their house on Swann Street, cutting Vivian's hair:

"You need to do this," he told her. "Each time." He kneaded KMS through Viv's hair, rinsed and began toweling it. She moved from sink to bedroom. Her mane glistened beneath the skylight, her figure lamped by the afternoon sun. Cortland dabbed a bit more, combed and blunt cut her split ends, then reached for his dryer. He spun warm currents about her head, fluttering hair across her shoulders. A line of perspiration appeared in that down above her lips and he blew it dry. She stood expressionless. He brushed her choppily, fanning the dryer, then settled into long, full strokes. The dryer hummed on the floor beside them, tumbling dust and fogging street noise. Cortland worked tight braids over her shoulder, a string of six. He wrapped one with green and red silk. Spotting splits, he candled them clean. The cabin was hot. Perspiration beaded in the hollow of Viv's chest. Cortland flicked it dry with the barrel of the dryer, then blasted it. The current disturbed tiny hairs on Viv's skin, about her breasts, in a way that captured sunlight. He moved the barrel to one tip and watched it lift toward the heat from down pressed flat by the current. He played air across her torso indiscriminately, drying then fluttering hair beneath her arms, spying moisture along her stomach, blowing

that clean, sensing a dampness below and teasing with quick flicks the odor mingling in her hair...They made love easily, gently, with no sound but the dryer's hum and the snap of her wetness. When they'd finished, Viv cleaned that hair below Cortland's navel which had become matted, and toweled sweat from his neck. The scent of her hair, freshly washed, and of their lovemaking, lingered.

Norman Mailer has written that "going back to a novel after a year and a half away is like going back to a wife after that much time separated—there's nothing automatic about it. But oh, what fun when you begin to hold hands again." As tender as this scene was, I could not rekindle its passion.

In a gasp at resuscitation, I drove far into the suburbs one night to have Ray Urgo cut my hair. He was on parole and working in Virginia at a Hair Pair, a shop so downscale as to be laughable in contrast to Bogart. Its design was Western bunkhouse, as I recall, with hitching rail accents. Urgo was chatty and well turned-out. I engaged him not so much as a customer but a writer, registering his moves, noting his patter, and eager to feel what it was like to have my hair cut by him, to place myself in his hands.

"Keep the sides full," I said.

He stepped back. "The length's not working for you."

"I like it long," I said.

"Your face..." And he complimented its structure.

"Actually, Ray..."

He walked round the chair, leaned forward and said, "*Trust me.*"

I've repeated his comment, as a punch line to the larger tale. But what it evoked had been anything but laughter. Urgo proved seductive (he cut my hair short) and his allure, his impulsivity and charisma, epitomized for me not only Georgetown, but everything I wished to distance myself from in the East.

I had begun to frequent the West, and found in its towns a sense of community I thought existed in the not yet gentrified quarters of Manhattan and Washington. I wandered New York's streets and those of Northwest DC, as I'd wandered those of Butte or the ghost town of Pony, Montana. I envisioned a life recreated in Washington's urban ruins. I had lived there as a child (I am a fourth-generation Washingtonian) and my relocation to suburbia is detailed in this volume's essay, "Living Alone." After the 1968 riots and during the 1970s I saw downtown Washington not as a fire-bombed ghetto but as a frontier. I was not singular in this. Fourteenth Street was categorized by many as a Wild West of drug trafficking and prostitution, and the term urban homesteader, regarding middle-class rehabbers, already had been coined. The streets lined with shade trees that overhung Victorian row houses resembled streets I'd seen in small towns of Colorado or Wyoming. There was peace in those side lanes, yet a war raged on the avenues that flanked them. As a culture, we were not that distant from the war in Vietnam. Who would say we were prepared to relinquish it?

I began writing about the city for the *Washington Post* and for *Washingtonian* magazine. I hiked 184.5 miles along the Chesapeake & Ohio Canal, from Georgetown to Cumberland, and wrote about that historic axis of the capital. I circled its beltway and patrolled it with a Maryland state trooper. I spent two weeks at the White House covering its irreverent press corps. I hung out nights at The Wall, Maya Lin's signature memorial to Vietnam Vets, and wrote about that. I revisited the nine years I spent at St. Albans, Washington's power prep for boys, in a piece that was early to catalogue abuses within such institutions. I researched the life of James Hampton, creator of *The Throne of the Third Heaven of the Nations' Millennium General Assembly*, the capital's pre-eminent work of art. For *Esquire* I profiled my classmate at St. Albans, Donald E. Graham, as he took reins of the *Washington Post*—first as publisher, then as chairman of the board—from his mother Katharine Graham. I toured

Washington's fish-larder estuary and wrote a sailing piece for *Outside*, titled "Gunkholing the Chesapeake." Other stories followed. Each explored some elemental thought about Washington, its region and its heritage. Later, I would profile Director of the FBI, William Sessions, a week before his firing by President Bill Clinton.

Much of this was in preparation for Manhattan. I'd been living in a 250-year-old log house on the banks of the Potomac. The *Metroliner*, Amtrak's high speed train running (at first) between Washington and New York, took me to the latter when I could afford it. *Metroliner* was a sleek, steel and plastic tube that hurtled through Baltimore and Philadelphia as if terrified to stop. Its contrast in modernity to the Pennsylvania Railroad trains I rode with my mother, during the 1940s and 1950s, with starched tablecloths in their formal dining cars and dignified porters who sold candy and magazines at one's seat, was stark. But I wrote of my uncle's pioneering in 1950s television, and his work with *Your Hit Parade*. For *Vanity Fair* I profiled writers Tom Wolfe, Norman Mailer, and Carl Bernstein; for *Rolling Stone* the television anchor Tom Brokaw, and for *American Film* Jackie Gleason; for *Outside* I profiled a striped bass fisherman, Guy DeBlasio, who at night stalked Manhattan's rotted piers, where he was threatened by street gangs, had his rods stolen, and was thrown into the Hudson. I moved to New York, a half-block from Central Park, and for *Outside* wrote about that patch of urban wilderness. I labored at other stories and book-length projects, but the core pieces are presented here.

Metroliner discontinued service on October 27, 2006 and was replaced by the *Acela,* a faster, more efficient train. That same month—nearly to the day—I left New York City and, with a summer house in Montana, moved home to Washington. A circle had been squared, the inner city gentrified, Urgo lost to the hinterlands and Kisacky thirty years in her grave. With a pistol shot, their era had closed. And a fresh one of mine had begun.

WASHINGTON

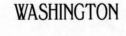

The Long Goodbye:
St. Albans School

In the spring of 1977, Canon Charles Martin retired after twenty-eight years as headmaster of St. Albans School for Boys. He was replaced by a thirty-seven-year-old Episcopal minister from Choate, an ex-miler gone to fat. You cannot begin to know what import that message carried unless you, like me, spent nine years under Canon Martin's tutelage. I have never met a post-1949 graduate of St. Albans School who was not profoundly affected by his association with the canon. Many admire him, some dislike him, most recall him with a mixture of bemusement and awe. Canon Martin never affected anyone lightly. In his twenty-eight years at St. Albans he *became* the school, embodying those characteristics that graduates remember as the school's most forceful.

The news of Canon Martin's retirement reached me in Montana. I was living in a railroad hotel, writing, hiking the Absaroka mountains, fishing, carousing in bars called the Wrangler or Longbranch, and felt, in brief, as insulated from St. Albans as an alumnus could get. Yet

Canon Martin's abdication shocked me. Weeks followed during which I fought off a piercing sense of loss. It was as if the man had died—indeed, the institution. After one too many evenings of slamming around cowpoke saloons, drinking and encouraging altercations, I realized it was no accident that the face I pounded beneath a high-crowned Stetson or watched fade to gray behind foul breath above my chest, shifted predictably to that of Canon Martin or stranger still, to that of the main school building itself.

I had passed St. Albans many times in the years since my graduation, but I had never visited the canon. I possessed no clear recollection of his appearance, save that which materialized nightly in dreams or beneath some obliging barfly's hat. I couldn't survive much longer provoking fights in Montana saloons with cowboys tough as pine knots. A few facts had to be faced. I didn't feel particularly hostile toward St. Albans School. If the truth be told, I didn't feel much of anything.

THERE IS A PHOTOGRAPH in the 1962 yearbook, a photograph tucked behind those of student leaders—prefects, vestry, student council, society of Altis, *cum laude*—that is slugged simply SENIORS. I am wearing a football jersey and a pair of dark khakis, my roommate, expensive corduroys, a starched collar, and one of those ribbed sweaters his mother knit for him. We are raking leaves. We are smiling. We are the only seniors in the picture, and there lies the joke, for we are in trouble, absolving an egregious breach of etiquette by working with the Cathedral ground crew. I cannot for the life of me think why I am wearing a football jersey; I never wore such garb off the field. But that's not what bothers most. It's the expressions on our faces. My roommate, today an Episcopal priest, sneers at the camera as if to flip it the finger. He holds his rake like a lance. I lean against mine more casually. I grin, and it is a broad grin, nearly impish. But it is forced about the corners. There's a cynicism, at age seventeen—a cynicism and world-weariness that startles me.

Not so, the photograph taken ten years earlier. We are C Former there, fourth graders, a gaggle of pudgy bipeds clothed in approximations of the school's dress code: coats and ties, more sackcloth than seersucker, scuffed oxfords, white socks about the ankles. We moon at the photographer like penned calves. We stare dumbly or glare in contempt, lined up before English Gothic windows in the Lane-Johnston Building: beginners. There is the arrogance of my roommate, already shooting a metaphysical bird, but in me there resides a capricious vulnerability. A little boy slumps in a forward row, a little boy with blond hair and a chubby face wondering where in god's name he is headed.

FOR STARTERS THEY called me Charles. It was my Christian name, granted, but I am a junior so it was foremost my father's name and I had never used it. It was also Canon Martin's name. Toby had been a nickname since birth—the gift of a great uncle too old and drunk to fight the Axis in other than the British Merchant Marine, where he could drink aboard ship and where Toby as a nickname had been popular. Charles was my father's, my great-grandfather's and another great-uncle's name, and it seemed appropriate that I be called that at St. Albans. One does not enroll in prep school of one's accord; one's parents effect the transaction. My parents had attended public schools and my father had envied what he believed to be the advantages of a private education. It was fitting that at St. Albans they call me by his and our progenitors' name. I grew used to it and learned to prefer it.

What a ragamuffin bunch we had been the spring of 1953, herded together for the first time, bent restlessly over entrance examinations that would determine our qualifications as candidates for the fall's academic year. What an oddity to think in terms of academic years in third grade. What perversity! They had escorted us that morning from Beauvoir (National Cathedral Elementary School) where all had been bright and airy, to the dim halls of St. Albans, where, beneath Gothic arches and in the shadow of stained glass windows, we labored several hours over arithmetic and vocabulary to prove our worth. This was not the first battery of examinations. Admissions tests had been required even for Beauvoir; I had endured a summer's tutoring between second and third grades to qualify there.

I had attended private schools exclusively but for second grade, yet I had a difficult time making Beauvoir. Beauvoir was an accepted predecessor to St. Albans, considered the most prestigious school in Washington. What I remember of public school was a girlfriend who was Jewish and a woman who taught me to write my name (my mother refutes this: "You were writing long before that!). I found a girlfriend at Beauvoir, which was coeducational—most girls matriculating to National Cathedral School for Girls, Holton Arms, or Madeira— and I was excelling in class with women teachers and in the company of females.

What I recall about that first year at St. Albans was no women, no girls, and a darkness concomitant to blue-chinned masters, navy blazers, and venerable wood paneling. I was not to know women again until adolescence, and then under that most strained of circumstances, dancing class. The campaign had begun.

St. Albans' admissions office boasts that 30 percent of its students come from families engaged in government, diplomatic, or military service, and I suppose our class approached that mark. Of the forty-odd boys enrolled in our fourth-grade class, only fourteen would survive to graduation. Of that original forty, I recall two officers' sons, one ambassador's, and a senator's, though we would pick up an extra ambassador's along the way, a defense secretary's, and a suspect in 1969's Tate-Labianca case (the Manson murders). Our class, as did the majority of St. Albans' classes during the 1950s, consisted largely of Washingtonians, sons of doctors, lawyers, ministers...

professional folk who could not be mistaken for workers "in trade." There were exceptions. We had a Marriott in our class, and on the journalistic side, a Graham.

But they were flotsam and jetsam to a nine-year-old. We would stumble together each morning at 8:25 to pledge allegiance to the flag, punching and gouging on the steps of the Lane-Johnston Building, awaiting a signal to move. Roll would be called and we would march en masse toward the Little Sanctuary, where morning services were held. Chapel lasted twenty minutes. It consisted of two hymns, a selection of prayers, and a word or so from Canon Martin. He invariably took the morning service, and I remember from the start how impressed I was with his severity. Life was somber in the Little Sanctuary; we enjoyed organ music and enthusiastic singing, but it was so dark in that tiny chapel one could hardly read the prayer book. I soon learned the prayers by heart. The seriousness of life and the ambiguity of resurrection in the arms of our savior were hammered home. I did not know Canon Martin at this point, except for his ministry in the Little Sanctuary. He appeared the sternest adult imaginable. Perhaps at 8:30 a.m. he felt as low as the rest of us.

By 8:45, first period would begin, followed by two others before recess at 11:00, when we would purchase cookies and milk from a white-jacketed man in a downstairs alcove. Albert Watson was that fellow's name, and he was part of an all-black staff that regaled us with a combination of affection and street-wise taunting that provided welcome counterpoint to the faculty's reserve. After recess we resumed class until lunchtime. The entire lower school gathered then, dining in a black paneled refectory, on black-oak tables, from black chairs. Walls above the black paneling were white, and a good deal of light shot about from tall windows. But black is what impressed me most; it was striking.

Lunch was a clamorous, jovial time, with confusion and an abundance of hacking around. We were reassigned periodically to different masters' tables and were-required, by turn, to wait on table, to clear and to serve. The kitchen was a bedlam of small boys with platters in hand, black arms and legs shuttling food with incredible speed, plus a cacophony of servant chatter, that approached babble. There was the scent of fresh rolls, the shine of stainless-steel trays, and the blur of starched uniforms, white constantly in motion. Mr. Alfred True, lower-school headmaster, would read administrative announcements; we would quiet for the thanksgiving, then shuffle to class. Upper school students, staring hostilely as we passed double-file by classrooms packed with the blackguards, would follow…as soon as staff scraped butter off the seats, French fries off window sills, and the detritus of two hundred little boys from fixtures about the refectory. The food was remarkably good.

After lunch followed several more periods, then sports. This was an eccentricity; Canon Martin believed in athletics from the earliest form, and was stern about his view. Each boy, unless ill, was required to attend daily sports sessions. Canon Martin decreed that "every boy is better for some exercise, exercise vigorous enough to shake up his liver and to make bed welcome and sleep come in a hurry" (Charles Martin, *Letters from a Headmaster's Study,* Oxford University Press, 1961). Above that, the canon believed in football: "Football gives a kind of elemental physical exercise that boys are better for having known." And, of course, it encouraged competition. In the fourth grade we were playing on teams that fought brother schools tooth and nail for conference championships. I personally found this contention fun, but there were others for whom it was disturbing…boys who were simply poor athletes. They were encouraged to try their best, but more often than not such encouragement led to humiliation. There is little sympathy in a healthy boy for his weaker classmates. His instinct is to devour.

Sports were exhilarating but took their toll. Part of that toll was the lateness of the hour one finished. We were rarely picked up before 4:30 or 5:00, which meant it would be 5:30 before we got home. In winter it would be dark. We always had two hours' homework. There was no time for play. We had little chance to associate with children outside the realm of St. Albans. At age nine, trussed up in coats and ties, we were miniature Ivy Leaguers keeping a university schedule, cloistered from the world by Gothic walls and a monkish workload.

THE FIFTIES WERE odd years to attend school in the shadow of a medieval cathedral. Off the grounds existed rock 'n' roll, finned automobiles, Harley-Davidson motorcycles...but across those sixty acres that constituted the National Cathedral Close hurried prelates toward theological seminars at the College of Preachers, European stonemasons toward gargoyles that would adorn Cathedral facades, and choir boys toward the Great Organ and choir practice beneath vaulted stone ceilings of the chancel itself. St. Albans was part of the National Cathedral Foundation (chartered 1893) and had opened in 1909 as the National Cathedral School for Boys. Harriet Lane Johnston, President James Buchanan's niece, had willed a sum of money to the Cathedral Foundation for establishment of a boys' school—with special scholarship privileges for choir boys, in hopes that her bequest would contribute to the advancement of church music in America. Cathedral choir boys still attend St. Albans on special scholarships, and each regular student is steeped in ecclesiastical music. My earliest memories on the Cathedral Close are of damp crypts, a drafty nave, and hours spent in hand-carved bishop's stalls before the Jerusalem Altar.

We were always singing, often coached by Paul Calloway, the Cathedral's choirmaster and organist, or his lieutenant, Richard Dirksen. St. Albans had been named for the proto-martyr of the English, and was attached sentimentally to the oldest public school in Britain—St. Albans, in Hertfordshire, approximately thirty miles north of London. A church had been erected there during the seventh century, a monastery during the eighth, St. Albans School during the tenth. St. Albans in Washington took its lead pedagogically from the public schools of Britain, emphasizing in its curriculum the goal of character-building through discipline, abstinence, and stiff competition. But above that, St. Albans remained a church school. Not so much through the doctrines it preached but through its mood. One never lost sight of the Cathedral and one rarely felt free of its pull.

OF COURSE, THERE WERE fiercely secular anomalies. Mr. Paul J. Graig was one. Master of my B Form (fifth grade) class, Mr. Graig was a gorilla of a man, blond, with a bullet-shaped head and grey eyes sunk deep in a pinkish face. Mr. Graig was an ex-sheriff from New York who carried a bristling masculinity to his manner—refreshing beside the calculated swish of other masters. He was charming, athletic, obsessed with pranks; everything a ten-year-old might wish to emulate. Yet some of his pranks were disturbing.

He liked, for instance, to shut boys in closets. One would misbehave and Mr. Graig would lock him in a closet. The class would continue, aware that up front and to the right of Mr. Graig's desk a boy sat cowering in darkness. Occasionally, Graig would shut three or four boys in there and make them whistle. It was quite funny. Except that he'd insist they whistle for upwards of an hour. If you were seated in the classroom, not much work would get done, but you'd stay amused. If you were one of four boys in a dark closet, gasping for air and whistling to stave off a gorilla's wrath, things weren't so amusing. Mr. Graig eventually locked up a boy with asthma, who did not fare well, and received a reprimand.

Another trick of Mr. Graig's involved soft rubber baseballs. He kept such balls on his desk, with a table knife from the refectory. During class he would stab the ball, then bang it against the desk, *ka-thunk, ka-thunk,* until the ball disintegrated. Then he'd start on another.

19

When Mr. Graig wasn't stabbing the ball with his knife, he'd surreptitiously palm it and wait for a boy to lose attention. Then he'd sling the ball fast at the offender's head, usually catching him off guard. Sometimes he'd throw an eraser. We got so we could anticipate these volleys and raised the tops of our desks to deflect shots. Mr. Graig wore skintight shorts during sports periods, really the first hot pants I remember seeing. These looked odd on a 230-pound man. He carried his fascination with balls to the gymnasium. One day he knocked a ten-year-old halfway across the court with a basketball to the head, which left the fifth grader senseless and reeling.

Mr. Graig was obsessed with appearance and dressed in a more contemporary fashion than his fellow masters. No Irish tweeds for Mr. Graig, no calfskin oxfords or subtle broadcloths. He wore sharkskin suits, thin ties, and shiny white shirts. He was fond of flashing the nickel-plated .38 he'd carried as a sheriff. He liked to masticate a four-pack of cheese 'n' crackers then display the glob on his tongue. I did not realize Mr. Graig was insane until one afternoon, seated on the front of his desk and in mid-lecture, he tore off a shirt sleeve and buffed his shoes.

It was not Mr. Graig's quirkiness that troubled us, nor its humorous manifestations. I found them entertaining, and for a time wanted nothing so much as to be like him. Graig's principal fault, obvious to a ten-year-old, was the fickleness of his affection. It was one thing for a class to incur a master's wrath and be forced to move all furniture into the center of the classroom, then march two-by-two about it for an entire period. That was funny and a diversion. What hurt was Mr. Graig's playing of favorites. If you did well in class, your grades up, your behavior keyed to Graig's temperament, you were granted privileges. The most visible being that you were encouraged to sit astride an upside-down trash can next to Mr. Graig's desk, literally at the head of the class. There he joked with you, petted you, and ignored the rest of his students.

Such special treatment kindled in me a hatred of favoritism and those who would practice it. Favoritism was a tactic several masters employed, but none so blatantly as Graig. To St. Albans' credit, Mr. Graig's career lasted but a few years. One morning he opened the scalp of a pupil with the ruby on his class ring, and that pupil (Breck Wilcox, later, Attorney General of Maryland) groused. Of course we'd all groused—or bragged—about Mr. Graig's antics. But the scalp couldn't be ignored. Mr. Graig retired.

St. Albans seemed oblivious to other forms of mistreatment. Lawrence Smith, My fourth-grade master, was kind and emotionally warm, but he showered with us after sports, clutching our nine-year-old bodies to his hairy chest, laughing, then holding us aloft. While creepy, such behavior was preferable to the other section's master, Charles Spicer, who disciplined pupils with excruciating neck squeezes and by standing them in a darkened cloak room.

We were fondled by other masters (one was our upper-school Latin teacher, William Hogan—affectionately known as "Homogan"—and treated by others as chattel. There was the atmosphere of being owned. If violence or hysteria were not explicit in a master's behavior, it churned beneath the surface. This turned boy against boy. For example, in eighth grade, during recess, I would be regularly if good-naturedly stomped. This seemed traditional—the Etonian way. As late as 1948, student prefect beatings of delinquent students, often with belts, had been common at St. A. And younger boys, "chosen apparently at random," a school history reported, "were walloped nightly with paddles." One day in A Form (sixth grade) a master glanced up, said "Look to the boy on your right, look to the boy on your left. In twenty years one of you three will suffer some form of mental illness."

Stanley Sofield taught my section of First Form (seventh grade). He was another anomaly, a Damon Runyon character from Columbia who had taught at St.

Albans since 1935. Sofield was short, squat, and abrasive with his New York accent. He resembled in fact more a cab driver than a prep-school master. Though Gore Vidal (a pre-World War II student) in his 1995 memoir, *Palimpsest*, would characterize Sofield as a closeted, frustrated gay, Sofield provided the masculine, worldly touch we needed approaching adolescence. He loved horses and lectured us often on the *Daily Racing Form*; he read us Damon Runyon stories, inculcating me, for one, with permanent respect for colloquial language and an appreciation of narrative. It seemed no accident that Mr. Sofield also taught Latin. He exposed us to our first Latin grammar, imbuing the text with that same low-life enthusiasm he brought to Damon Runyon. Sofield 's great gift was to show how English had grown from Latin, how foundations of the two languages were related. Sofield's infectious love of language was transmitted subtly, and I remained unaware of his chicanery until years later.

Sofield was infamous for his beer drinking, his piano playing, and songs he would write by the carload. Every year he composed a musical comedy for the First Form. Our year he fashioned a part for me based on an Elvis Presley character. I had become fascinated with Elvis and had acquired a guitar. Gyrating on stage, twisting, pumping, I growled out the lyrics Sofield had written:

I tried to be friendly to you all
But you wouldn't let me, not at all...
You wouldn't be friendly, not at all
I tried to be friendly to you all.

My future roommate played the devil.

TIME HAD BECOME crucial by now, time and the aware-ness of an increasing workload. St. Albans, as an Episco-pal school, encouraged its students to join the Episcopal church; thus a confirmation class had been fitted into the schedule for our First Form year. One was not required to attend this class. I did not. I balked not so much on religious grounds—I knew no religion outside St. Albans—but for the simple practicality of Too Much Work. I was obsessed by how much study was demanded of us; it haunted me. Although I was doing well, B's in most classes, I could not see taking on an extra responsibility. I remember approaching confirmation with a determined cynicism. It wasn't worth the trouble.

Mr. Sofield conducted something called a hash test, and it pinpointed a burgeoning competitiveness in academics perfectly. The hash test was informal, geared toward fun, and intended to nurture in us an awareness of current events. Sofield would pose questions off the top of his head—concerning politics, history, government—and the boy with the most correct answers would win a Hershey bar. The tests were given once a week. I looked forward to them, then dreaded them, then grew blasé. The same two or three students won the Hershey bar each week— usually Don Graham, Cliff Case, or another fellow with parents in public life. These were boys who not only rubbed shoulders with political figures mentioned on hash tests, but who were possessed of extraordinary intelligence. At the top of his class, excelling at all, Don Graham had the quickest mind I have encountered. He was gentle and unaffected, but he was touchy, nervous. There was something about St. Albans' regimen that ate even at him.

Pressure intensified that fall of 1957 with the cultural paranoia surrounding Sputnik. We were falling behind the Russians. Were our boys learning enough science, mathematics? Science and mathematics were my worst subjects. By Christmas of our Second Form year, I was swilling Maalox in class and sweating over the books. Also, for about fifteen minutes each noon, it had become accepted fun to good-naturedly slap old Charley around. I was getting the stuffing pounded out of me every recess, then collapsing at my desk, drenched with perspiration, to be called down by our form master for causing trouble. I

23

explained what was happening, but he would not believe me. Eventually, through the intervention of my father, summoned for a conference with the lower-school head, I was vindicated and the beatings stopped.

George Badger McGehee, our Second Form master, was a St. Albans alumnus returned to the Cathedral Close shortly after college. He had taught at St. Albans since 1922. He was set in his ways, cranky, dogmatic, and in poor health. He was considered a St. Albans institution, though, exposure to which was deemed obligatory and a privilege. He was largely responsible for the demise of six of my raucous friends, and if he'd had his way he would have sacked me. Mr. McGehee's most terrifying trait, I recall, was his habit of going round the room and telling, before the whole class, exactly what he thought of each student. This was psychological evaluation in public which on numerous occasions left the subject in tears.

THROUGHOUT OUR lower-school experience, Canon Martin had remained aloof. Whether intentionally or not, he associated himself almost exclusively with the upper school. We saw him each day in chapel and we heard him speak on special occasions, but our impressions were forged from a distance. They were fierce impressions, disconcertingly paternal—we knew, for instance, that it was Canon Martin who set the school's unwavering standards, abhorring lateness, sloth, and absence due to poor weather. The canon rarely, if ever, closed the school. This was a bullet to bite if you were a boy who loved to stay home and wallow in the snow. Especially when your public school peers often enjoyed two or three days straight with the sled and snowman. But such invariability was characteristic of Canon Martin's approach to education.

Canon Martin in 1949 had succeeded Canon Albert Hawley Lucas, as St. Albans' fourth headmaster. To follow Albert Lucas, an ex-Marine who had dominated twenty forceful years at St. Albans, must have been no easy task. Albert Lucas, by all reports, was every bit the disciplinarian Canon Martin would become. One alumnus wrote at his death that Canon Lucas seemed "in the direct chain of command from the Deity," and that "the mortal sin" in Canon Lucas's eyes "was not to fail but to have one's name posted as 'Poor in effort.'" It was Albert Lucas who had offered Canon Martin his first teaching job—at Episcopal Academy, Philadelphia, in 1927—and it was Albert Lucas who urged Canon Martin to accept the headmastership of St. Albans in 1949.

"At St. Albans we have always valued work," Canon Martin would later write. "I did not bring the idea with me or even develop it. I found it here."

Canon Martin had come to St. Albans after a seven-year interlude as rector of St. Paul's Parish in Burlington, Vermont. A New Englander's resolve permeates his *Letters from a Headmaster's Study,* and one is impressed by the good sense inherent in their majority. Virtues of discipline, hard work, reliability, respect for individuality, and the Christian ethic predominate. One is struck by Canon Martin's understanding of boys, and is hard pressed to find fault with his suggested handling of them. The prose is precise, elegantly sparse. His philosophies are sound. What one fails to derive from those early letters, however, is a sense of what it was like to toil under his purview.

It was vague. It was a world of study halls, upper-school prefects, boys who were men, a university-type schedule, five or six different masters where one had sufficed, a bustle between classes, sports, homework, and a lack of focus. The focus was intended to be college, but the prospect of four years' upper school kept college mercifully blurred. We had a Third Form master who was to hold things together, but we rarely consulted him. Canon Martin had taken over. Not readily available for consultation but omnipresent in the everyday workings of the school.

He remained aloof. As a symbol he was inviolate, but—the child of alcoholic parents, it was said, and a teetotaler—he held himself apart. The irony being that this was his furthest intention. Canon Martin lived to advise, to instruct, and to minister (his weekends were busy with visits to the sick). But his daily messages at lunch were confusing. What might begin as an announcement, to which we would listen attentively and with interest, after the first minutes shifted toward some ethical point, that might pique our curiosity, only to be dulled by a subsequent fifteen minutes of pontification. Canon Martin would start strong but finish holding his audience at arm's length. Expressions like "It does my heart good" and reference to "Our common life here on the Close" and the constant "Preparation for life" salted his oratory. These were clichés he would have never overworked in his writing; he would have hacked them from his prose for the fat they were. And he would have presented his ideas clearly. There was a good deal of eye rolling, from both masters and students, during the headmaster's speeches. It was a shame. One wished to be drawn close, but recoiled as if embraced by a sentimental drunk.

And there was explosive anger. It is lunchtime, 1961: the canon has completed a fifteen-minute diatribe against the ungentlemanly habit of speaking to a boy from a neighboring table without first asking permission of its head. He takes his seat. Within seconds a friend, Sandy Rock, is at my elbow, visiting without permission. "Rock!" the canon screams, slamming his fist against the table. The silverware hangs a good six inches above its surface as the refectory falls silent. "All I thought was 'Don't piss your pants,'" Sandy told me later. There, I remember thinking of the canon's outburst, that's better than preaching.

IT WAS THE YEAR of St. Albans' fiftieth anniversary. Fats Domino played for the midwinter dance and a black student enrolled as a C Former. Fats arrived wearing diamonds and in a lavender DeSoto with Louisiana plates. The nine-year-old wore a conservative sports jacket, and was chauffeur-dropped from a yellow Mercedes. Integration had been Canon Martin's doing. Writing of Albert

Hawley Lucas at his death in 1973, Canon Martin would cite what his predecessor had felt to be "the chief weakness of his leadership: He had failed to bring black people into the school...It was, he said, his awful damning failure." Canon Martin broke the color barrier (which had been stretched by the admission of Far Eastern, Middle Eastern, and Near Eastern boys, most with fathers in the Diplomatic Corps) at a time when it was still unpopular to do so. The private school was our last refuge from a liberal Supreme Court, alumni might argue. What's the point of spending two thousand dollars a year to send my boy to school with blacks, a parent might complain.... If any did, we never learned of it. We took the commotion in stride. There wasn't time for anything else.

The summer between my Third and Fourth Form years I spent working on a ranch in Montana. It was a tiresome job, pulling barbed wire, building corrals, cutting timber, but it offered a respite from Washington and the sort of stultifying extremes I was used to. I had been living a schizoid existence since third grade—commuting to the Cathedral Close for ten hours' association with Washington's elite, from Cabin John, where my good friends were sons of carpenters, bus drivers, house painters, and my best friend was a mentally challenged illegitimate. But Montana was different; it provided distance from home as well as from St. Albans, and it lent perspective. I was treated unfairly by my foreman, cheated of wages, accused of lying by a disturbed wrangler... behavior I by now considered the normal business of life. But at least in Montana there were no pretensions. I felt pretentious struggling through *Pride and Prejudice*, part of my summer reading, holed up in the bunkhouse. But I endured it. I was learning to accept contradictions. Besides, ranch work was putting me in fantastic shape. I had developed the chest and biceps of a fullback. Football the following fall would be a breeze.

Late that summer I was thrown from a bucking horse and smashed my forearm. It was a nasty fracture, snapping both bones at the wrist, jamming my right hand back toward my elbow. I had to be driven 180 miles to a hospital. It took the surgeon seven hours to set my arm, and he set it wrong. I had to have it rebroken three weeks later in Washington, then reset. Football season had started.

I can't remember what I did that fall for athletics— probably Troop Nineteen, a calisthenics class organized for the noncompetitively uncoordinated. In seven years at St. Albans I had not missed a season of football. I was light but quick, and consistently won my letter. Though I was to miss the contact, not having to play football proved a relief. The game had become too serious, I rationalized. It wouldn't be as much fun. Anyhow, I couldn't spare the afternoons.

The crush toward college had become overwhelming. Both administration and students wheezed under pressure. Each year several new boys would be freighted in—rarely athletes, always scholars; usually bespectacled, pale, and toting at least one extra slide rule. With every fresh admission my rank in class dropped. And as form masters warned, rank in class meant everything. The administration ran just as scared as we about harvesting a promising crop of Ivy Leaguers. The school's reputation depended on it. Though Canon Martin might quip that "St. Albans exists to help boys not into the Kingdom of Harvard but into the Kingdom of Heaven," his administrators would disagree. It became obvious to us they did. A fundamental schism had erupted in our eyes, between Canon Martin's humanism, his ideals of personal development and individuality, and the administration's push toward college.

I reacted to the pressure by flunking French and plane geometry. Summer school was in the cards. I was fifteen, drinking occasionally, and playing electric guitar in a rock-and-roll band—the Corpse Combo, my name. Drinking stayed experimental, but the music became life. Our band played for private parties and Catholic Youth Organization dances, an atmosphere that reintroduced the world of public-school funk and the women it afforded. I shook my head, took a look at the unsupervised lives these kids enjoyed, and led an entire contingent of St. Albans boys toward the women of Bethesda Chevy Chase. We'd been socializing with Madeira, Holton Arms, and NCS girls for several years—since Mrs. Shippen's dancing class had commenced—but public-school girls were another breed. I kept my electric guitar strapped high, hit resolutely from the bottle, and could not wait for our next gig.

The automobile had coughed into the picture. Every day after summer school a friend would pick me up in a 1954 Oldsmobile, fast, and another afternoon would unfold, filled with cold beers, public-school girls met at various pools, and drag racing wherever and whenever a challenge occurred. Ironically, I did better in summer school than I ever had in regular session. The pleasure freed me. My confidence was up, my libido was being fed, and an ease of concentration made study a responsibility rather than a chore.

Fifth Form (junior year) proved the most important of our career at St. Albans. It was the year of college boards, "activities," and the penultimate rank in class. Advisors scurried about, threatening, joking, making certain deadlines were met, applications filed. The night before those first college boards our band played for a CYO dance at Little Flower. I don't think the lack of sleep affected my scores. As for activities, I'd half-heartedly signed onto the yearbook staff, the Tea Dance, and Formal Dance committees. My marks were high-average, but I was resigned to a ranking in the bottom quarter of my class. Frankly, I did not believe I'd get into college. I'd spent eight years in a reputable prep school, yet remained convinced I wouldn't make the grade.

All I cared about, study-wise, was music. Music and that peculiar theatricality attendant to playing in a band. No music theory was offered in St. Albans' upper school. My study was relegated to the public sector. I had become hooked on jazz guitar and each Saturday would drive forty-five minutes from Cabin John to Eighteenth Street and Rhode Island Ave., NE, for an 11:00 a.m. session with Bill Harris. Harris was a black guitarist who had played blues, was an original member of the Clovers, one of doo-wop's first super groups ("One Mint Julep," "Blue Velvet"), and now concentrated on jazz. He was the only man in Washington teaching classical-style jazz guitar, the style I wished to learn. Eleven o'clock Saturday morning was dawn for a jazz musician; Harris stumbled downstairs most Saturdays groggy, still clad in pajamas, a cup of coffee in hand. What a contrast to those scrubbed-pink, Anglo-Saxon masters, hot to trot at 7:30 each weekday morning. Harris would hear my lesson, nod positively or negatively, then reach for the guitar. If I were lucky, he would sail off on a thermal of complicated riffs, melodic harmonies, and a half hour's calculated improvisation. To this day I have never heard finer guitar music. There was certainly nothing like it being offered in the Lane-Johnston Building.

To complicate matters that Fifth Form year, I got into trouble for skipping sports. Rather than endure Troop Nineteen, I had signed up for cross country, learning that it was next to impossible to keep track of twenty-odd boys strung out across an autumn countryside. My saxophonist and I drove every day to Tommy Tehan's, a seedy Georgetown University dive. We could drink there at age sixteen and never be carded; we did so for over a month. Finally our school absence was noticed, a sentence was served, and the long cool afternoons drinking beer and driving home on the sidewalks subsided.

My grades continued to seesaw. It was decided, in conference between my parents and the administration, that I should board the remainder of my Fifth Form year. This was fine by me. There were distractions at home and travel time between Cabin John and St. Albans each day was an hour and a half wasted. That was an hour and a half that could be spent with the books. I was studying every waking minute, often rising at four in the morning to cram for a test. St. Albans' boarding department was a relief. There was mandatory study hall each night, evening chapel (which proved meditative), good food, and a sense of camaraderie among the thirty-odd boarders previously unknown. I had a private cubicle in the underclassmen's bay; my grades improved and my moods leveled out.

There were some characters in the boarding department that spring. Al Gore was there, and I recall finding him asleep on the couch the morning after 1960's Kennedy-Nixon election. Another boarder was Ordway Burden, of the New York Burdens and son of the former ambassador to Belgium. Ordway was bespectacled, nonathletic, shy, but saddled with a remarkable wit and a mind more complex than any boy's in our class—he would enter Harvard as a sophomore. Ordway was the first person I knew to learn speed reading; he bused downtown once or twice a week to study Chinese. These courses he took above the work he did for St. Albans, in which he excelled. Ordway's first automobile, a gift from his family, was a supercharged Triumph sports car with the license plate MAINE B. It was a joke around school as to how much money Ordway was worth. He fueled such speculation good-naturedly. On Sunday evenings, after returning to the dormitory, he would stroll past lower Formers' cubicles, making certain he drew a crowd, then spin at the end of the hall and hurl pocket change down the polished linoleum. Lower Formers would dive like beach boys for the coins.

My future roommate came to board about then; he likewise had distractions at home, and the two of us, between obligations, shared laughs. Tommy Adams was a funny kid, cocky, good-looking, and bred to wear expensive clothes. I was something of a clothes horse myself, so we traded garments. We were about the same size. We'd been together at St. Albans since the fourth grade, but it was touch and go as to whether we'd graduate.

I was doing better at athletics that junior year. Despite

a soccer coach who openly despised me, I won my varsity letter. I would letter in varsity baseball. Tommy also lettered in soccer and would letter that spring in golf. That team was something of a joke at St. Albans, even though it often enjoyed the school's only championship season. The golf team practiced at Chevy Chase Club, which led to a certain amount of hacking around. Tommy would talk Ordway into joining the team so they could drive to Chevy Chase in style.

My attitude that year was agonizingly hostile. Rereading report cards for various periods, I am struck by the masters' comments: "If Charley spent less time talking and acting out his frustrations, he'd do better...." Insubordination through manner. "I am most disappointed in the caliber of Charley's work, in his effort, and his class attitude...he is wasting time in class...his mind is on something else. He should do less complaining and more work...it used to be very encouraging to see him make progress." Jesus, I was busting my ass! But it was true: There was something in me not programmed for academic success. "I wish I taught Charley Thompson guitar playing, bluegrass music, or any subject in which he were really interested," my English teacher wrote. "Charley's got the stuff in him," Canon Martin added. "He also has temperament. We shall be rooting for him...."

Canon Martin consistently wrote nice things about me to my parents. Why he couldn't communicate that affection to me, why he didn't take time to try to figure what was eating me, remains a mystery.

What was eating me? I'm not sure. Part of it was an inability to succeed in an atmosphere fraught with the stiffest academic competition—twenty boys from our class of forty would become National Merit finalists or receive letters of commendation; seventeen would go to Harvard, Yale, or Princeton. Part of it was living in the cloistered world of a small private school, where every activity was monitored. Part of it was being sixteen years old and wild, with no girls at hand. Part of it, no doubt, was some nonspecific craziness I carried to St. Albans in the fourth grade.

By fall of our senior year, college board scores had circulated and my results were bleak. I was more convinced than ever I'd be left out of college. Tommy and I shared a room, that we decorated in an outrageous manner; everything from papier-mâché decoys to antique flags, to sabers from Tommy's summers at Culver Academy, to a modest Winslow Homer from his parents' apartment. Dean Stambaugh, the art teacher, would escort students upstairs to view it. Coffee would spill, soccer balls would fly, yet that Homer survived. More than can be said for us. We were five-day-a-week boarders, which meant we vacated the premises on weekends. I would head home, pick up a car, get a girl by my side, and roar. Tommy, more often than not, would stick around school. This was against regulations, but certain regulations might be stretched. One Saturday I dropped him off after a party, and we lifted two beers from a master's upstairs icebox. I disposed of the empties by tossing them beneath the hallowed Glastonbury Thorn.

The Thorn was a tree at the center of a traffic circle that fronted the Lane-Johnston Building. It was a cutting from a historic tree at Glastonbury, England, said to have sprung from the staff of St. Joseph of Arimathea, who'd brought Christianity to Britain in 43 AD. The Thorn bloomed whenever English royalty visited the Close. It had a good record, the Queen customarily arriving in spring. It was special, and Canon Martin parked his station wagon next to it. The following morning he arrived for an early service, discovered the beer bottles, and exploded. A modest amount of detective work was required to determine our guilt. This was no minor offense. Two years previous several seniors had been expelled for drinking *off* the Close. I was certain we were finished. Nine years' study down the drain for twenty minutes' foolishness. I telephoned my father and he drove down immediately for a conference with Canon Martin.

Tommy and I, in the company of our Sixth Form master, were brought in.

My father had taken a drink. "It's not like they knocked somebody up," he said. Canon Martin stifled a smile, responded philosophically, then segued into a discussion of Tommy's and my peculiarities as individuals. I remember raising my eyes from the floor, shocked to realize the canon had been discussing Tommy's clothes. How well dressed young Adams was! I was incensed. Tommy had borrowed and wore one of my Brooks Brothers sports jackets.

We were placed under house arrest, or its equivalent, and required to live on Close for three weeks, working each afternoon with the Cathedral ground crew. Weekends we spent polishing silver and mopping floors in the Cathedral. But not before we were forced to sweat out our fate, to ponder the inevitability of expulsion and enrollment in public school, then plead to the brink of tears lest we be cast to the sharks. That pleading scene, monitored by the assistant head and our form master, was ugly. I recall with loathing the manner of things I was forced to say. The Cathedral ground crew—a ribald band of ne'er-do-wells—was not bad, though; in fact it proved enjoyable. We raked leaves, dug ditches, and buried a bishop and his wife in the Cathedral's crypt. The Cathedral was a fascinating institution, its ground crew even less responsible than we.

Despite the pressure, I made Honor Roll with a B average, and sidled toward the Canon's graces. I continued to take chances—meeting girls on the Close, necking astride the Peace Cross (nearly as hallowed an icon as the Glastonbury Thorn), pushing curfews. I was just... crazy. Canon Martin bestowed a dubious honor upon me, however: the custodianship of his bulldog, Marc Antony. This was an honor reserved for troublesome boys. My predecessor, Fred Houghton, had been wild with cars, booze, and ten years later would be convicted of murdering his wife.

Canon Martin had kept a bulldog as long as anyone could remember, The dog was his symbol and the school's mascot. It was my job to dress Marc Antony in his St. Albans sweater, handle him during football games, and keep him off parents' legs. He was a randy little devil. Before each home game, snare drums would roll, a bugle would sound, and I would hurl a football toward the center of the field, releasing Marc Antony. He would bound after the ball, batting it about until he gained control, then unabashedly hump it. It was my duty to reach the ball before this might occur, leash Marc Antony, and trot him toward the sideline. I was not always quick enough. Nor was I 100 percent successful with the leg assignment. I am pictured, in my senior cartoon, wearing letter sweater and hip boots, holding Marc Antony at bay. We await the kickoff.

Canon Martin taught us Sacred Studies that year; it was the first time we had encountered him in a classroom situation. The course consisted of primarily theological reading: Reinhold Niebuhr, Martin Buber, and the like. We had been required to take a course in Sacred Studies each term since fourth grade. But this class was different. Canon Martin demonstrated the breadth of his mind and the depth of his religious thinking, but he could not curb his wont to pontificate. After the first weeks' sessions, I for one paid little attention. Few boys did. The canon brought Marc Antony freely to class, allowing him to wander about the room. Kidders discovered that by feeding Marc Antony chalk they could make him vomit. Approximately halfway through the hour, a cough would sound, Canon Martin would look up and say, "Take care of that for me, would you Thompson?" And I'd slump downstairs to the men's room for paper towels and disinfectant.

None of which made any difference. Earlier that fall, a representative from the University of Delaware had come to St. Albans, hot to recruit a first student from so hallowed a school. I attended the meeting with one or two other doubtfuls on the Ivy League circuit. The

Delawarean was impressive. I was invited north for a visit. Delaware's campus proved attractive (it was modeled on the University of Virginia's) and I was convinced nothing better lay in store for me. I applied and was accepted before Christmas. The pressure was off. I had been accepted at college before anyone in my class and could relax.

My grades improved. I did better at athletics. Don Graham hosted the football party that fall; there was plenty of beer and good music, and I danced with a most sensual date. I intensified studies in jazz guitar with Bill Harris. I was researching my senior paper on the evolution of New Orleans jazz—an essay the canon would take time to read. "This is very unfamiliar ground to me," he wrote. "The vivid, stirring, rhythmic music that is jazz comes out of a life or culture which is more than the degradation of the dives with which we frequently associate it. I suppose what I'm saying is I don't understand it and I would like to understand it...Charley, I am going to miss you."

I played first-string varsity baseball that spring, batted well, and in our last game drilled a fastball into the trees at Landon, to cinch the conference championship against a pitcher who was being scouted by the pros. Only two other St. Albans boys had put one into the trees at Landon, both legendary athletes. "How does it feel to travel in such fast company?" someone shouted on the bus. "It feels like they deserve it," I answered. The team fell out.

I threw the senior party that spring, a cathartic revel enjoyed by all. On graduation day in the Cathedral, bolstered by trumpet voluntaries and washed clean by sheets of organ music, I accepted my diploma from Bishop Creighton with no thought of looking back.

Men of the future, stand
And watch each fleeting hour,
To make your lives what God has planned,
To spread abroad His power.
In work, in game, or play
Suppress all fear and hate;

Show forth a spirit generous true,
For God and for the State.

St. Albans hymn

IN CANON MARTIN's final parent letter, mailed last spring, he spoke of the many lessons he had learned in twenty-eight years as headmaster of St. Albans: "The most important...is how little I know...I mean know about the fundamental business of headmastering: understanding people." He added, "There was a time when without any doubt I knew what was right and what was wrong on almost any moral question.... That time no longer is, thanks somehow to St. Albans...certainly I have come to know: when I am sure I am right, I can be sure I am wrong."

Canon Martin went on to quote a letter from an alumnus of the 1960s who vilified St. Albans but who praised Canon Martin as one who "truly cared."

"And I did care," Canon Martin reflected. "Caring is the one great certainty I have wanted in my school and, indeed, in my life. I would even hold that it is the ultimate in life. That I have come to believe."

I TOOK MANY THINGS from St. Albans, not the least of which was a willingness to study, bludgeoned into me from years of practice. But I never felt that anyone cared. Except perhaps Canon Martin. In that regard, St. Albans prepared me well for college, where no one *did* care. It also instilled a primary sense of written English—one of Canon Martin's goals—and an ability to interpret literature that stood me in good stead throughout my university career. It took a decade, however, to feel that anything my mind produced was of significance.

Several years after graduation, I received a letter from my Sixth Form master, John C. Davis, in response to a note I had written him concerning St. Albans boys at the University of Delaware, where I happened to be doing honors work: "I feel quite certain that you were one of the ablest students in your class," he wrote, "and I am including some of the quick brighties like Case and Burden and Graham. But somewhere along the line, St. Albans manages to convince some of the students that they are not able, and that is something else I'd like to put an end to. Somewhere…you made up your mind that you couldn't or wouldn't compete with the boys with the books, and then irrationally decided that you were stupid, or at least not book-bright.

"Your ability would have responded to more sensitive handling by faculty, and here we fell down. We didn't engage you sympathetically in the process of education, and you went elsewhere to do your growing. The personality of a master can mean the difference between success or failure for a boy in school, and this is the area in which I am most concerned, both for myself and for the educators who feel that the problem of training can be solved by building more classrooms....

"I should like to hear whatever else you have to say about Delaware, for I feel certain that more and more St. Albans boys can find there a sense of ease and an opportunity to excel, both of which are necessary for a person to have in order to enable his native intelligence to function unhampered by things that chain a person in places like St. Albans. Regards as always...."

I SAW CANON MARTIN two weeks before the close of school. I wandered into St. Albans' crowded refectory during lunch, as Canon Martin was offering the thanksgiving. At first I stood confused. It was some kind of Mardi Gras day, students were dressed in every sort of costume, and the canon himself wore paisley Bermudas, yellow knee socks, and a yellow Lacoste. I could not recall seeing him at mealtime in other than his clerical collar. I was the only person in the refectory dressed in coat and tie.

As the revelers filed out, I stood by, waiting for Canon Martin. He smiled upon passing, but did not appear to fix me. I introduced myself.

"Thompson!" he said, grabbing me by the arm. "Come into my study."

There he stared at my face reflectively and asked, "How's the author?" He reached behind him for an alumni directory, and thumbing to the class of '62, started at the list's top and recited what each man was doing and where. When he had finished, he snatched off his glasses, sucked pensively, and spoke:

"In many ways we met your needs here," he said. "In others we did not."

That was succinct. I awaited some pontification. None was forthcoming. We spoke casually for several minutes, then Canon Martin clasped me by the arm and ushered me toward one of the new buildings. A recital was underway, various seniors completing their musical year with a curiously informal, yet formal, presentation. Boys dawdled in long hair and outrageous costumes. Girls were in evidence, students from NCS who now shared numerous classes with St. Albans boys. Canon Martin listened attentively. Students scuffed past, greeting Canon Martin with arms about the neck. A boy wearing shoulder-length hair began a guitar rendition of "Satin Doll," a piece I had played for an assembly fifteen years before. I slipped out the door.

In the library, a book I had written sullied an alumni shelf sagging under the novels of Gore Vidal, plus obscure tracts by obscure authors on military and naval history. But there were books by Brit Home, James Reston, Jr., John Casey, and the astronaut Michael Collins. I caught a sense of belonging. A leaflet announced a series of one-act plays presently underway in the Trapier Theater. Boys trotted by carrying kayak paddles and rock-climbing gear, hustling toward a bus marked ST. ALBANS VOYAGER PROGRAM.

All this was Canon Martin's doing. A thirty-seven-year-old minister would be taking his place as headmaster, a black man would succeed William Creighton as Bishop of Washington, old masters were dying or retiring, Frances

Sayre was stepping down after twenty-six years as Dean of the Cathedral, Paul Callaway would retire after thirty-eight years as organist and choirmaster. The order was changing. St. Albans' new headmaster would speak of improvements he desired: coeducation at all levels of study, an alternative to mandatory athletics, courses in television, etc. But it was evident that Canon Martin had started the ball rolling.

"The 1960s made it plain even to those slow learners among us that in education, the richer the curriculum, the greater the opportunity for a student to develop his interests and own unique gifts," he had written. Outside, I again encountered the Canon. He escorted me toward Trapier Theater. Students grinned and called hello. Canon Martin seemed to have begotten some elemental change. He was the same man, not much grayer, a little more stooped, but I failed to recognize him.

"If I looked long enough," Canon Martin said, as if reading my thoughts, "I'd probably recognize you." Then we ducked into the darkened theater.

Postscript

WHEN VICE PRESIDENT Al Gore (class of 1965) accepted the Democratic nomination for president on August 17, 2000, he quoted one of the canon's prized homilies, that a test of moral character is the willingness "to choose the hard right over the easy wrong." Gore said: "But the presidency is more than a popularity contest. It's a day-by-day fight for people. Sometimes you have to choose to do what's difficult or unpopular. Sometimes you have to be willing to spend your popularity in order to pick the hard right over the easy wrong."

Washingtonian, 1977
Vanity Fair, 1989
St. Albans School, The First Hundred Years, 2010

A Walk on the Wild Side:
Chesapeake & Ohio Canal

"Strong drink for strong men;
only babes must be fed on milk."
Old Canal Motto

"I wished I never seen you," the fat woman said. "I wished I never seen you and I tried to be nice." We had come off the towpath at Brunswick, Maryland, scrambling across rail yards, packs stooping us over, and the first thing we'd asked was how many bars there were in town.

"Sixteen," a gas-station attendant had answered. "Sixteen...and eight churches. Now you decide." If we hadn't hit all sixteen, we'd managed a good dent. We'd started slowly, at My Sister's Place, gulping cold beers before a hundred-year-old front bar, gnawing Polish sausages, playing the juke, eavesdropping on fire calls from a squawk box behind the back bar ("Got a little barn far up-country"), chuckling as locals leaned off stools to watch the Amtrak sail by, marveling at Easter decorations among the Slim Jims and pickled eggs, though Easter was nearly a month away. And making Darr's Bar, the Metropolitan, and others before checking into Railroad YMCA for our first night off the ground in three days. Not that we required the night off the ground, but seeing how drunk it was out, the decision appeared reasonable.

Now we were haggling with this checkout clerk at Railroad Y, and she was making us feel small. "I wished I never seen you," she repeated. "You come in here last evening late and I give you my only two rooms, charge you members' rates when I never ast to see your cards, give you a locker to store gear, no charge, and you say dollar refund. Dollar refund on a four-dollar room just 'cause the 'lectricity don't work. I offered you this flashlight. I said we'll change rooms if we can, but you talk a dollar refund."

Her face crinkled into a taut grin, the sort of terrifying grin only a fat woman can muster when she's really displeased with you.

"I wished I never seen..." she continued, shaking her head.

But Fox cut her off. "Lady," he said, "if you'd just total what we owe and throw in a tin of that Stanback, we'll be on our way." The fat woman commenced to figuring.

Fox looked terrifying himself: The pack he was wearing boosted him from six-four to over seven feet. His toes stuck out of his Topsiders where he'd trimmed the canvas back, his face was swollen pink, his hair matted, he was obviously hung over, and he carried a two-and-a-half-foot chocolate bunny under his left arm like an Oscar. My memory was vague as to where that bunny had come from—some tavern in town, because that's all we'd hit. I seemed to recall a scuffle. Railroad Y's café was packed with breakfast eaters, mostly Chesapeake & Ohio railroad men in CHESSIE SYSTEM windbreakers and twill pants. All night they'd called each other to shifts—*bam*, "John, it's four o'clock, John," *bam bam*, "Huh, you need me?"—underscored by the clatter of trains, the clang of bells, the hoot of whistles. A stench of fried ham and eggs was making me sick. Railroad Y was uncomfortably busy.

Both chairs in its barber shop were occupied, and retired railroaders sat in squads before a huge color TV, ogling cartoons. A few lounged in what passed for a lobby, studying whomever came and went. Fox paid our tab; we shuffled toward the street. Brunswick was a railroad town and we had no business lingering there.

Fox carried that two-and-a-half-foot bunny strapped to his pack, and as we hiked through Brunswick he drew stares. But I was too beat to react. We were fifty-five miles out of Georgetown, with 130 miles left to Cumberland. That may not sound bad, but when you're 130 miles from *anyplace* and your feet start to go, a single mile is an interminable distance. Of course, we'd worn the wrong boots. We'd each brought moderately heavy, Vibram-soled hikers that we'd planned to change occasionally for Topsiders, but after the first twenty miles we'd strapped those "concrete galoshes," as Fox called them, resolutely to our packs.

"Sonsabitches are fine for car-to-bar wear," Fox said, "but out here on the trail they're worthless."

And he was right. Vibram soles proved much too stiff for your everyday towpath—essentially a hard-packed dirt road—but were fine for rain until they cleated up with mud, great for shale if you were hiking the Rockies, perfect for Georgetown when you wanted to impress someone with the authority of your gait.

"I'd throw these mothers in the goddamn canal if they hadn't cost me half a week's pay," Fox complained. I felt nearly as bitter.

We tested our newly doctored Topsiders while we slunk through Brunswick, neither of us certain he'd achieved the right orthopedic solution. Fox had hacked the toes off his, just ripped the bastards apart. I'd dropped some coin in Dr. Scholl's slot by adding two pairs of insoles and a set of arch supports to mine. I'd switched to thin socks, having carpeted both feet with moleskin. In addition, I wore over my right little toe a tiny pink cup of foam that looked like one of those novelty condoms you buy in men's rooms.

"Damn, Bob," Fox had said, eyeing my feet at Railroad Y. "Gets any worse and you'll do your next hike off one of them rolling wooden dollies."

"It's a killer, Bob," I'd answered, fingering a blister. "Damn sure a killer."

We'd been calling each other Bob for about forty miles. What had started as a joke now possessed an odd kind of utility: To call each other Bob was to fuse identities in a way that ameliorated pain. It also helped us forget there existed two real fools with real names who'd conceived of such a venture in the first place.

I SUPPOSE IT WAS my fault for initially bringing it up. I had always wanted to hike the towpath from Georgetown to Cumberland. Of all Washington's variegated escape routes, I had long considered the Chesapeake & Ohio Canal to be the most alluring. To hike its 184.5 miles in winter, with no leaves to impede the view, no bicycles to crowd the towpath, and no Boy Scouts to foul the campsites, had been a dream since childhood. I had lived by the canal in Cabin John for twenty-six years, and I knew the stretch from Georgetown to Great Falls like my own driveway. I had hiked many other stretches, jogged and bicycled more. But I'd never walked the whole way.

Fox had been ready for anything. It was New Year's Eve in Washington, barely fifteen degrees outside and desperate. We'd had a few drinks. We'd been avoiding resolutions. "No more whining," a member of our party had offered, and we almost drank to that. But the pure desolation of Columbia Station's barroom warned against such folly. Washington was deserted, empty, about as cheerful as a weekend in Warsaw. There had been a soiree we'd tried to locate, maybe two, and a lot of high-speed driving through vacant streets, slamming down one-ways the wrong way, heading oncoming vehicles onto sidewalks, roaring up Eighteenth Street in the far left lane—all that crazy driving Fox loved and was so graceful at. I must have proposed the hike then, since I recall Fox hollering, "Let's go!" as we rolled over a curb, "Let's go tomorrow!" Then he'd hauled the Powerglide into low and spun out facing traffic.

We hadn't got started until March. There had been complications, not the least of which was the severity of Winter 1977. Also, there was the matter of Fox's job and the fact that he had a few cars he wanted to sell. Fox Person always had a car or two for sale. The Department of Motor Vehicles had served notice that if he sold any more cars this year he'd have to apply for a dealer's license. Fox was the kind of guy strange characters would approach in a bar and say: "Got the title to that Mercury yet?" Fox had a day job, sure, but his real passion was automobiles, and what he could do with them during the evening. What he did was restore, repair, trade, or sell them, and those he kept he drove disturbingly fast. Fox cared for automobiles the way young men of another age cared for horses. He groomed them, coddled them, mended their ailing parts. Then he rode the absolute bejesus out of them very late at night.

"Look at that Nash," Fox mumbled as we trudged determinedly through Brunswick. "Look at that Chevy '55. Look at that Studebaker! I could turn six hundred bucks on her in a New York minute if we were only back in DC."

ALAS, WE WERE NOT. And had not been these past three days. First day had been glorious—about forty degrees, sunny. We had hiked unblistered and strong, noticing everything: that stately lock at Pennyfield with its weathered farmhouse, white with black shutters, a red sleigh in the yard and a girl in a red shirt who'd herded sheep over the crest of a hill ("I want to marry her," Fox had sighed); the aqueduct at Seneca, first of eleven, that carried the canal across Seneca Creek; ruins of an old stone-cutting mill where red Seneca sandstone had been cut and shipped to fashion such structures as the Smithsonian Castle, Cabin John Bridge, and numerous canal locks; an absence of people; Chisel Branch campsite, short of Edward's Ferry, where two boys on horseback appeared from nowhere, laughed about fetching us a case of beer, then disappeared. A clear first night by the fire. Sipping one hundred-proof J. W. Dant, the backpacker's friend. Some small-plane activity this close to Washington, many airliners. But a quietude threatening to pervade. The clearness dissolving into rain by morning; still cheerful inside our tent, but with a sense of gloom descending. A slow start. Fox having forgotten his rain gear. Fox breaking camp with a plastic garbage bag for a coat, my extra hat. Fox having forgotten his hat. A slow trek to White's Ferry, where the grocery was not open and a ferryman proved oblivious to our plight (just one cup of coffee for the trail, mister). A bevy of canoeists paddling in before the primitive ferry—150 years old, last regular ferry along the Potomac—bailing out of crummy weather. "Nothing but mud on up," they'd warned, shaking woolly heads. A slogging through drizzle and muck to Monocacy Aqueduct (constructed 1833), a magnificent structure 516 feet long that portaged both towpath and canal across the Monocacy River on arches of white and pink sandstone. Aqueduct closed for repairs, with a six-and-a-half mile detour—but we'd finessed that, climbing across anyhow.

There we'd camped at the confluence of two rivers and in the shadow of Sugar Loaf Mountain. The wind scary, screaming down a long bend in the Potomac to bowl me over at one burst, send my fifty-pound pack sailing off a picnic table like an orange Frisbee. The light striking, dull as steel but with an edge to it lent by the wind. Our tent rattling and popping in the ten-degree chill like a three-master before a hurricane. Me warm in my heavy down bag, Fox nearly freezing in his Sleepy Owl Comfortsack, a lightweight synthetic he'd borrowed off God-knows-whom back at work. "Wait 'til I catch up with that sonofabitch," Fox had moaned, scraping ice off the coverlet. "Slap his ass in a box and mail him somewhere."

We'd cooked breakfast in a Park Service outhouse, the wind remaining strong, and limped off toward Brunswick feeling mean.

THIS MORNING WE hiked in silence, ruminating upon failure. Myself, upon failure of the canal, a fact brought to focus by our evening in Brunswick, largest railroad town between Georgetown and Cumberland. The railroad had killed the canal, had rendered it obsolete before its 184.5-mile length was completed. These railroad folk were no pals of ours. The B&O Railroad had reached Cumberland eight years before the C&O Canal, though both ventures had commenced the same day, July 4, 1828. Both had sought to link a rich Ohio Valley with the Eastern seaboard via an economical transportation route. Both succeeded, but the canal, with its primitive barges drawn by mules and piloted by captains whose entire families lived on board, was quickly eclipsed by the speed and efficiency of the rail. It had cost $22 million to take the canal as far as Cumberland—a million per year to 1850, when the last stretch was finished. The dream of another 180 miles to Pittsburgh was scrapped, and the B&O headed westward. By 1924 the Canal Company was bankrupt; its magnificent ditch with seventy-four lift locks, twenty-four lock houses, eleven aqueducts, eight bridges, seven dams, 162 culverts, and a 3,118-foot tunnel stood ravaged by floods, irrevocably in want of repair.

By 1938 the federal government had acquired the canal property, leaving it far from safe. Plans to tarmac the towpath for a highway were blocked by public sympathy in 1954 as a result of Supreme Court Justice William O. Douglas's celebrated hike. Six years later the canal became a national monument and was presumably saved. In 1971 it became a national park. On May 17, 1977, the C&O Canal would be dedicated to Justice Douglas.

Of this I reminded Fox. "They should've gone ahead and *made* it a road," he said. "I mean, this backpacking's for jerkoffs."

A NAP IN THE SUN south of Harper's Ferry. In a meadow at the foot of the Appalachian Trail, where Fox ate lunch and boiled coffee on our tiny gasoline stove. A nap that laid a compress of sweat across my forehead but erased fatigue. Forty minutes of blue sky through veiled eyelids, wind still screaming but buffeted here by tall, warm grass and the sunlight. Dreaming of rafts in summertime. Sleek rafts that would bear us effortlessly upstream, defying current. Turn in half-sleep and feel oneself swimming. Warm water to soothe aching feet. Warm sweat in the sun and waking to find Fox grinning.

TEMPERATURE DROPPED opposite Harper's Ferry to perhaps twenty degrees with wind chill. The Potomac ran high and flat and very swift. We ducked into gusts tearing across the Shenandoah, yanking at our scarves. Fox was telling stories. I had asked him for a story, begged for anything short of bitching to distract the pain. I felt cold and brittle as an old nail. My feet ached deep inside the arches. My pack was freezer weight. We could lean into the wind for support, but made no more than one and a half miles an hour.

Fox spoke of his father. We passed under the B&O bridge and shuddered as a freight train throbbed off toward West Virginia. Fox told of his father, dead two years, and it was a sad story. Harper's Ferry cropped up on the opposite shore, squatting like a Victorian urchin. The wind bore down. Fox told of his sister, an older one who'd died in a house fire. Harper's Ferry lay to port, a specter of its nineteenth century solemnity. I mused upon John Brown and his capture of the federal arsenal there. I recalled his hanging. I remembered tales of Stonewall Jackson potting Union troops "like fish in a barrel" from heights above the city. I wondered at Thomas Jefferson's oft-quoted declaration that the view from Harper's cliffs was worth "a voyage across the Atlantic." Today Harper's cliffs were every bit as romantic as those facing Manhattan from the Jersey shore. Same gray dominance. Same soot of industrialism.

Fox told of watching his sister burn, and tears inched down my face. They evaporated quickly to salt in the stiffening wind. Fox noticed and stopped, hiking along in silence. We trudged past ruins of the Salty Dog Saloon, where old Spence Weaver had headed a tri-state syndicate during Prohibition, got drunk one night and backed his car into the canal opposite Lock 33 and drowned. We read aloud from Captain Tom Hahn's guidebook, absolving the site; we laughed.

SIXTEEN-OUNCE BALL JARS of Schlitz at a bar in Shepherdstown, West Virginia. Sixteen-ounce Ball jars fading fast as we caroused with two mountain girls, one skinny, one fat, in the town boasting a bridge named for James Rumsey. Rumsey somehow made it seem important that we visit Shepherdstown and entertain these girls. Most assuredly that we drink his health. James Rumsey had designed the earliest canal locks at Great Falls—for George Washington's Patowmack Company, a predecessor of C&O—inventions hailed by many as the principal engineering feat of eighteenth-century America. He had been an early supervisor of Washington's company, handpicked by George himself for his brilliance as an engineer. Moreover, Rumsey was a pioneer in steam navigation, having launched a steamboat into the Potomac from Shepherdstown Ferry some twenty years prior to Robert Fulton's 1807 adventure on the Hudson.

We had a little head of steam up ourselves.

Our packs crowded the aisle where we scrunched into a wooden booth with these two mountain girls, and Ball jars were stacking up. We were grungy, raucous, and sampling one of everything on the menu. Socks hung off the straps of our packs. There was mud all over the floor.

Nobody seemed to mind. These two mountain girls had just gotten off work and they were thirsty. They'd been working construction.

"Whole lot of restoration going on," the skinny one said. "Trying to make this into a miniature Georgetown."

We had noticed antique shops and boutiques.

"Don't see many people wearing backpacks in Shepherdstown," she continued. "Not this time of year. That's why I come over. To talk, I mean," she said. And gave us a smile.

Fox called for another round: The jukebox was a steady blare. "Tell us about West Virginia," Fox said, relaxing but eyeing the fat one hard. "Tell us what it's like growing up hereabouts."

There was a silence. "I couldn't rightly say," the fat one muttered. "My daddy owns a bank in Chevy Chase, my momma one of the biggest hardware chains in Washington."

"Would you marry me?" Fox said, drawing the mountain girl close. "I mean—we could settle down."

LATER, MUCH LATER, hiking across James Rumsey Bridge, a pickup's taillights flash as the back end rides up on load-leveler shocks. The driver shifts to reverse and burns rubber accelerating back in our direction.

"You boys'll want a ride 'cross this bridge," he says matter-of-factly.

We climb aboard. It is cold now, perhaps twenty-five degrees. But the sky is transparent. We have the stars and a good buzz on, which we hope will hold us the three miles' hiking to Killiansburg Cave. The pickup truck sails across Rumsey Bridge at a hundred miles an hour, sweeping back under the span in a matter of seconds. We climb out of the flatbed opposite the canal, where there's a footbridge leading to the towpath.

"I used to sleep out on cold nights like this'n," says the driver. "When I was young once't, like you boys."

The driver cannot be nineteen years old. We stand in

the noise of the idling pickup and trade pleasantries.

"How about a drink of sour mash?" Fox offers, reaching for the J. W. Dant.

"Naw," says the driver, fishing a jug from a stack of tires lining one end of the cab.

Then he whoops. "I'm gawn down the road, meet my woman and drink this wine!"

MILE 75.2: Killiansburg Cave. Where citizens of Sharpsburg hid during the Battle of Antietam. Now a hiker-biker overnighter, typical of numerous others along the towpath, outfitted with picnic table, fireplace, and sickly green crapper. Cold. I raised up on one haunch and reached for the water bottle, which was frozen. Twenty-nine degrees in the sun by my pack thermometer. An inch or so of ice glazing the canal. Fox shivered in his Sleepy Owl Comfortsack and reached for the Dant.

"It's a killer, Bob," he said, bubbling her good. I tried to squeeze a little water from the frozen plastic bottle; enough for one cup of coffee. We seemed miles from any living creature. The silence was awesome, no doubt intensified by the cold. I got the stove started and boiled water slowly in a tin cup. Fox dug out the aspirin he carried in a Bionetics specimen-collection bag. In 75.2 miles we had encountered six people along the canal; two of those had been surveyors, one a park ranger, the rest bicyclists. We had beaten the redhots to the campsites, and for that I was grateful.

Barely a foot of water in the canal at Killiansburg, par for most of the battered ditch's length. The canal had traditionally been drained during winter—for repairs and to guard against flooding—so that didn't seem wrong. Ice had usually halted boat traffic about Christmas, so engineers drained the entire ditch west of Georgetown, and left it drained until April. In that sense we were seeing the canal as it had been. Canal captains had either camped on their boats until spring or retired to canal towns like Williamsport to wait out the thaw. Their mules were let to pasture. Everyone gorged and had a good old time. So it was in theory.

Except for numerous trees growing from the canal bed, this morning might have been March a hundred years ago. Fox wore his yellow down jacket zipped tight against the cold, but his toes, in heavy wool socks, protruded from his Topsiders. His river slides, he'd come to call them. I wore a navy down jacket and vest, Topsiders and a red watch-cap. Both of us puffed up like barristers beneath several pounds of feathers.

"Oh, Daddy, won't you take me back to Mont-gomery County," Fox sang, his voice rebounding sluggishly off cliffs lining the berm. Then, more upbeat: "There's rednecks and white socks, and Bradley Exxon." Bradley was a gas station near his apartment.

We were really up-country now. A school of fish spooked in the sunlight below a thin layer of ice, and I thought they might be trout. That did not seem inconceivable this far north; a number of cold springs dripped off rocks into the ditch. We followed the school fifty yards upcanal before losing them in brush.

The river here flowed high, wide, and extremely muddy. Several dilapidated houses appeared around a bend: Taylor's Landing. Two old people, a man and a woman, strolled toward us. The old woman wore a long gray overcoat and an orange wool cap pulled tight over the back of her neck. Both old people were toothless. They were the seventh and eighth humans we'd seen on the towpath in five days, but they obviously lived nearby and hardly counted.

"Them's suckers," the old man said, dodging my question about trout. Then he hustled the woman along.

Taylor's Landing was disturbingly remote. It could not have changed much in the hundred-odd years since construction of the canal. Primitive houses, animals in the yards, ruins of an old bridge. Taylor's Landing lay along the canal's far bank like the displaced frontier community it was.

Every quarter-mile or so a pair of wood ducks would get up and screech off toward the river. Except for fish, they were the only wildlife we'd encountered. "I've seen more birds than this at Rock Creek Nature Center," Fox complained. There was no need to remind him it still was winter. Our breath steamed out before us in reams.

Below Dam 4, Fox spotted a COLD BEER sign on a grocery up the hill; we headed for it. It was a tough quarter-mile up that hill, our packs straining at every step, arches howling, each toe a tiny anchovy of pain. A hand-printed sign on the grocery's front door read CLOSED FOR WINTER. The soda machines stood empty and unplugged. I gave the front door a solid boot. From inside came the sound of a TV set and the barking of a small dog.

"Goddamn them anyway for hanging a beer sign like that," I said, collapsing in the debris that fronted the store. "They ought to *drape* the sonofabitch or something." A broken doll's head lay in a mound of pop-tops near my left foot. I kicked it toward the gasoline pumps. "Especially since it's winter."

We hiked another three miles, then ate a rectifying freeze-dried lunch on an overlook facing Dam 4.

Just above this dam, constructed 1832, the canal had dropped into the Potomac. There remained an inlet lock where canal boats had switched to the river, and above that was fifteen miles of slackwater running to Williamsport. Dams along the Potomac had once served a threefold purpose: they had diverted water from river to canal, filling the ditch and assuring steady levels; they'd controlled some flooding; and they'd calmed water upstream for Potomac navigation. A canal boat could enter Big Slackwater at Inlet-lock 4, and cruise unencumbered to Lock 41, about three miles upstream. The towpath narrowed to a trail here, mules pulling canal boats against the current, mule and mule driver plodding several feet from the flow.

Freshets being in, we hiked past the high water with trepidation. Fording several stretches. Climbing over rocks, wading through puddles, negotiating cliffs in some spots where river had encompassed towpath. It was a tough three miles. We bitched and changed to boots and bitched again. But it was undeniably beautiful country. The river curved hard, so that sunlight switched metronomically over our shoulders. The river ran flat and Mississippi-like, its cliffs imposing. Wind continued to blow, however; as evening bore down we feared never getting through. Cottages lined the Maryland shore but none seemed occupied. Above McMahon's Mill our path was blocked. We broached a private staircase, nearly plunging through rotted timber, and stepped among the cottages themselves. All were vacant; an eerie loneliness prevailed. The sky had taken on a steel-gray countenance, and sweat pasted cold to our shoulders. We hiked up a dirt road sullied with scrub trees, feeling ominously alone.

We cut back to the path where water would allow, but we repeatedly sought higher ground. By Lock 41 we were soaked with perspiration and our teeth chattered. Here the canal emerged from the river, sidling comfortably inland. Happy for once to retrieve the towpath, we collapsed against a lift lock and drank deep from the Dant.

"YOU YOUNG FELLOWS hiking the canal?" an old man said from a corner in downtown Williamsport. "Got any questions, I'd be glad to answer 'em."

It was 2:00 p.m. and we'd been guzzling beer since noon when we'd limped off the towpath at the hundred-mile mark. We were tired and discouraged in places that alcohol couldn't touch. We hurt. Fox had been unable to locate any size-13 sneakers to replace his river slides. I feared he might mutiny, might hitchhike home. I longed for a hot bath. It was Saturday afternoon in Williamsport, Maryland, a classic canal town; we couldn't have cared less.

"I used to drive mules on that towpath," the old man said. "Hoggees, they called us." Immediately I perked up. "Go on, ask me anything," he said.

"I got a question," Fox said, slipping the straps on his pack. "What in hell did you people wear for shoes?"

"Shoes?" the old man repeated, as if he hadn't heard Fox right. "Never had money for shoes. We walked barefoot."

Fox groaned. For a moment I thought I'd lost him.

The old man lounged at the corner with a group of his contemporaries, but somehow he stood out. He was better dressed, for one; he wore a dark sports coat, pleated trousers, cardigan sweater, and a vinyl porkpie hat. He carried an aluminum cane with an odd twist at its center-that Fox later said looked like the curb feeler to a Mack truck. But more than that, he possessed an air.

"I'm Hooper Wolfe," he said by way of introduction. "I wrote a book all about it."

I'd heard of Hooper Wolfe. Had heard about him just minutes before from a fellow named Jess Brown, who'd lived on Williamsport canal boats until he was seven—his daddy, old Charley Brown, being one of the last Canal Company captains. Jess and I had been knocking back a few beers at Potomac Tavern, lamenting various lost ways of life, when Hooper Wolfe's name came up.

"Hooper Wolfe's fulla sheet," someone had offered. Jess hadn't seen fit to contradict.

Hooper's book, *I Drove Mules on the C&O Canal,* was a standard reference, one so popular that I'd been unable to locate it in bookstore or library. Hooper Wolfe at eighty-three was a sought-after lecturer, considered by many to warrant his nickname, "Mr. C&O Canal." I had thought to look him up in Williamsport, but not today. Not in this mood, with this tiredness, with this hiker's fear.

Hooper took Fox's arm, leading him down Potomac Street to the combination general store-apartment building that bore the Wolfe name: Old Taylor Hotel, Hooper explained, which he'd acquired in 1924 and converted to various businesses.

Hooper still kept an apartment upstairs. His wife had

died and Hooper lived alone. But he had children in town. We stood in the sunshine on the square opposite Wolfe's and talked. Hooper prated on about Williamsport, filling us with local history—how Williamsport for twenty-eight hours in 1790 had served as national capital but because of hazardous river navigation had lost its permanent bid to Washington; how the first canal boats had reached Williamsport by 1834, the town already prominent as a shipping center for George Washington's Patowmack Company; how Hooper's great-grandfather, a stonemason, had emigrated from Ireland to help construct the canal; how Hooper himself had quit school at age ten to drive mules along the towpath, working for his brother, who owned a boat, later for anyone who required his services; how they'd labored for eight dollars a month and how, during winter, times were so hard that stealing became an accepted way of life.

"We had to worry about keeping warm, collecting firewood, and the like," Hooper said. He tapped his cane against a curbstone for emphasis. "Wasn't no welfare or Mr. Jimmy Carter to take care of everybody. Wasn't no longhairs like this'n," he said, pointing at Fox. "Everybody worked."

"Hey, Hooper," a fellow shouted from a passing station wagon. "Stop telling them boys all them lies."

Hooper flinched. "That's our Scout leader," he said. "I donate a lot of money to his troop."

Hooper proceeded to relate how successful his book had been, how surprised he was, how he divvied up royalties between his investments and the Williamsport Lutheran church. "Only two publications I read anymore are the *Bible* and the *Wall Street Journal*," Hooper said. Then he shifted from Williamsport history to the rewards of organized religion.

I listened to Hooper Wolfe rant on about his health, various operations, longhairs, presidential politics, and Jesus, because here was an old-time canal walker and I believed he held some vital information. I let him have his head before coaxing him back toward canal topics, but finally I had to break in. If not, Fox might have hailed a cab.

"Where can I buy your book?" I said by way of interjection. Hooper caught my eye. "I tried to find one in Washington but couldn't."

"Right here," Hooper answered. "I'll sell you a copy right now."

I wanted to see where the old man lived. There is something in me fascinated by lairs, particularly those of old scholars. Hooper unlatched the downstairs door to the Taylor Hotel and led us through a musty lobby. The passageway was dim, but the old man marched confidently to the staircase and ascended. He stopped at the first landing, giving his key any number of misthrusts before hitting the lock.

Inside was another narrow corridor, backed by a combination kitchen-study awash with canal memorabilia. I was overwhelmed. Photographs covered the walls— photos of Hooper, of the nineteenth-century canal, of the canal today, with Hooper presiding. Clippings hung framed or strewn over tabletops. Tape recorders and cassette tapes added to the clutter—he must have owned five tape recorders. Several stacks of Hooper's books lay against a wall. Except for a bit of food, there appeared nothing in his apartment unrelated to the canal.

I handed Hooper ten dollars for his book and requested that he sign it. He did so in flourishes—with a pen filled, he assured me, with water from the canal. Then he played a cassette of himself reading a chapter from his book, describing how the old lift locks worked. He'd colored the reading with sound effects of dripping water, explaining that "this was how it was down inside" when canal boats locked through.

Fox shifted back and forth on sore feet steaming with agitation. Hooper followed that tape with another reminiscence, also in his voice, capped with the signature: "This is Hooper Wolfe, your old C&O mule driver, telling

how it was in the good old days on the C&O Canal."
He cued up another cassette—this one of a woman
reading from his book—that Hooper explained was a
library rendition for the blind. The old man sat listening
to rhythms of his own prose, nodding, evidently quite
pleased with himself. Here time lost was time recaptured,
and he had done it. Through this room flowed a history
of the canal, and Hooper was hearing it. Fox flipped shut
an album of canal photographs, growing angrier by the
minute. If I didn't rescue him he'd start destroying the
place. I limped to Hooper's bathroom, washed my face
for the first time in five days, and yawned.

KIDS JOCKEYED BICYCLES across Conococheague
Aqueduct at the foot of Potomac Street. Couples hung
lines off the weathered abutments and fished—from john
boats in the structure's shadow. Here was life. Yet this
aqueduct, like every other along the canal, stood ruined.
A boy on a bike with monkey bars and a banana seat
cut doughnuts across a parapet, leaving blue tire tracks
on the limestone. The sun was out. It was warm and we
had a little load on. Yet there was something ultimately
funereal about the whole scene. There was something
ultimately funereal about the entire canal. Forget the fact
of its failure, that it was doomed from the start by an age
of mechanization. One could nearly overlook that. One
couldn't overlook what remained, however—not when
hiking 184.5 miles of towpath. What remained was this
endless ditch, filled with water in some stretches, merely
damp in others, but linked by a succession of masonry
structures called locks, culverts, and aqueducts. It was
this masonry that proved unmistakably funereal.

The stones were big, massive, reminiscent of stonework
in the Great Pyramids of Egypt. In fact, a large proportion
of lock architecture was Egyptian in style. Some of the
world's first canals had been constructed in Egypt, as
early as the seventh century BC. A style of architecture
known as Egyptian Revival had enjoyed popularity in

the United States from about 1820 to 1850, roughly the period of the canal's construction. Egyptian Revival had flowed in the wake of Napoleon's campaign on the Nile, encouraged by a cultural madness for all things French. It was employed by symbol-conscious architects to suggest structural permanence but found its forte among patrons as a style that radiated gloom. It was widely used for prisons, mausoleums, cemeteries, banks, and insurance companies, and was popularly associated with incarceration or death.

More important, Egyptian revival was a neoclassic style, an offshoot of Greek and Roman revival—the last such styles to suggest direct sympathy with the neoclassic mind. The neoclassicist was of eighteenth-century persuasion, a person who saw nature as a force to be ordered, to be tamed. Westward expansionism in the United States, of which C&O Canal Company was no small stockholder, held that belief as a basic tenet: The Allegheny Mountains must be conquered, even as the continent, and the rich produce of the Ohio Valley made accessible to the Tidewater. All this was well and good. Georgetown and by association Baltimore were geographically the closest links to a Midwest which, it had been demonstrated by the Erie Canal, could be accosted by canal water. Encouraged by favors of free enterprise—one must remember that the C&O Canal Company remained private, and though funded occasionally by federal money was never a federal project—the neoclassicist saw the Potomac Valley leading to Cumberland as another wilderness to be civilized and ultimately exploited. The railroad glimpsed a similar horizon, and the irony is not that rail power beat the mule by eight years to Cumberland, but that the Canal Company continued its losing venture so far.

Perverse things were happening to the Victorian sensibility during this period of the canal's construction; industrialism and its fruits had turned the neoclassic mind a little wacky. Feats loomed out of proportion, and there seemed nothing in the natural world which could not be brought under harness. Public monuments saluted invincibility with the massiveness of their construction, architecture became intricate in design, self-consciously literate: One did not occupy a building so much as read it like a book. Gothic, Italianate, and an overweening eclecticism smothered neoclassic styles. A less than subtle longing for anything picturesque had swept the country by 1845. This was the age of influential landscape architects such as Andrew Jackson Downing, "cottage" architects such as A. J. Davis. This was the period of stunning mood pieces such as the Smithsonian Castle. This was a turning point in the completion of the C&O Canal.

Could it be that elders of the Canal Company had finished their magnificent ditch out of some macabre fascination with the picturesque? That their neoclassic resolve to tame the Potomac Valley via an inland waterway of heroic dimension had succumbed to romantic fascination with that waterway's impracticality? One need only approach any number of remaining locks to confront the possibility. A country path following a scenic river, bending as the river bends, ducking inland toward a forest where sluiceways trickle through piles of decaying masonry; a stone lockhouse overlooks rotted beams of the ancient lift-lock itself, a brace of weeping willows frames the whole. Where the canal still flows, the picture becomes more Gothic; one feels the loneliness of boatmen, the Charon-like gloom of hauling cargo through stone locks as pharaonic as Egyptian pyramids. Was it pure coincidence that blocks of Seneca sandstone—blood-red, the very essence of Gothic—so resembled stones of the Great Pyramids? Had Canal Company elders become so saturated with defeat by 1850 that they continued their heroic venture from a perverse obsession with picturesqueness? In all probability, one had only to stand back at Point of Rocks or Harper's Ferry, lean against the tow line beside one's straining mule, and watch the steam engines puff by, to wonder.

Today this courtship of the picturesque was an attitude

far from unfashionable. The National Park Service might ask Congress for $34 million to reconstruct major artifacts of the canal, but nobody in his wildest dreams believed the entire 184.5 miles would be restored. Nobody really wanted it restored. It was much more satisfying to remember the canal as it must have been—the canal was more picturesque in disrepair, less accessible. It was most attractive as a romantic ruin, to be poked around in like Stonehenge or the Coliseum. No one wished to be reminded of the fact that it had been built largely by slave labor—by Irish, Welsh, and German miners and stonemasons who worked in unspeakable poverty, suffering disease and devastating epidemics, only to be shot or have their heads and eyebrows shaved if they bolted from indenture. Nor to be reminded that the canal did as much to encourage rape of the Potomac Valley as any other vestige of nineteenth-century industrialism—displacing wild game; luring farmers closer to river banks where they stripped the land, causing runoffs and uncontrolled flooding; tempting loggers to devastate whole forests in search of lumber; and polluting the Potomac for the first time in its history with acrid drainage from the Cumberland coal mines.

Apologists like Hooper Wolfe never seemed to remember the meanest facts. To them the past was romance, a rounding of edges, a forgiveness of transgressions. Never mind that Hooper Wolfe's great-grandparents had most likely worked the C&O Canal unwillingly. Never mind that they had most likely worked hungry and sick, that Hooper himself had hiked barefoot through his share of muleshit. The canal was the past, and the past was them good old days. Like Hooper had said: "My daddy always swore he'd give the man twenty-five dollars who could tell him where he was to die, 'cause then he'd never go there." A history remained of the C&O Canal. But most of that history was dead. The canal was less the sum of its historical parts than how we encountered it today. And today was rough.

WE BROKE CAMP AT Hagerstown Filtration Plant around nine and hiked into a cold but splendidly bright Sunday morning. Four miles above Williamsport the towpath skirted a bridge abutment sporting the legend HITLER WAS RIGHT, scrawled in large, hand-painted letters. We were out in the woods where the ground was just warm enough for a bit of game to be moving: ducks, squirrels, muskrats, rabbits, even a turtle or two. People were fishing. The legend was grotesque.

At Dam 5 we took a break, resting in the sunshine with fifteen Boy Scouts and a couple of Scout masters. The only person nursing bare feet, besides us, was a Scout master toting the same brand of boots as Fox.

"How you like those boots?" Fox asked.

The fellow blushed. "Fine. Real comfortable," he said, eyeing his charges.

"Wait until you get down the path a ways," Fox laughed. "Be so comfortable you can't stand 'em."

Several Scouts sat on a stone parapet facing the dam and watched a man dip for fish. The man used a long, boom-like pole with a minnow net attached to its tip; he wasn't catching much. He was with his young son. They were dressed in tattered coveralls and were very country. The man worked his rig hard, paying little attention to the Scouts' questions.

He was rude.

The son walked over our way.

"What you dipping for, boy?" Fox asked.

The son looked up, poleaxed, and said: "Thuckers." He let the word drip from his lips like pabulum.

"Walk over there and tell your old man he's an asshole," Fox said. And bit the head off a Slim Jim.

The wide parking lot at Four Locks was crowded with vans. Rank rock wheezed through velveteen interiors, mussing sweet things' eardrums, tugging at haltertops, keeping everyone's nerves jangled in Sunday fettle. Dirt bikes screamed up embankments, idling *putaputput, puuuuuut,* to accelerate again. Sunday boat jockeys disembarked passengers from the Four Locks ramp, embarked others and *rannnnngged* back toward the river.

We paused for lunch in the grass by Lock 47 and observed. Our kingdom for a bazooka, a howitzer, or a laser gun. String up the idiot who'd invented the two-stroke engine, hang his ass from a tree limb, feed his nuts to a catfish. We passed close by one van, asking directions, hinting for a boat-ride upriver. Nobody knew anything. Nobody offered squat. One bottomfeeder dipped a Diet-Rite from a cooler packed high with Pabst Blue Ribbon, poking it our way. The music was so loud she didn't hear what Fox called her.

We hiked past Fort Frederick and Big Pool, picking up Interstate 70 at Licking Creek Aqueduct around dusk. Interstate 70 ran parallel to the towpath, which here was dark and overgrown. We startled four deer below Little Pool. They'd been feeding along the berm and were trapped between I -70 and the canal. One was a buck, extremely large and abnormally shaded, like a Holstein. Spotting us, the herd crashed to and fro, confused as to an escape route. Finally it broke downstream, making a great noise as the deer tore through the brush. You could barely hear it over the roar of traffic.

That night it grew cold, but the sky stayed clear and exhilaratingly full with the sound of trucks, trains, and night birds. We pitched camp slowly and got a fire going. To our rear lay Interstate 70, then the canal, then fifty feet of campsite, our tent, the Potomac River with the B&O Railroad at its far bank. We were camped amid two centuries of hysterical transportation, four different modes—five, if one counted an occasional airplane. Fox took several heartless tugs on the J. W. Dant and retired to his Sleepy Owl. I built up the fire and dissolved toward night. I knew it would be a long one. Lulled by trucks, shaken awake by trains, I was musing upon similarities between television and flickering firelight when the rain started and I crawled toward our tent.

"IF YOU AIN'T CIRCLE-track racing," someone hooted, "you depriving yourself of one of the greatest pleasures in life." Fox was arguing cars with various rain-idled construction workers, nodding, and making points between huge bites of double cheeseburger. Triangle Motel's bar had been packed since morning with every sort of Hancock entrepreneur, Hancock, Maryland being that sort of town where you either entrepreneur or starve. Interstate 70 bypassed the little village, and so did the canal. Between 1818 and 1850, Hancock had been a major stop on the National Road. She'd been a notorious saloon nexus, remaining so well into the nineteenth century. But the railroad killed that, even as it would kill the ditch. Drivers along National Road had been a special breed of wild man. They'd captained boat-shaped Conestogas, drawn by six fast horses, from Baltimore to Wheeling and back, with hardly a stop but to carouse in taverns and harass pretty women. They'd been legend throughout the valley, as proud and crazed as buccaneers. Young men once had longed to drive the National Road as others later would dream of piloting Spacecraft. These Hancockians were descendants—in spite of Interstate 70, in spite of the railroad.

They'd been drinking Rolling Rock drafts and snowshoes since morning, though, because the rain was a torrent, because it was Monday and nobody felt right anyhow. A sign behind Triangle's bar read:

EASTER SPECIAL
MOGEN DAVID
$1.75 A FIFTH

Easter was still two weeks off, but all of Hancock was decorated with bunnies and baskets, Day-Glo eggs, and jelly beans. We'd hiked down Main Street before settling into Triangle, and every door had boasted some Easter finery. Hancock was a rough little town with many handsome houses unspoiled by the restorer's greed. I'd liked it immediately. We'd bought dry T-shirts at Hancock Rescue Mission for a half-dollar apiece, and these drafts we were drinking, fat twelve-ouncers, cost a mere thirty cents.

What the hell *was* a hoggee, anyway? Hooper had been a hoggee—muledriver on the towpath—but that hardly explained the thing. What kind of man would spend his life hiking through muleshit at two miles an hour, or, for that matter, riding aboard a canal boat—not a ship, not a wagon, but a hybrid every bit as unattractive as the mules that pulled it? What the hell was a canal captain? Not a sailor, not a teamster, not even a drover. After all the literature I'd read and all the people I'd spoken with, I still couldn't tell. Didn't have an inkling. They must have been strange men, dull as the life they led—plodding, familial, irrevocably harnessed to commerce. A stagecoach driver or a privateer I could fathom, but a canal boat captain seemed beyond comprehension.

A kid in a complex head-and-neck brace took the stool beside me. He ordered a beer. He raised it to his mouth carefully. His brace was steel, and ran from his hips to the top of his head.

"How you doin'," I said.

The fellow swiveled, back immobile, and smiled. "I'll make it."

"Where'd you collect that wire? If you don't mind my asking."

"I don't mind. Don't mind one bit. I flipped my Camaro, got hung up in a ditch."

I bought him a drink. Outside, rain still blanketed the Westvaco lumberyard and only an occasional truck pulled by. A tame mallard waddled down Triangle's walk, disappearing into an adjacent game room. Someone in there was ringing hell out of pinball machine. Here inside Triangle's barroom it was very smoky, steam rising off damp Hancockians in billows, jukebox throaty, food hot, and the beer ice-cold.

Fox was conversing with a sandbagger named Rust. All they seemed to talk about was kicking ass; but friendly. There was a little old lady at the far end of the bar who had to be ninety. I moved off in her direction. Back in our room were two soggy packs, three clotheslines strung with wet gear, a tent that stunk like oatmeal, a TV set, and several books about the C&O Canal. I wanted to hear some stories.

"YUP," FOX SAID, sipping from a cup of dehydrated soup, "my one ambition is to open a used car lot, somewhere like the Midwest where the cars don't rust."

We were up around Dam 6, reclining against a moss-covered log overlooking a dangerous stretch of river, and Fox's comment took me by surprise.

"What's that?" I said. "What, Bob?"

Then let it drop. After eight days on the trail we'd reached that point where either we traded ideas hysterically or walked long miles in silence, bracketing rest stops with non sequiturs. I was chewing a Sycamore branch, contemplating the view, and saw no cause for a rejoinder.

I was thinking about Dam 6—how right here in 1842 the Canal Company had run out of funds and halted construction. How Mile 134 had remained the canal's western terminus for eight crucial years; during which the B&O reached Cumberland and pushed on to Pittsburgh, effectively sealing the ditch's fate. The canal above Dam 6 ran fifty miles to Cumberland, the toughest of its length. Ten million dollars had been spent to reach Mile 134, another $12 million required for the last fifty. It was here that the canal had truly died, and what survived, Dam 6, seemed a fitting headstone.

We saddled our packs and hiked toward a region that mirrored this death. Cliffs pressed closer, rocks took on a sharpness, mountains and rough foliage reached about us. The landscape was like some allegorical passageway in a Hudson River School painting: overlarge, romantic, a testing ground for *wunderkind*. A black swamp oozed from the canal bed, its water thick, miasmic, aswarm with reptiles—snakes, spotted turtles, a chorus of frogs. A light drizzle would start, stop, then begin again. The towpath proceeded purgatorially, minus any sign of humanity or hope.

We pitched camp at Lock 57, quickly laying a fire. After supper and several nips of sour mash, we felt stronger. But the countryside stayed spooky. Two houses faced our campsite from the West Virginia bank; we saw no activity in their yards. They sat smack up against the B&O tracks, and as a freight train roared through the final gloaming two shotgun blasts barked and an air whistle screamed maniacally.

"I THINK I KNOW something of what you talking," the wan fellow said. He spat out a limp toothpick and bent closer. "I once walked six and a half months from Georgia to California. Wore out four pair of them tennis shoes. I carried a pack. Never ate much. Got so hot I wound up hiking at night, slept during the day in brush swales—like a hawg."

Fox and I set down cold drafts and started at this apparition grimacing from the dark end of Bill's Little Orleans bar. "I never called home or nothing," the fellow added, then ambled slowly toward the door. He was white as pastry, soft as pudding, and looked like maybe he'd been hit in the head.

"For real?" I asked the barmaid.

"For real," she said, and drew another beer.

Bill's place was a combination general store, saloon, hunters' oasis, museum, dance hall, and restaurant. At 10:00 a.m. we were Bill's only customers, but the place looked like it might hop later in the day. The building was 150 years old, formerly a warehouse and supply depot for C&O boats. It had originally faced the canal, but had been moved a hundred yards inland in 1905 to make way for the railroad.

Guns dripped off the walls, hung from every available inch of space: shotguns, rifles, pistols, automatics. They did not seem out of synch, as quite a bit of rioting had occurred at Little Orleans, rioting among canal workers in 1838 following a secession of payments by Canal Company officials. No doubt justified rioting. Irish laborers, angered when German workers were shipped in as scabs, clubbed at least one to death with shillelaghs, roasting another over an open pit. That had led to skirmishes with state militia, the acquisition of more than five hundred guns by the Irish, and rioting from Little Orleans to Paw Paw—today's destination. The guns at Bill's were apropos, but not reassuring.

It was a hard sixteen miles to Paw Paw, and the vibrations here were discomfiting enough. I girded up with cold beers and a new pair of socks, Fox with cold beers and a 75-cent fishing cap. Somewhere Fox had lifted a STROH'S IS LOVE bumper sticker; he wore it slashed across the back of his pack.

We had been nursing sore feet and bitching about the final forty-four miles to Cumberland when this wan fellow had spoken. His comment had cut us to size. If we hadn't been hurting so bad we might have sloughed it off. But we were damaged. There is an ailment called a march fracture that afflicts hikers' arches, and I feared I might be suffering from it. Fox had pulled a groin muscle and the blisters covering his feet were pitiful to see. No question, as level walkers we were rubes.

I was worried about my arches and scared that Fox wouldn't make it. What's worse, might bolt. He'd started nipping Dant at every rest stop. I'd caught him nudging gear out of his pack just to break stride and guzzle a drink. All he could talk about now was cars. Cars, Hooper Wolfe, and hitchhiking.

We had Paw Paw Tunnel coming up—a premier attraction along the towpath—and I was damned if I would let Fox miss it. At Paw Paw bends, the canal skirted six miles of meandering river with a 3,118-foot tunnel cut through rock. We had seen the canal ford rivers, we had seen it hug impossible cliffs. But we had not seen it flow through a mountain, and if I had to kick Fox like a football he was going to make it. Paw Paw remained sixteen miles uptowpath; I had my work cut out for me.

Fox was already a little delirious.

North of Little Orleans the countryside stayed ominous, the canal lagoon-like and fetid. Fox kept raving about "gobs," spooks and "haints" that might accost us. As long as I held him to automobiles, things sort of stabilized. We speculated about car washes for backpackers—how you'd hand a man a dollar and hike on through, getting that much-needed shower without missing a beat. We joked about Park Service golf carts. The towpath grew insistently macabre. "I don't want to die on this Hooper Highway," Fox groaned. "I want to go out like an American—in the front seat, by the bottle, or with cancer of the rectum." Dark shale overhung the towpath, and the canal wound back and forth, making it difficult to ascertain direction. We were deep into mountain country, beneath cliffs and precipices that truly resembled the Catskills. The sun would darken, drop behind a mountain, then we'd catch it again on the far side. We hiked through periodic showers.

It was well after five when we reached Paw Paw gorge. Locks ran close together here, raising the canal dramatically in a very short distance. Construction equipment lined the towpath, and restoration work was underway. Massive slides of shale filled the canal. Bulldozers rested in two feet of water; heavy trucks and earth movers blocked the towpath. A half-mile short of the downstream portal a sign announced that Paw Paw Tunnel was closed.

I took the empty pint of Dant and slung it hard against that part which read NATIONAL PARK SERVICE. We were sore and hurt, and the only alternative was to hike uphill an extra mile over the mountain. It was getting dark. We had our adrenalin up. There were two feet of icy water in the canal for a couple of hundred yards ahead, and a barrier to climb, but I thought we could manage it. The tunnel's mouth was around the bend. We were deep in a gorge, shaled cliffs above us, implanted at the face of the mountain. We climbed down a catwalk and hiked into the canal.

We crashed through its filthy water, stumbling across shale. But our heavy boots kept our balance. Those damned boots! If we slipped in this water, wetting parkas and sleeping gear, we'd be in trouble. We considered very little of that. The tunnel's maw was before us, a tiny speck of light at its center. We crawled over a barricade, shaking water from our jeans. Then we were inside.

It was absolutely black. There was the trickle of water dripping off walls and the clump of our boots. It was cold. The towpath ran elevated inside the tunnel, with the original wooden rail at our right hand; restoration crews had not touched that. We used flashlights, but they shone dimly. We could make out damp brick walls. We could see the canal bed, black, where Lord knows what manner of creature lived. Fox was silent in a way that communicated terror. Halfway through, the light upstream seemed hardly brighter.

There was a history to the tunnel that I thought to relate, but it paled in comparison to the desperate elation we felt. I searched for details to lighten the mood, but every fact seemed to enunciate pain. Pain was the name of Paw Paw Tunnel. The pain of indentured service, pain of canal company failure, pain of fourteen years' digging, pain of mules and hoggees and backpackers. It wasn't picturesque, it was painful. It was far from romantic, it was horrifying. Fox wasn't even dropping jokes about the Lincoln Tunnel.

After fifteen minutes we were through, scrambling across a ten-foot fence and hoisting backpacks to each other. We were out of the mountain. Immediately the landscape changed. It was not our imaginations, the canal simply spread out. Cliffs retreated, vegetation

overpowered shale, and stretching to Paw Paw there was
light, blessed light.

BENNY CLARK'S TAVERN was the worst-looking redneck
joint I'd seen, but we'd hiked a mile for a drink and there
wasn't any way we weren't going in. Benny's was the only
bar near Paw Paw, West Virginia. We'd pulled up a long
hill to reach it—cussing, sweating, dragging crippled legs
behind us-and I sort of wished someone would mess with
us. I was tired but felt tough as leather; I was ten pounds
underweight but what I carried was all muscle. Paw Paw
nurtured a reputation for violence—from canal days and
workers' riots to present-day residents shooting up state
police. But its reputation was no more riotous than our
mood.

I hit Benny's tavern a hundred yards ahead of Fox. Still
wearing my pack, I walked to the bar and called for a
beer. I called for two beers. I was bearded, smelly, clad
in T-shirt and muddy jeans, and water squished audibly
from my boots. I had that hair you love to touch. Four
or five of the roughest-looking hillbillies I ever saw stared
at me in silence. I drank off my first beer and dove for
the second. I ordered three Polish sausages and a sack of
chips. About that time Fox limped in.

"You boys been trappin' groundhog?" a man beside
me asked. He had no teeth, was unshaven, dirty, and
looked even mangier than us. I glanced around the room.
Nobody looked any better than us. "You oughta *try* that
young groundhog," the fellow drawled. "Bread it up
good, fry it crisp, tastes better'n chicken."

We were among friends. Pretty soon we had our boots
off, were skating around in stocking feet, trading stories,
chugging countless beers, and punching pocketsful of
quarters into the juke. There were two fat mountain girls,
a pool table, and any number of good old boys to kid.
We crunched up in Benny's beat wooden booths and
absorbed. There was a train wreck north of Paw Paw,
threatening to leak chlorine gas, but nobody at Benny's

appeared concerned. That motherhumping railroad. There were little kids poking our packs, and pickups raking out of the parking lot. There was Paw Paw's sheriff loping in, big and jovial, his hair longer than mine, and there was Benny Clark's wife boiling water for our freeze-dried dinners.

She'd never seen one. We sat shoeless, eating supper from a plastic bag, and folks couldn't have cared less. Toward midnight Benny collared a fellow named Bud, who owned Paw Paw's Sunoco station, and got him to run us back to camp. We hadn't even asked. But Benny Clark knew. Fox bought a bumper of Stroh's and we piled into Bud's Bronco.

It was our last night on the trail.

A STORM BROKE about 3:00 a.m. I awoke with the first thunder, in time to watch a mountainous cloud darken the sky. It drew blackness across our moonlit meadow like a shade. We were camped near a canal workers' graveyard, on the stone porch of a deserted log house, and long before the storm reached us I could see hail and wind and rain tearing up the grass. Then the entire house trembled. We were huddled at porch's center under a flimsy roof; oddly, we did not get wet. The rain swirled and spat hail all about us from a sky as dark as a tunnel. But we stayed dry.

Next morning we hiked back through drenched grass to the towpath. We were fuzzy from all that beer, but the air was clean. We hiked past last evening's derailed train, its cargo of chlorine gas presumably secure. Scores of workers skittered across its belly. At least there'd be no agitating rail traffic this afternoon.

There wasn't much of anything. There were fewer people along the towpath here than at Taylor's Landing. All around us were mountains, stiff wind, and the canal—little more than a trickle. At Town Creek Aqueduct we faced another detour; since workmen were about, we saw no way to finesse it. We limped onto Highway 51 and stuck out our thumbs.

At Oldtown we banged on the pickup's rear window, signaling the driver to stop. He was heading into Cumberland. We hiked resolutely back toward the canal. But not before eating a leisurely lunch outside Lewis's Grocery, rancid hoagies exacerbating gastric distress.

At Oldtown Lock the canal had been watered. Not just watered but stocked with bass, crappie, even a trout or two. Several fishermen braved the March wind; no one appeared to be catching much.

Above Oldtown the canal resumed its characteristic level...one or two feet deep. The landscape continued to soften, however. Mountains receded, the path was less rocky, and a deciduous warmth overwhelmed the scrub.

By early afternoon the day had grown warm. Wide meadows separated canal and river, cattle grazing to the towpath's edge, ducks and strange birds exploding from the ditch. We took frequent breaks. Fox lolled on the bank, poking carp with a stick and exclaiming, "Them's suckers, Bob." It was the first time I'd caught him showing interest in wildlife.

A mile short of Spring Gap—the day's destination—Fox suggested another break. The spot was gray and thickly wooded, but the sun shone warmly enough to make things comfortable. We broke out our little stove and boiled water for coffee. I dozed in the high grass, hat pulled over my eyes, parka open to the sunshine. That night we would sleep at a friend's farm, in beds, with clean sheets. Tomorrow we would ride the last ten miles into Cumberland on horseback; we would dutifully note where Western Maryland Railroad station squatted within the ancient canal basin at the towpath's western terminus. We would endure a weekend of unparalleled revelry—followed, Lord save us, by a train ride home along the route we'd just hiked. We would begin to recover. It made no sense, but here in the warm grass, with our stove hissing and coffee bubbling, we didn't want the trip to end.

I raised up on one elbow and sipped from a steaming cup. Fox stared meditatively across the canal bed.

"You know, Bob," he said. "You know..."

I leaned forward.

"...Soon as I get home I'm going to shed these boots, hop in my car, and drive all over town barefoot."

Washingtonian, 1977

The Beltway

Before Interstate 495 there was Route 240. Heading north. A calm road, linear, minus a circle to confuse, 240 ran straight to Frederick above restful pastureland, placid Guernseys and a dotting of red barns, to an actual Midwest beyond. The Midwest was presumed actual, though never perceived, for Frederick was the finish...a spot for negotiating U-turns.

Archaic automobiles bobbed atop the bubbling macadam (it was always midsummer on 240): sleek plesiosauri with undulating fins, subcaudal blinker lights in tear-drop or mortar-point trim; boxy pickups and tractor-trailers after the old style, scuttling north with deliberate gustiness, as if self-propelled from weed patch to bridge piling, thankful to make cover. There was a 1959 Bonneville with a 300-horsepower engine, 389 cubic inches nested into the widest, longest passenger frame Detroit produced. There were white vinyl seats with aqua trim, a bright chromium instrument panel canopied like an F-series jet's, and more interior space than six slightly hysterical teenagers could fill. It was a car built for the open road, and 240 was that.

A cooler of beer, Mighty Mo wrappers from the Bethesda Hot Shoppes, damp loafers or discarded tennis sweaters, wet bathing suits, hot fudge ice-cream-cake cartons, music from WDON, and the cruise control set at 120. Route 240 catapulted that Bonneville to Frederick in less time than it took to chugalug a six-pack of malt liquor. One hundred twenty miles an hour with the radio loud and the air conditioner on high. Weaving through a wagon train of lesser vehicles traveling just half one's speed—like negotiating a lot full of parked cars at sixty.

The road was straight and faraway, the activity ecstatic. There was a circle at the Bethesda Shoppes, where one made his play, and there was the U-turn at Frederick. Often one sat at the Shoppes and allowed himself to be circled. A 1949 Jeepster was prime for that, the piss-yellow Willys, good to whip up on an occasional Falcon or Corvair along Rockville Pike, but inadequate for 240. Zero to fifty she was quick, but much over that and you risked throwing a rod. Perfect for the Shoppes, though… top down, summertime music, seeing and being seen as a caravan of outrageous vehicles lapped the premises.

Then there was a 1962 Corvette, and the circle began to constrict. White, fourspeed box, 300-horsepower mill, with a frame so stiff that the whole seemed a block of fiberglass. The circle narrowed to Connecticut Avenue, a perpetual lapping of that Hot Shoppes, the inevitable rumble and squeal as Traction Masters sighed, dual Holleys spilled fuel about the pavement, and a scent of scorched oil hung above the special sauce, the Hot Shoppes' French fries after midnight—rare perfume.

There were short sprints from a stoplight at Macomb, more deliberate challenges along three ridiculous lanes of Reno Road, timed mini-prix the length of Normanstone (Little Monza), plus occasional hegiras to Aquasco Speedway or 75-80 Dragway for the legal test.

But street racing predominated. It sped one south along 29-211 to Charlottesville and university parties never to be forgotten, it blasted one to Richmond, east on Highway 60 to Williamsburg and half an hour of one hundred mile-per-hour cruising through pine forests so sparse they threatened to hypnotize with ten thousand flickers of sunlight. Then a cross-continent drive to San Francisco so redolent of *Route 66* as to approach fatuity. Home, and rumors of a new road-to be opened in a few years; it would encircle the city. Sixty odd miles of high-speed Interstate that would *circle the city.* Could the soul comprehend? A natural Le Mans in the night, sixty-odd miles of Le Mans being constructed *legally* by the state for our delectation. One awaited not so frantically the date, August 17, 1964, when the Capital Beltway would open, but an evening sometime before: the monster asleep without a truck on its back, lying like a great serpent enveloping the city, burning nary a light, macadam as yet unlined, exits blocked, no police, an open road to nowhere, an invitation to emptiness. And speed.

TROOPER DAVID WASHINGTON hung in the shadows near call box 217 and watched Beltway traffic swim by. Green numbers flashed across his face as he studied the radar and his mirror...58, 62, 60, 67...cars plummeted downhill on that last wide stretch north of the Cabin John Bridge, sprinting for Virginia.

"This is a good spot," Trooper Washington mused. "Always seem to speed up a little here." He sat quietly, watching radar blip through the darkness of the patrol car...59, 62, 73. *"Seventy-three,"* Washington muttered, "that's a ticket." His big Plymouth exploded, 460 horses powering toward an outside lane in a fusillade of red and blue lights, whooping sirens, and flashing emergency signals; the acceleration proved unnerving, seventy, eight in less than ten seconds, Trooper Washington on the violator's bumper, a black Cutlass with pinstripe trim, Maryland tags, and slowing—Washington calling in the vehicle's tag number and approximate location before hitting disc brakes and slamming to a stop in a shower of gravel and ice. Red light spinning, traffic coursing by, Washington strutted to the driver's window, adjusting his sidearm for access and his hat for aplomb.

The driver handed over license and registration without being asked; Washington walked back to the patrol car. Five minutes later he had written a ticket for forty dollars and his sleek yellow Plymouth was inching again toward the shadows.

BY 1965, EXPLORATION via motorcycle had become the psychic mandate of all those who looked to the Beltway for darker sustenance. A 305cc Honda, fine for darting through traffic in daytime sprints, soon was found wanting. A 750cc Norton took its place, an English machine of such grace, such power and suppressed rage, that to pilot it once around a block was to experience the incongruities of the fatherland.

After midnight one swept toward Virginia, crossing the Potomac at Cabin John astride an insidious swath of molecules; hair askew, lips parted, shirt open to the waist, Levi's torn, feet sockless and barely covered by Wellingtons trussed up with tape. There was nothing like protection, just sweet vulnerability. At eighty, one shifted lazily into fourth gear and the brutish machine throbbed from foot peg to handle grip. Close to ninety, one's teeth set on edge; there began the whine of dentist's drill. The Beltway remained dark but for porch lights of farm houses—no monolithic apartment complexes had then been constructed, no chthonic shopping malls—and as one flew past Vienna, past Fairfax toward Alexandria, one knew the wind, the blackest rural night, and a kinship to speed that approached the elemental.

One sensed that what Einstein had discovered of matter—that through velocity, mass might ineluctably be altered—had been considered old news by every farm boy who had pushed a modified stocker to its limits along a deserted country road.

The lights of Alexandria snatched one temporarily

toward the city, and as the Norton hurtled over water for a second crossing, the Washington Monument buoyed to the north like a giant Maypole. Past Woodrow Wilson Bridge the countryside opened; one flattened to the seat and cranked it on: 100, 110, 115 miles per hour...no sound but the whir of a cyclotron, no drag on the bike but an oblique centripetency. One did not forget the sight of Washington's monument, nor lose the tension of its pull. It was as if one rode leashed. Deep in concentration, negotiating the slalom west of Connecticut Avenue at 105 miles per hour, the great white obelisk stayed fixed on the retina, exerting force.

Later, above Great Falls near the foot of Falls Road, one rested against the Norton and gazed downriver at Washington's monument. Like a communication tower it stood against the night, red beams constant, white marble bathed in artificial light. It drew one mysteriously toward the center with the inexorable pull of tide. Yet the center was what one fled.

"YOU'VE PROBABLY SEEN this on *Emergency,*" the young lieutenant said, opening a left rear compartment of Bethesda-Chevy Chase Rescue Squad's $85,000 Kenworth crash truck. "It's a Hurst tool. For extrications."

The lieutenant gestured toward a thick, two-pronged device elongated like a hemostat, its painted iron scarred.

"A pair of mechanized pliers, actually, capable of parting ten thousand pounds of wreckage." He shut the cabinet smartly, walking to the opposite side of the truck. "Here we have an acetylene torch, for extrications requiring the cutting of metal. These hooks are for dragging wreckage from a precipice, for clearing an accident site. These eight floodlights are for illuminating the scene or to assist in fighting fires. Like I say, you probably know all this from *Emergency.*"

A series of alarms sounded within the building and several tall Rescue Squad doors raised automatically. One of the smaller crash trucks hurried into the night.

The young lieutenant cocked his ear to the various signals. "That's an automobile accident now," he said, vaulting casually aboard the idled rescue truck. He fiddled with a length of rope, as if pondering how best to conclude his tour.

"Sounds like it may even be a pinning."

WHEN PIERRE CHARLES L'ENFANT composed his plan for the city of Washington in 1791, he specified a monument to be placed at that point where two principal axes, north-south and east-west, were to intersect. It happens that these axes crossed near the exact center of George Washington's ten-mile square. Though the Washington Monument was later constructed slightly off kilter—due to marshland at L'Enfant's preferred location—the great obelisk today, for psychological intents and purposes, stands at city center. If one studies almost any traffic map of the greater metropolitan area, with George Washington's original ten-mile square stenciled over Arlington and Alexandria, one will see the Washington Monument likewise near dead center. Standing farther back, one will notice the Capital Beltway, in truth more circular than amoeboid, encompassing the whole...Robert Mills's 555-foot Egyptian obelisk sprouting inscrutably from the pith.

L'Enfant's original intention for the spot was a gigantic equestrian statue of General Washington in full regalia, astride a blustering charger. Robert Mills's obelisk, in his 1836 design, boasted at its base a circular building one-hundred feet high, topped by neoclassical columns and statues...that included a chariot drawn by four horses abreast. These architects' fantasies of motion and circularity were not shared by George Washington in his plans for the federal district. He envisioned the seat of government quadratically: as a square. Though the Residence Bill of July 1790 had authorized selection of a site "not exceeding 10 miles square," it was for George Washington to choose a tract and ultimately to decide its parameters.

Symbolism of the square could not have been lost on General Washington...freemason, classicist, and scion of the Enlightenment. For the seat of a new government, one of history's few planned capitals, the square must have been an obvious choice. The square symbolized stability, firmness, and definition. It appealed to rational intellect. It conveyed the permanence of earth, of its four seasons, four elements, four points of the compass, the four seasons of man's life; his four humors, four temperaments, four virtues. It suggested organization and construction, and was inextricably tied to symbolism of the number four. Ternary symbolism, and the symbolism of odd numbers generally, was to be shunned. Odd numbers suggested circularity, were too dynamic. In Eastern symbology, the circle represented activity or the masculine principle, as opposed to the black square, representing earth and passivity, the feminine principle. The circle stood for heaven and things spiritually empyrean, too flighty a symbol for a federal district.

George Washington went with the square.

His architect, the Frenchman L'Enfant, showed a marked proclivity for broad vistas and epigraphs of circularity. Like Thomas Sutpen's "French architect" in Faulkner's *Absalom, Absalom!*, L'Enfant had been virtually plucked from polite civilization and hurled at the wilderness, to be flicked away once his usefulness had ebbed. L'Enfant's original plan had called for grand avenues up to 400 feet wide and a mile long, that would radiate like spokes of a wheel from strategic circles. Each circle would contain a monument at its center. These circles worked as a cautionary measure—they broke the city into defensible segments, stood at the head of avenues to ward off dissident mobs or marauding armies—but their primary intention was symbolic.

The circle or disk, especially when surrounded by rays, was emblematic of the sun. To an eighteenth-century artist, the sun symbolized many things, not the least of which was a heroic principle—courageous and spiritually active, aggressive, intellectual, violent, yet curiously suggestive of a source of life and the latent wholeness of man. L'Enfant's vision for Washington City was born of the Enlightenment, an age that failed to notice irony in the amalgamation of government and truth. Once L'Enfant had been fired—hounded from his job by landholders who did not share his passion for the symbolic, not at their expense, and had been dismissed by General Washington, whom he had sought to honor—perhaps he saw a soupçon of irony then. Perhaps L'Enfant cultivated that irony during the thirty subsequent years he spent designing gardens around Washington City, his plan—but for the Capitol and White House—uncompleted. Possibly L'Enfant felt nothing and barely smirked from beyond the pale when Boss Alexander Shepherd re-implemented his plan in the 1870s, embellishing it to a Victorian T. Probably L'Enfant's ghost managed a smile during the 1960s when nameless technocrats from administrative think tanks enveloped the ten-mile square with Interstate 495, a grand avenue worthy of the Frenchman's vision.

OF THE 63.8-MILE LOOP of the Capital Beltway, Trooper David Washington patrols approximately a fifth, from the Maryland state line at Cabin John Bridge to the Montgomery County line west of New Hampshire Avenue. This stretch, according to Bethesda-Chevy Chase Rescue Squad chief, David Dwyer, is as dangerous as any along the Beltway. "It's those curves," Dwyer says. "People tend to speed into a curve, and when Beltway curves are wet they're slicker than glass."

A disabled tractor-trailer from New Jersey perched along such a curve near call box 417, nursing a broken wheel bearing and a comfortless load of rock salt. "We try to get round this Beltway just as fast as we can," the driver said. He spoke with an Australian drawl. "You have no truck stops, no spots to get service, so we gas up good before coming 'round and hope to make it through."

The Australian rested against the back seat of Trooper

Washington's patrol car and sipped a cup of coffee.

"Laurel has one or two truckstops off Interstate 95," Washington said. "Frederick off Interstate 270 has a couple, but the nearest service for any major truck repair is one-hundred miles south, near Richmond." He swiveled toward the back seat, looking professionally sympathetic. "I'm afraid you're in for a long night."

The Australian snorted and scuffled back to his rig, tractor idling, heater laboring against the ten-degree chill. Trooper Washington slipped his Plymouth into gear and prepared to renegotiate the stream of heavy evening traffic. Over the past hour he had responded to the Australian's call for assistance, chauffeured him to a public telephone, paused at a coffee shop for the driver's convenience, chauffeured him back, then had to repeat the same basic maneuvers when a trucking firm in New Jersey demanded further description of the trailer's damaged part. Trooper Washington was clearly annoyed. He accelerated powerfully as the Australian climbed back into his cab and bedded down for the night.

"We're out here to serve the public," Washington said, "but that kind of inconvenience is ridiculous."

He leaned forward and switched his AM radio to a rhythm-and-blues station in the District. Funky disco strains filtered through the squawk of the police band, settled over the sparse interior, seemed to soften harsh paramilitary fixtures.

Trooper Washington began to hum.

A thirty-year-old black man, stocky, good natured, diligent in his work, Washington could laugh when fellow troopers joked about the Capital Beltway, calling it "Congo Bypass." He had been raised in Foggy Bottom, had graduated from Roosevelt High School, and had attended the University of Maryland as a communications major.

"Broadcasting," Washington said, still moving to the funky beat. "Broadcasting is what I was about."

A roughened billy club hung from the dash, a pair of

handcuffs lay hooked over the emergency-brake release, a heavy black flashlight sat on the front seat next to Washington's ticket book, and a Sylvester the Cat incenser dangled incongruously from the turn signal. "Sometimes I'll burn a little incense," Washington said.

It was warm in the patrol car. Safe. We hurtled through and around traffic with impunity. Suddenly Trooper Washington's conversation broke and his gaze began to stiffen. He pulled into the passing lane, tracking a rented Capri for perhaps half a mile before sounding his siren. Fourteen points over the speed limit. Another forty-dollar ticket.

"I rarely get offered bribes," he said. "But there's something about people from Illinois. They'll slip you a twenty with their license and registration, not think anything about it. 'Course there's no way I'd jeopardize my job for that. Can't imagine how much money it would take to bribe me."

An all-points bulletin shot across the police band, concerning a twenty-nine-year-old white male wanted for questioning in the homicide of two West Virginia troopers. David Washington listened solemnly then shook his head.

"People are crazy," he said.

It was well after midnight, so Washington wore his Safariland armored vest and, in addition to the standard Colt .38 Police Special, carried a 9 mm Beretta in his jacket pocket. With each stop he made, even for a routine traffic violation, he radioed in his call number, approximate location, a description of the vehicle, and tag number before he stepped out of the patrol car.

"Should have been with me last week," Washington grinned. "Detained a guy for speeding, turned out to be driving a stolen car. Made the arrest but I encountered some trouble. You can't ever tell what you'll run into out here."

A shadow swept past along the shoulder, and Washington braked, backing carefully until a solitary hitchhiker crept into view. Washington hit his lights and motioned the man toward the car.

It was close to zero outside, yet the hitchhiker was dressed in bluejeans and a light Levi's jacket. He had reasonably long hair and a beard, and as he hit the patrol car's back seat he failed to even shiver.

"Where you headed?" Washington asked. The young man handed over one or two pieces of plasticized identification.

"Ohio. Barberton, Ohio."

"Where you headed from?"

"Portsmouth. I got a friend down there."

"You know it's illegal to hitchhike on this road?"

Silence.

"You know how cold it is outside tonight? You have any money?"

"I got some money."

"Well, maybe you better spend it on a bus. Too cold to hitchhike tonight. Farther north you get, worse it will be."

The young man sat without moving under the interior light as Trooper Washington cleared his identity with the Rockville barracks.

"Barberton, Ohio," Washington said, handing back the young man's ID. "I got some relatives there." The young man looked surprised but said nothing. "Tell you what," Washington said. "I'll run you a ways up 270 and you can hitchhike off that ramp near the Rockville barracks. That's a police installation, so if you get too cold you can walk down and warm up. Now, I don't want to catch you back on this Interstate."

The young man said nothing, and when we stopped at Route 28 he quietly got out.

Ten minutes later we heard over the squawk box another trooper radioing in the young man's identification, having stopped him for hitchhiking again.

"People are crazy," Washington reiterated. "I mean you could *die* out here."

We snaked through the turns west of Connecticut Avenue, the wide Beltway deserted, moonlight slicing off riverbeds of ice that were the median and shoulders, winter sky transparent so that walls of the Mormon Temple shown white as alabaster, stained glass windows bright as neon beer signs.

At a 7-Eleven outside Wheaton, Trooper Washington swigged anxiously from a large cup of cocoa and looked around him. The 7-Eleven was empty but for a clerk. Its interior was disconcertingly bright, fixtures helplessly immobile after the patrol-car's velocity. This was the first break Washington had taken in nearly four hours. He looked as if he could not wait to get back underway.

"Let's move," he said, striding impatiently toward the door. "These damn places are always getting robbed."

EXPOSURE TO THE CAPITAL Beltway affects people in different ways. Tom Daniels, sculptor, who secured his reputation in "drag art" by chaining a junked washing machine to the bumper of his van and dragging it across the Delaware Memorial Bridge, toll booths included, relaxes by dragging old toasters about the Capital Beltway—then marketing the end product as sculpture.

Another conceptual artist, FP, has written an experimental novel, *Dead Dogs on the Beltway*—a narrative of indescribable carnage and psychic displacement. Patricia Sherman, president of Happy Hooker Ltd., has painted her tow truck a shocking pink, applied for accreditation by the Maryland State Police, and awaits whatever calls to Beltway service might drift her way. Hers is a twenty-four-hour towing service. Bruce Springsteen, composer—heralded for lyrics such as "The highway's jammed with broken heroes/On a last chance power drive"—on the occasion of his first appearance in Washington, drove around the Beltway a time and a half before he could muscle out of the fast lane and force his way in toward the center.

Washington's most ecstatic entertainment has, for some years, appeared outside George Washington's ten-mile square. Desperate little clubs such as Fred and Sully's, the Birchmere, the Crossroads, the Italian Gardens, the Red Fox, the Psychedelly, and others have served Beltway mavericks cold beer at acceptable prices, and have offered Washington's most successfully experimental bands—those playing country-rock—a more enthusiastic audience and more relaxed surroundings in which to gig. It was at Beltway bars that the Seldom Scene, the Rosslyn Mountain Boys, and Emmylou Harris honed their acts to near perfection, establishing the basis of their local following. It is in Beltway bars that inner-square groups such as Liz Meyer and Friends, the Country Gentlemen, the Nighthawks, and Danny Gatton have fled to experiment with broader sounds. All that heavy energy pouring off I-495 each night, a new crowd every show, or stranger still, familiar faces the circumference of the 63.8-mile loop...out there tracking laps, swooping off at an exit here, an exit there, for a hit of musical resuscitation.

It is at the Capital Centre, near Largo, that I-495 has hosted the weirdest musical extravaganzas of recent years: concerts by the Who, the Rolling Stones, Kiss, the Band, and Bob Dylan—who responded to the salute of a thousand lighted matches by screaming, "It's good to be back in old DC."

Outside George Washington's ten-mile square exist the city's tallest broadcasting towers; they soar toward the moon of a darkened evening like red-lighted space vehicles, Christmas trees on the launching pad. Music from Washington's most exuberant stations—WHFS, WXRA, WETA—wafts out over the Interstate, fueling visions, lubricating psychic impaction. None of the inner square's repetitive rhythms here, no restrictive funk, no debilitating disco. Just the wide-open slide of a pedal steel guitar or the caterwaul of a talismanic banjo.

When one accepts the premise that Washington's Beltway is in fact circular, experience dictates the qualifier "magic" to be not altogether inappropriate. *Mandala* means "circle" in Sanskrit, an ordinary enough word, but when applied to those orbicular images composed under the hand of religious contemplation or frenzy, one acquires a larger meaning. In psychology as well as religion, mandalas are "magic" circular patterns that may be drawn, painted, modeled, or danced. Carl Gustav Jung spent much time studying mandalas, and was fascinated by their utility in the treatment of psychiatric patients. He found mandalas to appear simultaneously in dreams, states of conflict; and cases of schizophrenia. Tibetan Buddhists had used ritual mandalas *(yantras)* as objects of contemplation for centuries, but Jung established the reproduction of typical mandalas to be archetypal psychic fact. Similar magic circles containing similar symbols and arcane sets of shapes recurred in different patients from different backgrounds, indeed, different parts of the world. They were often identical to centuries-old religious emblems, and Jung believed them to spring from some communal psychic pool.

These orbicular patterns compensated for the disorder and confusion of various psychic states and invariably turned on a central point, or epicenter, to which everything psychological was related. To reproduce a mandala was an *"attempt at self-healing* on the part of Nature," Jung wrote, "which does not spring from conscious reflection but from an instinctive impulse." Patients were encouraged to draw mandalas, and to use them as instruments of contemplation, as did Buddhists and other religious groups.

The goal of such contemplation was an awareness of the mandala's center, correspondent to a center of personality suggestive of some deity or archetypal "self."

"There are innumerable variants of the [mandala] motif," Jung wrote, "but they are all based on the squaring of a circle."

This squaring of a circle Jung canonized as *"the archetype of wholeness."* Strictly speaking, squaring was a "circling of the square," for a circle formed the image's outermost border, and was employed in meditation to experience unity in the material world—equating two fundamental cosmic symbols of heaven (the circle) and earth (the square).

So contemplate again George Washington's ten-mile square, hypnotically encircled at points Falls Church, Alexandria, Seat Pleasant, and Silver Spring by the greater mandala of Interstate 495; recall L'Enfant, and cock another ear to Bruce Springsteen, who would sing: "At night we ride through / mansions of glory in suicide machines…"

The Capital Beltway is referred to concomitantly as "Washington's Main Street" and a "Road to Nowhere." There is a bit of truth in both monikers. No question but that Interstate 495 has made accessible more suburban neighborhoods to more diverse groups of people than any road in the city's history. Diminutive towns such as Tysons Corner, Springfield, Landover, Largo, even Wheaton and Silver Spring, have blossomed as centers of commerce and mass culture. The Capital Beltway is that main street that links these various enclaves, but not precisely in the manner of small-town main streets across the continent.

The small-town American main street has traditionally served its community as a route to somewhere and to no place at all. Accessibility has been its chief appeal—the accessibility of shops in a row, the convenience of nine-stop shopping—but romance has been the tickler that has kept them coming back. All those false-front buildings, branch stores of nationwide chains such as Sears or Montgomery Ward—with the same delightful products for sale that some New Yorker or Washingtonian might be purchasing this very moment—a town's best restaurant, its finest saloon, an Art Deco movie theater, a jewelry store, a sad old hotel…all practical and there to serve the public, but suggestive of escape, romantic flights of fancy, the possibilities for a richer life somewhere down the pike.

Not for nothing are main streets referred to as main drags. People cruise. Old people in 1937 Packards, five miles per hour, window shopping before every store front; young people in hemi-headed Dodges and ram-charged super Novas, drag racing between stoplights, gearing down the length of the strip in symphonies of straight exhaust, turning and cruising the main drag again. Only rarely do folks slip to a side street, only occasionally do they break off to a highway. Main Street is where it's happening for small-town America. Everything and nothing at all.

Interstate 495 may be Washington's main street, but there is a paucity of false-front architecture, or its equivalent, to be viewed from the highway. There are few electric signs, few advertisements for commerce to draw one from the flow. Beltway architecture tends toward the monumental. It is psychically oriented. Apartment complexes either squat mausoleum-like (Goddard Space Village near Greenbelt) or soar in stunted posture, veritable Stonehenges of thwarted spirituality (Promenade near Bethesda or The Château east of Silver Spring). Shopping malls are shapeless masses that suck one toward their viscera; their only architecture is interior, they are great caves of negative commerce, drawing one irretrievably underground. Indoor tennis courts pulse under bubbles of polyurethane like primitive organisms. The Capital Centre at Largo hovers like a somnolent space station, a vast puddle of concrete and steel, exhaling pneumas of the musically harmed, stout armies of inebriated sports fans.

Significantly, 495's three major pitons of psychic draw—the Mormon Temple at Kensington, the Masonic Temple at Alexandria, and the Washington monument at city center—bisect Washington's greater mandala in a nearly sigmoidal line. The sigmoid line as diameter, in Eastern philosophy, has long symbolized flow of communication, and suggests rotation—a magic spoke of transgressable boundary between forces celestial and telluric.

One does well to keep in mind the metaphors of "Main Street" and "Road to Nowhere." Interstate 495, for all its practicality as a major traffic artery, is nonetheless absurdist if one drives it in circles. Absurdist unless one views such activity as nonsensical to the purpose of acquiring sense. Think again on the circle and square. Washington is, if anything, square. Its cultural activity, bureaucratic thrust, its original shape...all square. Washington lies enclosed by Interstate 495, a circle of astounding dynamism...the outer rim to a mandala that Jung might have described as a ring of fire, "the fire of *conscupiscentia,* 'desire,' from which proceed the torments of hell." It is quite a journey inward from that frenetic outer rim. A psychic step or two from the "horrors of the burial ground" traditionally depicted there. But a garland of lotus leaves and the perfect center waits. The devoted jams that sonofabitch into second gear and pastes a little rubber on the monster's back.

WHAT IT MUST HAVE been like to drive I-495 the evening of July 4, 1976, the nation's Bicentennial. To hit Woodrow Wilson Bridge and spot a devilish green laser beam cutting across the night from the pyramidal tip of Washington's stone obelisk. To have shied at fireworks exploding above city center where a million people, mostly Washingtonians, huddled on the very spot L'Enfant designated as center of the square; where a medieval crafts fair had crouched all summer, where music representative of the entire nation had soared to bathe the obelisk, where an Old World itself had paid homage. To slam across Woodrow Wilson Bridge and be caught astride that laser. To ride it like a tether out toward Prince George's County, where CB'ers chanted dipsomaniacal mantras blessing every and all with a bountiful holiday, where broadcast towers for once stood muted, thwarted in their power to distract, diminished in their crane-like imperative as sculpture—no red lights on this night to dim the magnetic force of that laser. To feel nothing but *centripetency*, not a centrifugal eon to the breeze. No pulse beating off I-95, no pull toward Dulles and the mystery of that extreme, no compulsion for Beltway music and the bars that bartered that relief; instead, a gradual tightening of the leash, a drawing toward the center where a million people had taken to the streets—Washington's square standing shattered, circled keenly if you must—and all quandaries of government, race, and discordant culture absolved themselves in an orgy of focused chaos. One would have fought toward the center on that night if it meant 9:30 the next morning before traffic let up. One would revel through the darkness, dancing across L'Enfant's wide avenues under that cathartic laser, having forgotten where one's car had stopped, crushed against the petrified traffic as if crashed head-on. One would drink with policemen, strumpet with adversaries, debauch upon the very steps of Justice itself. A bull's-eye had been scored. For an evening the archer drew back.

Washingtonian, 1978

Forgive them Jody:
A Week in the Life of the White House Press Corps

A White House outsider, approaching the northwest gate, may not feel so disaffected as that citizen positioned there, she of suburban demeanor who petitions President Carter from behind a bed sheet slashed red, with fliers that proclaim her *torture from being sprayed by chemicals, all sorts of gas mace fumes, day and night, that burns blinds and paralyzes a person, poisons the blood, chokes and burns the lungs and body...is an invasion of privacy, interferes with work and daily life, includes mail, and ruins the wardrobe,* but an outsider is likely to sense something awry. The notion insinuates itself with a presentation of credentials, via a glass drawer that pinches, then retracts. It is intensified by an electric buzz that imperspicuously releases the gate; then is bolstered by uniformed guards who baste the outsider's estrangement with volleys of profanity while he sits to file his security card. It calcifies with the clipping of a plastic visitor's badge to the lapel, and nips determinedly about the outsider's ankles as he strides toward the West Lobby.

A television set plays inside the press enclave.

Several sets, to be precise; one in the briefing room proper. Technicians lounge in Jacobean armchairs and taunt the monster. They prate at game show hosts like kindergartners to playground monitors. Photographers draped with Nikons lumber past, cursing snow and Egyptian President Anwar Sadat, whose presence in Blair House is cause for exterior vigilance. Minicams wrapped in garbage bags droop toward the carpet. "Just enough snow to mess up your lenses," someone says.

It is Monday, February 6, whitened by snow but blue as the bluest on record. Reporters stride by, plucking handouts from glass bins toward the press enclave's center, skimming for questions. The daily news briefing will soon commence. Everywhere people wait with that blend of Monday-morning optimism and anticipatory dread that categorizes bureaucracies nationwide. The briefing room, with its droning TV, sibilant technicians, and sonorant reporters, is like a lounge in a new-car dealership where everyone has gotten in early for that minor repair which, despite promises, no one expects to have remedied so quickly.

An electronic voice announces the impending formality, and reporters hustle to attention. One or two scurry toward the front, whistling "Hail to the Chief." Others lay aside crossword puzzles and flip reporter's notebooks open to blank pages. Technicians persist in ogling TV, remaining at the briefing room's rear. A class divisiveness begins to assert itself. Reporters regard the blaring set with disdain. A technician cuts it down but not off. Reporters harumph; others fail to notice. Among these are recognizable personalities, phantoms from the evening news: Bob Schieffer and Robert Pierpoint of CBS, Bob Jamison of NBC, Ann Compton and Sam Donaldson of ABC. They perch above other reporters, the faceless bylines or rumpled wire service jockeys, like cotillionettes. Pinched in at the waist and blown dry, they fence among their peers with voices familiar as dreams.

Press secretary Jody Powell emerges from a corridor,

taking the podium. He lights a cigarette. Dressed in shirt sleeves, loosened tie, and charcoal vest, he grips the lectern professorially. An intense man—authoritarian for his years—he leans toward the unsettled class and drawls across two microphones: "I know many of you would like to get out of here so you can get to the Press Club...." Which quiets everyone but technicians.

Powell pledges to keep the briefing short, appeasing a majority of reporters. Sadat has spent the weekend at Camp David discussing a possible peace treaty with Israel, and will address the National Press Club this afternoon. Reporters are eager to learn details of Sadat's meeting with President Carter. They crowd about Powell's feet, on the floor, on blond captain's chairs, deep in the folds of matching leather sofas.

"Jody," they cry, soliciting attention. "Jody, I—"

Powell fields some questions cordially, others he juggles with phraseology such as "I am not aware" or "I'm not in a position to interpret." Little enmity is apparent. Fraternal sparring is the rule. Powell speaks breathlessly, but with respect for his adversaries. Questions hone in on Sadat, on the weekend spent at Camp David ("Jody, did the President order anything in writing?" Powell: "Maybe another cherry tart during the movie"), on weather emergencies, on this morning's Cabinet meeting. Others are more elliptical, prodding a nerve.

"Jody, today is the deadline for signing of the so-called child-porn bill," Sam Donaldson asks. "Do you know if the president has decided to sign it?"

"I don't," Powell says. "But I think he's concerned about its impact upon the press." Laughter.

A newcomer to the White House beat as of Carter's occupancy, Donaldson is Powell's sharpest foil. He and Powell clash with freshman vibrancy. Powell, an adviser throughout Carter's campaign, remains his unshakable ally. Donaldson, frustrated after years of comparative ease covering the hill, is cynical, ever on the attack. As to what precisely is expected from Powell on a day-to-day basis, Donaldson has remarked: "Nothing. Absolutely nothing. The press secretary will say no more than he wants to. You may chisel and pry, which may yield a little comedy and some anger, but very few answers will be forthcoming. Attack someone personally, as with [advisor] Hamilton Jordan, and that just pulls them together. It's very much an us-against-them world so far as the president is concerned."

TECHNICIANS LOLL TOWARD the briefing room's rear, gossiping among themselves, chortling and grunting in amplified banter. Chris Curle recites news copy from the TV set, in counterpoint to Powell's offerings. Most reporters are oblivious. Questions-drone, a malaise has nested. "I'm not aware.... I have no information on that." A stenographer records the double-talk for posterity.

Then one of three women in this group of forty reporters speaks. She is middle-aged, frumpish, dressed in a light-green pantsuit and a fuzzy gray hat. Her name is Sarah McClendon—a press corps icon and occasionally a buffoon. In her outfit she resembles a dandelion.

The reporters' mood shifts from one of tolerance to fragmented annoyance. McClendon phrases a complicated series of questions concerning Senate confirmation of a Georgia woman named Omi Walden, nominated by the president to a newly created, $50,000-a-year post as assistant secretary in the US Department of Energy. The thrust of McClendon's question is personal; ears perk around the briefing room. How qualified is Mrs. Walden? How friendly is she with Georgians on the president's staff? How friendly is she with Jody Powell? Laughter and admonitions to withdraw the question explode from fellow reporters. "What are you getting at, Sarah?"

McClendon repeats that she wants to know how well Mrs. Walden and Powell know each other, how effective her administration as director of Georgia's Office of Energy Resources has been (misappropriations of emergency fuel within that department have been alleged), and whether her relationship to Powell is connected with her nomination to that high-paying federal post, for which McClendon obviously feels Mrs. Walden may not be qualified.

Powell waits, furiously impatient. "I...don't want to prolong this any longer. I say this in as gentlemanly a fashion as I can: If there is something to the implications that you raise or seem to raise here, it strikes me that we ought to deal with it in the same forum that the things are raised. I think it is one of the unfortunate aspects of public life that you sometimes are not in a position to deal with those sort of things until it becomes a matter of public record. If you think the trend of the question is irritating, you are correct."

"What implications do you think she raised?" a reporter blurts.

"I don't know. What do you think?"

"You are the one that mentioned implications. What implications do you think she has raised that haven't been dealt with?"

"I don't know."

"I don't understand your last comment," a reporter says.

"If you have nothing more to say on the matter beyond what you said, then that is fine. If there is anything further that you would like to explore in specific, I would like to give you an opportunity to do it," Powell says, fuming.

"That is fine," McClendon counters. "When will we have the opportunity?" Denunciations of McClendon's impudence resound across the briefing room.

"Let her speak!" a reporter shouts. The room quiets.

McClendon restates her question, sidestepping pitfalls of direct confrontation. She inquires how well Powell knows Omi Walden and whether their relationship is cause for her appointment. Powell professes friendship for Mrs. Walden but denies that friendship or cronyism has led to her nomination. McClendon shrugs, promising to follow the matter up. Atmosphere inside the briefing room is atomic. McClendon has gaffed reporters' interest. They regard her with a mixture of hostility and apprehension. "Thank you, Jody," the senior wire-service jockey sneers, closing the briefing. There is apology in his voice; he has sided with Jody Powell.

Several reporters corner McClendon and probe the matter further. "Sarah's holding a briefing now," Sam Donaldson laughs, striding away. Who is this Omi Walden, reporters want to know. McClendon spells the woman's name, adding that she is "thirty-two, married, and good-looking," and that her department may have authorized special allocations of emergency fuel to presidential brother Billy Carter. Her nomination is questioned on the Hill. The administration stands terrified of another Bert Lance—who in September resigned as chairman of the Office of Management and the Budget, amid corruption allegations.

"Is Jody sleeping with her?" a reporter asks.

"You saw how sensitive he was to the issue," McClendon answers.

A hint of scandal has brightened the day. Reporters scatter to file stories, none of which will mention Omi Walden. But that does not hinder frolicsome tinkering with the matter. As newsmen retire to cubicles, network booths, and telephones, details of McClendon's questions are shuttled about the premises. What the hell did she say? A statement is misinterpreted here, a detail warped in translation there. Rumors clatter, facts shifting through reamplification like retellings of a joke. Within fifteen minutes the entire incident lies bogged in distortion. But spirits are high.

"*Omi, Omi,*" a reporter singsongs...*give me your answer, do...I'm half crazy...*

TUESDAY, FEBRUARY 7. "President Truman was a terrific guy," an old-timer reminisces, back by the plaques and beaten photographs of press corps past. "Kennedy liked his women, but he never brought it home, never to

Hyannis anyway. Nixon ran the best campaign...." This old-timer is suited-up three-piece, affects a bow tie, and looks authentically Speed Graphic. His face is bludgeoned from hard campaigns; his earlobes stretch to his shoulder blades. He leans against a shelf by a row of telephones as if bellying up to a bar. Reporters dally. One-liners spit the air. A leering correspondent accosts Ann Compton with the caveat that "you destroy seven hundred brain cells a day by remaining celibate."

There's a good deal of horsing around this noon. It has snowed four inches and the mini-blizzard conditions have reinforced camaraderie. Sam Donaldson—who has been waiting outside for US envoy to China Leonard Woodcock—bustles in with an ABC crew, quipping: "How much wood is a Woodcock worth?" Rubbing hands together and bullshitting a mile a minute, Donaldson plays class clown to this fettered assemblage. Malaise has deserted the press with the passage of blue Monday. "We're gonna chew Sarah alive," Donaldson growls.

But McClendon fails to appear. The briefing room is crowded. Reporters huddle about the podium, sit along coffee tables, squat around the floor. Powell opens the briefing, visibly disturbed.

"Why so on the muscle today?" UPI's Helen Thomas asks, after Powell's third acerbic reply.

"Didn't mean to be," he says, looking surprised. Then more carefully: "You can't hold your tongue in your teeth forever."

"Is the president going to [speaker of the house] Tip O'Neill's *roast* tonight?" Donaldson inquires, in his richest Gore Vidal voice. This wins a laugh. Powell admits he hasn't heard.

Questions track news of the day. Powell hangs up on every issue: American support of human-rights violators abroad, the president's reaction to Sadat's Press Club address, official position on an annoying Joe Kraft column concerning an alleged slowdown policy toward Sadat.... "I'll say this and that's *it*," Powell groans. Or: "We've been over that ground; I'll not waste other reporters' time." This hedging continues to briefing's end. Reporters retreat, subdued. Some bit of life has been sponged from the air. Newsfolk clutch Styrofoam cups and fudge about the wire tickers, sniffing for leads. Light is piquantly bright from four tall windows illuminating the briefing room, but a dudgeon has portcullised the afternoon.

What a drain to endure this every day.

WEDNESDAY, FEBRUARY 8, summons the corps early. President Carter is slated to introduce a proposal on financing higher education, and open coverage will be available in the briefing room. Open coverage means "for broadcast." Technicians are flung from their lethargy. They press toward room's front like offensive linemen. Warm-up jackets flapping, gum snapping, they cajole each other from complex matrices of equipment, elbowing reporters aside.

"Get those cameras set up," Donaldson barks, the mock drill sergeant. Photographers are out of control. "Everybody and his *dog* is here," Donaldson says.

Most reporters have yielded to this onslaught, taking position behind the line of fire. Others squat resolutely before cameras, clutching their notebooks like revolvers. Hot lights assault the walnut lectern. Numerous outsiders are in evidence—reporters wearing day badges, TV faces one recognizes but cannot fix. A good seat, claimed early, is stage left beside the stenographer. Perhaps a hundred people crowd the briefing area. The bustle and profanity approach bedlam. Reporters scowl at technicians, who look ready to throw a punch. Everyone jostles carnivorously. It may be Ash Wednesday elsewhere in Christendom, but here among the press corps, one notes a marked absence of humility.

President Carter takes the podium...to a dulling of commotion. A thousand tiny Sonys begin to whir. Jostling continues as Carter deigns to speak. "Let's have some respect!" Donaldson mugs. Carter pretends not to have heard.

"Good morning, everybody."

Carter speaks for two minutes and two seconds. His remarks concern middle-income families his proposed bill is to aid, and serve to introduce HEW Secretary Joseph Califano and members of Congress who have worked on the program. Reporters study Carter; they know his transcribed statement will be forthcoming, courtesy of the press office. What may be observed during this brief address is Carter's demeanor toward a captive audience. From the waist up he supplicates with that passive reserve familiar to television viewers; from the waist down he threatens, legs spread, left knee popping, with the autonomy of a Georgia line coach.

Carter relinquishes the podium to Califano. Cameras lead Carter toward the wings. Photographers climb walls, knocking framed prints to the sofa. Reporters curse. Donaldson simply gets up and trails Carter down the hall.

Secretary Califano speaks, followed by Senators Pell and Williams, Representatives Brademas, Thompson, Biaggi, Ford, and Perkins. How grotesque these public figures look under the lights. Questions rebound, but there is no sustained interest once Carter has left. Regulars prattle among themselves. When Califano's question period has finished and the line of congressmen has exited, the official stenographer inquires of an outsider: "Who was that guy on the end?"

Jody Powell calls the news briefing to order. Lights have dimmed and Powell cautions reporters that this segment is not for broadcast. Technicians are rolling up cords; photographers have retreated to the soft-drink machines. Regulars stretch and settle in.

Powell announces open coverage of President Sadat's departure from the South Lawn at 3:00 p.m. He cites deployment of troops to assist blizzard-torn New England. Powell is confident today, in a better mood. He is relaxed. Repeating a telephone number for blizzard updates, he jokes in announcerese: "That number again is…First three persons to call will receive a Vegematic." To polite laughter.

Not to be outdone, Donaldson adds: "Next two, an F-5E." Then: "The fact that [presidential son] Chip is not being sent, does that mean it's less of an emergency than Buffalo?"

Others get their two cents in. Donaldson jabs with heady questions about Sadat and Mideast summit talks. A seriousness threatens. Someone asks if departure dates for an upcoming presidential trip are available. "Not yet," Powell allows. "That's a cheap story; you can do better than that."

"Don't be too sure," Donaldson sighs. The briefing winds toward its close.

THE SOUTH LAWN IS crowded for Sadat's departure at three. Press has been escorted from its lobby in squads, past taciturn Secret Service, whom no reporter will test. "I'm not pushing that guy. He's packing a gun." They have been roped off in bleachers facing a podium where the two presidents will speak. Reporters endure this rope-a-dope mischievously. They cavort with unobstructed view…on a platform high above technicians who squabble for a better shot.

Donaldson jabbers incessantly. "Sleazy affair," he complains of Tip O'Neill's roast. "Second-rate dinner— *no one* was there."

It is after lunch. The probability exists that reporters have imbibed. Everywhere Marines stand at parade rest. Ceremoniousness of the occasion is marred by reporters' capering. They gamble at liar's poker, placing bets and passing dollar bills overhead. The South Lawn is imposing, even intimidating to an outsider. Military regalia, limousines, the Secret Service, boxwood emitting subtle perfume, the mansion so white at this remove.

Reporters take it in stride. They are like church-school kids who've forgotten they're hacking on consecrated turf.

The army's herald trumpets proceed up the drive, casting flourishes. Presidents Sadat and Carter, their wives, emerge. Reporters duck toward notebooks. Minicams hum. Sadat speaks first. His remarks are gracious. Some joking can be heard among reporters.

Carter speaks, praising Sadat as "the world's foremost peacemaker."

"He says that to all the boys," Donaldson whispers. Strangled guffaws.

The presidents embrace, bussing each other on alternate cheeks. TV lights blanch, flashbulbs pale...per usual, the image is distorted.

Sadat's limousine drives off slowly. The press, unleashed, bounds toward telephone and courier to disgorge its spoils.

THURSDAY, FEBRUARY 9. Reporters grope blearily for handouts in the wake of Sadat's departure, struggling to focus on this morning's activities. "We milked from him the last drop of news," Donaldson gloats. Correspondents shuffle from coffee machine to glass booths; bylines from toilet to syndicate cubicle, barking their shins on that *World Book* dolly that juts into the narrow corridor like a kiddy car. "He got what he came for," Donaldson harps, of Sadat's request for American jets. Reporters test a laugh.

They cluster at Powell's feet, confused. The verbal grab-ass continues, but jokes fall short of their mark. Donaldson mumbles something to automatic tittering, but his humor is forced. "Strike Sam's sexist remark from the record," Powell asks of the stenographer. Then he introduces Jessica Tuchman of the National Security Council staff, who holds a special briefing.

Reporters clutch thick transcripts of a treaty with the International Atomic Energy Agency regarding nuclear safeguards. Tuchman fields questions on the treaty for twenty minutes. Bickering flares. The press nearly comes awake. Tuchman relinquishes her podium to Powell and the regular briefing proceeds. Prefaced by a humorously arcane discussion of Indian land-claim settlements in Maine.

"Pronounce the names of the two tribes," Curtis Wilkie drawls. A southerner—mustached, long-haired, wearing red lumberjack shirt and Frye boots, Wilkie approximates a breaching of social boundaries between reporters and technicians. A figure in Timothy Crouse's *The Boys on the Bus*, about the 1972 campaign, he is White House correspondent for the *Boston Globe*.

"I don't even have the names here," Powell says. "I'm sure if the *Globe* can spell it right I'll be able to pronounce it." Pause. "I'd like to see 'em spell it from your dictation over the phone." Hawr-haws.

Donaldson spearheads a further assault with questions on Prime Minister Begin, which Powell jocularly stalls, then dodges. Sarah McClendon, last noticed Monday, solicits Powell's attention. "Jody, Jody...." Powell extends his remarks on Begin. "Jody," McClendon persists. Finally she is recognized.

"I'd like to reframe a question I put to you earlier in the week, concerning Mrs. Omi Walden. I do this out of fairness to you. I was asking my question as part of a fishing expedition, and I still think, despite the opinion of one of my noted colleagues, that this is a valid question and certainly it's a valid subject for questioning here. The subject's now working on the White House staff, at times has been sent out as representative of the White House to speak on energy in other states. I asked what you did know about her and what was your relationship, and you feel, I understand, that that carries certain implications. I was just after information, but in fairness to you, who denied any relationship other than friendship with a former fellow Carter staffer, I wish to reframe the question to you. When did you first learn she was being considered for the energy post, and how well qualified do you think she is for a $50,000-a-year job as assistant secretary of the Department of Energy?"

McClendon has recited her question from notes, speaking precisely: Reporters have listened poleaxed. It is difficult to gauge their feelings. Powell responds formally, dismissing any hint of impropriety—and encouraging McClendon to meet with him privately for specifics on Mrs. Walden's qualifications. One has the impression they already have met and have thrashed this thing out.

"Jody," a reporter interrupts, shifting subject matter. McClendon sits quietly. Powell speaks with calm authority for briefing's remainder, answering queries where he can. Questions focus on Carter's TV image, a possible shift in tactics there; on Jewish response to Sadat's remarks of yesterday...Powell is evasive ("I'm not qualified—"). A perfidious ennui settles over the press corps. Reporters cradle their heads and slump. Correspondents sag. It's as if the whole entourage has shot up with curare.

"Thank you, Jody," someone clacks. The tableau shudders to life.

FRIDAY, FEBRUARY 10. Sam Donaldson is edgy. At a presidential photo session he has snapped at the escort and demanded that his crew be allowed a better angle. Here in the briefing room he has pulled a captain's chair directly before the podium, where he sits alone. To an electronic voice, announcing that presidential remarks to members of the Federal Regional Councils will shortly conclude, he snaps: "When is the *briefing?*" He hunches before the vacant podium like a leper.

Last evening Donaldson appeared on ABC News as interviewee. He ranted animatedly after the fashion of his posture here—behavior normally masked by the coolness of his television demeanor. Donaldson took part in a 1957 nuclear stress test, similar to that at Jackass Flats, Nevada, which precipitated the leukemia of one participant, and, it is feared, may have contaminated others. Donaldson, a soldier assigned to the test, witnessed the explosion from six thousand yards, then was marched toward ground zero, "where pieces of whitened, black ash rained upon us as the wind shifted." The fourteen-kiloton atomic blast, code named "Keppler," was thirty kilotons lighter than "Smoky" of Jackass Flats.

Still, Donaldson has reason for concern. "They herded us out of there, stripped us down, hosed us off, and said everything would be fine." Donaldson sits frozen before the podium.

A Friday-morning restlessness enlivens others of the press corps. Antsy, they squirm like lower formers anticipating a holiday. Their joking takes on aggression the moment the briefing begins.

Deputy press secretary Rex Granum officiates today. Powell is not present. Rex Granum wields considerably less authority. Very much the substitute, he vacillates where Powell would not waver, attacks where Powell would absorb. Donaldson plants the earliest barbs with tough questioning on Mideast talks. Other jabs concern an infusion of Cuban troops into Ethiopia, the White House's posture toward that; the sale of military aircraft to Egypt; a presidential meeting with Dayan; Carter's authorization of warrantless television surveillance and the possibility of his having exceeded constitutional authority. Granum is defensive through most of this. He is hostile. Reporters pick at his vulnerability. They vent weeks of frustration, gorging on recompense.

"Why *won't* Hamilton Jordan return our calls?" And then: "Wouldn't it be lovely to have Hamilton for a press conference?"

To a persistence on the question of Begin's meeting with Carter, Granum's reticence coagulates. "I'm trying to be helpful and responsive to the question," he stutters. "I could very easily just come up here and, and, and—"

"Stonewall?"

"That would be the easy thing to do," Curtis Wilkie says. "But it would be wrong."

Tumultuous laughter.

The last vestige of control flees the briefing room. Further barrages ensue, flecked with heckling at Granum's expense. Tough grilling about warrantless surveillance is served. Sam Donaldson plucks at a misstatement: Carter has referred to himself as "a former president."

Why so, Donaldson inquires.

"I'm sure there are occasions in all of our lives in which we wish we were now out of our present occupation," Granum snorts.

"Does the president wish this?"

"I really couldn't tell you," Granum sniffs.

"Now, wait—" reporters cry.

Granum has attempted to slough the question off. His intentions have backfired.

"Thank you, Rex," someone screams. The briefing is closed. Yet wags persevere.

"Is he still the president, Rex?"

"Rex?"

AT A 1:00 P.M. photo session in the Cabinet Room—where Carter is meeting with national editors—Donaldson glances about, scans technicians' faces, and bays: "Where are the writers?"

It's true, not one byline is present.

"What if he *resigns?*" Donaldson sputters. Then he laughs, twitching his shoulders, intrigued by the prospect.

PRESIDENT CARTER WILL depart for Camp David at 3:00 p.m. and reporters are grouped beside a narrow awning leading to the South Lawn. Presidential effects are piled nearby, awaiting the helicopter.

Among these are a pair of violin cases.

"*Two* violins!" Ann Compton exclaims. "There'll be music this weekend!"

Correspondents have been observed at Class Reunion's bar over lunch break, and their Friday hijinks abound, lubricated. Someone broadcasts a classical sonata over a tape deck. Others shout fantasy reprobations toward the vacant awning.

"What about Somalia?" Donaldson hollers.

"What about the F-5E?"

"What about ERA?" Compton says.

All quite jovial and clubby. Carter's son Chip, in blue jeans, and his wife Caron holding their child, wait on the Truman Balcony. Aides, a butler, and a white-suited chef are in evidence. Fire trucks crouch on either side of the helipad. Hamilton Jordan instigates a snowball fight near the Rose Garden. A dullish throb is heard as the chopper banks over Jefferson Memorial and pushes toward the South Lawn. Reporters duck, Donaldson covering his head like a primitive or a man doused too often. The tail wash hits as the chopper turns, spraying dirt and ice. Hats soar.

Rosalynn, daughter Amy, and assorted functionaries materialize beneath the awning. President Carter strolls from the Oval Office, striding casually over grass with the air of a man who has put in a solid week. He stumbles tentatively in a patch of snow, is met halfway by an Air Force aide, and escorted toward his family.

"What's the point of covering this?" Ann Compton is asked. The affair is ceremonial but inconsequential.

"In case he trips on the top step and breaks his neck," she says. "Ford tripped so much it got so they didn't want us to film it."

Rosalynn and Amy mount the ladder confidently, followed by the Chief Executive. No sound can be isolated from the throb of blades, no feeling from the surge of wind. Carter trots up the steps looking straight ahead.

"A wave!" Donaldson howls in consternation. "A little kiss!" Apparently Carter will not recognize the press this afternoon. At top step he fails even to turn.

"Nothing!" Donaldson screams, as the big chopper lifts. "Nothing, nothing, nothing!"

Washingtonian, 1978

Postscript

On September 17, 1978, President Anwar Sadat and Israeli Prime Minister Menachem Begin signed the Camp David Accords. President Carter was instrumental in bringing about these agreements. They were signed at the White House, but were the product of thirteen days of secret negotiations at Camp David. The second accord, Framework for Conclusion of Peace Treaty between Egypt and Israel, *resulted in the 1979 Egypt-Israel Peace Treaty, for which Sadat and Begin shared the 1978 Nobel Peace Prize.*

Night Watch:
The Wall

The Vietnam Veterans Memorial was conceived at night—founder Jan Scruggs brooding in his kitchen over whiskey and flinching as mortar rounds struck in a battle that was ten years past. He'd seen *The Deer Hunter*, but the soldiers he sought in his mind's eye, broken and gutted at Xuanloc, were buddies, real. "The names," he thought and later wrote, "the names. No one remembers the names."

They descend in ranks, 58,156 of America's dead or missing, toward the vertex of a black chevron that has become Washington's most-frequented memorial.

Four million tourists a year visit the wall, to place mementos, to leave notes, to commune with the dead. Many are Americans for whom Vietnam was their generation's pivotal experience, and who confuse a mourning of war dead with grief for their own lost youth. But others are veterans who feel comfortable at the wall only at night.

There are regulars among these night visitors. Some, like Jan Scruggs, come every other weekend before sunrise. Others are drawn to the wall each night. The darkness offers camouflage against those daytime tourists whom Scruggs calls "almost an obscenity." But night time worries others. The police officer who shot himself to death at the memorial was a nightly visitor. And a veteran who wounded himself there with a handgun did so at night, explaining that "I wanted to die with my men." Jan Scruggs says, "If l had the money, I'd hire counselors to be here every night."

The dead seem closer at night. The wall shimmers behind campfire spots that light the names with a special radiance.

"Night is the best time," says John Holland, a retired sergeant major who spent four and a half years in Vietnam, and who works with the memorial's MIA Vigil. "You can *feel* the wall better. "

To follow the names down a slight, cobblestone incline, 250 feet to the wall's vertex—pitched ten feet below ground—is to descend into a mass grave. Over and about are the names. The greenish tint, in sunlight, of the black granite reflecting grass is lost at night. As is the impulse among the uninitiated to seek logic in the circular rather than alphabetical arrangement of names. The night watch accepts circularity.

It is late, and a mother searches for her son's name. Family members attend, a young woman saying, "so *that's* where all the men are," another wondering if so many names might not fill "a city directory, a city of the dead." The mother finds her son, high on a black panel. To touch his name she must reach overhead, pressing her entire body against the wall. Her reflection leaps out at her. And her breath leaves a mist on the stone. For a moment she hesitates. Then she moves among the names, touching her son's first with a finger, then with a rose, that she tucks into a crack in the granite.

Lydia Fish is a folklorist who's spent eight weeks and up to thirty-six consecutive hours at the memorial. She likens it to pilgrimage sites such as Lourdes. "Time spent there is time out of time," she says, "when the living confront the dead."

The same petitionary letters and votive offerings as are left at Lourdes are left at the wall. Fish is most impressed by Maya Lin's impulse, in designing the memorial, "to cut open the earth," to create "an interface between the sunny world and the quiet, dark world beyond that we can't enter."

The notes speak to the dead. "Dear Don, it's been a long seventeen years and not a day goes by when I don't think of our last firefight together...." The mementos are placed there almost exclusively at night. They include baseball caps, swords, cowboy boots, cans of beer, panties, and teddy bears—objects that might be of some comfort to the dead. These mementos are collected by the Park Service and stored in Maryland at a facility called MARS (Museum and Archaeological Regional Storage). Curiously, on Elvis Presley's grave at Graceland—which six hundred thousand of the faithful visit each year, ranking it with the memorial as a pilgrimage site—notes, flowers, and teddy bears also are left. War and rock 'n' roll: shrines of one generation's principal concerns.

An offering is being tendered now. Before the wall lies a wreath from the 196th Light Infantry Brigade, embellished with a combat Zippo, brigade patches, a folded camouflage jacket, and a cane. An inscription below a rubbing of two names reads: "They shall not grow old as we that are left grow old. Age shall not weary them, nor the years condemn, at the going down of the sun...." The Zippo, jacket, and cane belong to Dan Dinklage, a bearded Houston vet in jeans and a Rockin' Robin T-shirt who stands nearby.

"Those two died tryin' to save each other," he says, nodding toward the rubbing. "In sixty-nine, thirty-five miles north of Tamky. I'm here for brigade reunion. And to have a brew for the boys. It's therapeutic. I'll sit up on that hill tonight, do some drinkin' and thinkin'. I'm *compelled* to be here. This is our church. There's a couple our fellas can't yet face the wall, so I'll help 'em down later. Last night one bawled louder than a bull buffalo. It's hard to watch them big boys cry."

A man near the tree line is blowing taps on a harmonica. The sound is blues-bent, ratchety, and it rakes the tent flaps of the MIA Vigil, where a veteran in a three-piece suit is trading unit histories with a regular. "It's been ten *years*," he argues emphatically, "they're dead." Then he makes a fifty-dollar donation.

A two-hitch Special Forces captain, he is experiencing the wall for the first time. "I don't know if l can handle it," he mutters. The regular draws a cigarette from a flak jacket and bums a light. "You can do it," he says. The captain eases down the cobblestones. As the names envelop him, he begins to shake. "You can do it," the regular coaxes. The captain stands at the wall's vertex, where the dead from 1959 and 1975 meet, and weeps quietly. Then he continues up the west wall toward the flag and statue, its uniformed figures intent behind their thousand-yard stares.

"Don't never forget," a voice in the darkness calls, "them names on the wall."

Washingtonian, 1988

The Throne of the Third Heaven of the Nations' Millennium General Assembly

He was a street artist, like his father, the son of a black gospel singer and itinerant preacher—also called James—who left the rural South at nineteen to make his way to Washington. He walked the side streets of this city with a gunny sack and child's wagon, collecting discarded light bulbs, jelly glasses, and gold foil as material for that work that would ensure his salvation. He was a short-order cook and janitor, a veteran and a foot servant to bureaucracy. He was a junk sculptor who worked in the detritus of his adopted city. He was a visionary, a black William Blake, whom Jesus met each night at the head of an alley to escort past the junkies and winos to the unheated stable where he performed his holy tasks. He was a craftsman of such unconscious sophistication that the most accomplished artists of his day would hail him as peer. He was possessed of a postwar consciousness as reflective of the 1950s as that of Rauschenberg or Chuck Berry. Above all, he was a Washington artist. He was Saint James, "Director, Special Projects for the

State of Eternity" and creator of *The Throne of the Third Heaven of the Nations' Millennium General Assembly*— one of the great puzzles of contemporary sculpture— which critic Robert Hughes has suggested "may well be the finest work of visionary religious art produced by an American."

James Hampton's *Throne* sits in Gallery 3-D, of the Smithsonian's National Museum of American Art, in an explosion of light. It perches there, vibrant, like a giant bird—filling one whole room with its assemblage of gold foil, silver foil and efflorescent parts. Its every limb is winged, a frail rope all that restrains it from collecting itself onto its haunches and taking off.

Moments pass before one can see that its pieces are, in fact, stationary. It is difficult to think other than of some massive bird of prey. One is awestruck at first viewing, speechless. And what one perceives, ultimately, to be an altar backed by a winged throne with its legend *Fear Not* does little to ease distress.

It is comforting to think of Hampton's *Throne* as art, convenient now that the piece lies enshrined in the Smithsonian. But imagine it as it was found, in a brick stable behind 1133 Seventh Street NW, one month after Hampton's death in 1964, by an impatient landlord who forced a padlock and flung open the doors to this glittering display.

Meyer Wertleib was no art critic. He was a white pawnbroker and merchant in a black ghetto, and he had rented the stable to Hampton since 1950, at fifty dollars a month. But even he could guess that this assemblage of pulpits, lecterns, standards, altars, plaques, and crowns— more than 180 pieces—was worth saving. Hampton's sister, who had come to claim his body, did not want it. So Wertleib contacted the *Washington Post*. "You can't just destroy something a man devoted himself to for fourteen years," he told a reporter. Hampton had once said, "That's my life, I'll finish it before I die." *The Throne* was apparently incomplete. "It seems to me an example of the futility of life," Wertleib reflected. He advertised the stable for rent, with vague ideas of selling *The Throne* or tossing it out as junk.

For junk it was, a meticulous concatenation of light bulbs, desk blotters, glasses, armchairs, tables, newspaper, and foil hustled from the whiskey bottles of bums. Ed Kelly, a sculptor in search of a studio, answered Wertleib's ad and, visiting the stable, suffered a typical response. "I was overwhelmed. Hampton had a dozen 500-watt bulbs around the ceiling, and everything shone." Kelly caught a sense of *The Throne* as art, and contacted Alice Denney, a collector and art figure around Washington, and she likewise was astounded. A number of art folk such as Leo Castelli, Ivan Karp, and Robert Rauschenberg were in town for a Corcoran Biennial, and she brought them down to see it. Rauschenberg, particularly, was impressed. *The Throne* was so close to what he had been doing in mixed media with found objects and junk surfaces, he could not believe his eyes.

Alice Denney was eager to save it. She was Vice Commissioner of the Venice *Biennale*, had been Assistant Director of the Washington Gallery of Modern Art, and would found Washington Project for the Arts—she had clout. She dragged anyone she could to the stable for a viewing: artists, ambassadors, congressmen. Limousines trailed through the alley back of St. Stephen's Baptist Church in platoons. Denney contacted Hampton's sister and attempted to gain legal possession of *The Throne*, but before she succeeded, Harry Lowe of what was then the National Collection of Fine Arts paid Wertleib his back rent, and acquired the piece for the Smithsonian.

Harry Lowe's reaction to the first sighting was predictable: "It was like opening Tut's tomb."

What added considerably to the spookiness of *The Throne* were its accouterments. There was a loose-leaf notebook with the title, "Archives of the State of Eternity." There were tags on several pieces with the inscriptions, "This is true, that the great Moses, the giver of the 10th

116

commandment, appeared in Washington April 11, 1931." And, "This is true that on October 2, 1946, the great Virgin Mary and the Star of Bethlehem appeared over the nation's capital." And, "This is true that Adam, the first man God created, appeared in person on January 20, 1949. This was the day of President Truman's inauguration." Everywhere were references to the Book of Revelation and the word "dispensation." In a small book and on plaques around the stable were elegant hieroglyphics, hand printed in stark contrast to Hampton's childish penmanship. The figures were symmetric, or Oriental. They were indecipherable. On many pieces of *The Throne* was an inked symbol, likewise inscrutable. It was shaped like a rocket, or a plane. Tacked to a bulletin board in one corner of Hampton's stable was the message, "Where There Is No Vision, The People Perish."

That Hampton was a man of vision, no one could refute. But what was his vision? On one level, *The Throne* was visual interpretation of the Book of Revelation, where God, flanked by his angels, sat upon "a great white throne," to judge the quick and the dead. Hampton believed in the Second Coming. He had written, "the word millennium [sic] means 'the return of Christ and a part of the Kingdom of God on earth.'" He considered himself "Director of Special Projects," a verger to the holy bureaucracy. He had seen Moses, Mary, and Adam with his own eyes, and believed God oversaw his work each night in the stable. That work was both a warning against and a preparation for apocalypse. Hampton called himself Saint James and had been photographed wearing a golden crown. Who was this prophet of Seventh Street?

Few people in 1965 knew. The newspapers reported that Hampton had been a laborer for the General Services Administration, and had died at age fifty-three. Wertleib remembered him as a quiet, unassuming man who paid his rent promptly. He was small and bespectacled. He lived in furnished rooms. He was the sort of man who, in death, generated more curiosity than in life. And that curiosity was intense. Professors James L. Foy and James P. McMurrer of Georgetown University's department of psychiatry wrote a paper about him for a scholarly journal. The Throne traveled to museums in Williamsburg, Minneapolis, Boston, and Montgomery, and to the Whitney in New York. The contemporary art world, figuratively speaking, was at his feet. But it was not until the National Museum of American Art put an intern named Linda Hartigan on the case full time that an inclusive portrait of Hampton emerged.

He had been born April 8, 1909, in Elloree, South Carolina. His father, in addition to singing and preaching the gospel, had pursued a life of crime and worked on chain gangs. He had abandoned his family. At nineteen, James Hampton left South Carolina and joined his older brother, Lee, in Washington. From 1939 to 1942 he worked as a cook before landing a job with the government. He was drafted into the Army and served with the 385th Aviation Squadron at home and on Saipan and Guam. His duties as a noncombatant included carpentry and maintenance of airstrips. He was awarded the Bronze Star and honorably discharged in 1945. In 1946, he was hired by the GSA as a janitor, a job he retained until his death.

The most remarkable events in Hampton's life were the visions he had and his work with *The Throne*. They seemed inextricably linked. His first documented vision had occurred when he was twenty-two years old, the last when he was forty-one. These visions were not dreams, but personal visitations. God and his subordinates spoke to Hampton, directing him in his work upon *The Throne*. Hampton did not advertise these visitations, and he never proselytized for his beliefs. He showed acquaintances, mostly women, his work and tried to interest a few churches in accepting it. But he was no hysteric. He seemed reconciled, by the end of his life, to anonymity. Perhaps he would found his own church: "The Tyler Baptist," named for a pastor Hampton admired.

Linda Hartigan worked for nine months on Hampton's

history and came up with little. Yet there was something haunting about the man's life. He was so anonymous. His service and government records had been lost in a fire in St. Louis. His brother, Lee, had died mysteriously in 1949. What family Hartigan could locate were reluctant to provide information. They were intimidated by calls from Washington and vaguely frightened of *The Throne*. It was a powerful item. Hampton never married, and his closest friend was a woman with whom he shared a car pool. She remembered him as diligent and religious, a reserved and humble man who showed his work modestly and believed that one was rewarded in heaven for what one accomplished on earth.

If there was a key to Hampton's vision, some "Rosebud" that might explain his life, it lay with *The Throne* itself.

The earliest viewer of Hampton's *Throne*, still alive, is Otelia Whitehead—she visited Hampton's workplace during the 1940s. Whitehead, a registered nurse and a cosmopolitan woman, suffered this reaction:

"I was speechless. A cab driver brought me to the alley, saying there's something here you really must see. Mr. Hampton opened the door and it was like the wings of Gabriel were beating in the extremely bright light. Mr. Hampton showed me each piece, speaking of the millenium and Armageddon. 'You might be here when He comes again.' Mr. Hampton was sleeping in that space, on a couch, with an electric burner for heat. Despite the poorness of the surroundings, I felt the presence of some unknown force. I returned to visit Mr. Hampton on a dozen occasions. No one could sit on *The Throne*, but he would permit you to approach it on your knees. I knelt before the Mercy Seat and it was like praying before a great altar."

Last year, Whitehead, who considers herself psychic, was pronounced clinically dead. She was resuscitated, but in that limbo between life and death she had a vision of James Hampton. He was standing beside a man who may or may not have been Jesus, and he was motioning her back.

"My work was not done," Whitehead said. "I've thought and thought about his meaning, but I always come back to *The Throne*. There are mysteries there which have not been solved."

In a storage bin off Harry Lowe's office at the National Museum of American Art is the notebook in which James recorded his secret language. It is titled, *The Book of the 7 Dispensations* by St. James, and the word "Revelation" is written on every page. It is this notebook that Otelia Whitehead believes may hold the key to Hampton's vision. The Smithsonian already has had several cryptographers try to decipher it. The have been unsuccessful. There are priests at Catholic University to whom Whitehead would show the book, and Linda Hartigan has considered submitting it to the Vatican. If all this begins to sound like *The Exorcist*, take heart. Research is often the stepchild of speculation.

Sticking to the notion of Hampton's *Throne* as the result of his close reading of the Bible, the *Book of Dispensation* finds its niche. When God previewed the Second Coming for John the Divine, he commanded him to write what he saw in a book. Thus, the Book of Revelation. Hampton may have considered himself a latter-day prophet, but his vision, unlike John's, seems to have been incomplete. Empty notebooks were found with the *Book of Dispensation*, as if ready to be filled. It seems Hampton's secret language was either some psychic shorthand for the visions he'd had, and expected, or decorative art.

The use of secret languages and cryptic symbols is not unusual among visionaries. Hampton saw something, that he tried to describe, but it may not have been the Lord.

In all of Washington, the object most resembling *The Throne* is not sculpture, not environment, not architecture, but the lunar module from the Apollo Space Program, displayed in the southeast corner of the Air and

Space Museum. The LEM, with its gold and silver skin, its aluminized plastic films to deflect sunlight and cold, is like something from James Hampton's dreams. That it was designed to perch at the tip of a Saturn rocket, rather than in the nave of a church, is telling. The third heaven Hampton envisioned may have had less to do with religious ecstasy than physical space.

The conflict between UFOlogists and fundamentalist visionaries, as to who experienced what and why, is as old as the Bermuda Triangle. UFOlogists contend that biblical visitations may have been ancient meddlings of extraterrestrials. Fundamentalists scream, "Heresy." Suffice it to say, the symbol Hampton drew, in its field of shimmering energy, may or may not be a rocket. The crowns that were strewn about the stable, and upon which the symbol is sketched, may or may not be protective headgear. And the wings, that seem ready to lift *The Throne* like a prehistoric bird, or a vehicle, may or may not be functional. People have visions and attempt to reconstruct them through language or art. Something from another world may have visited James Hampton, and whether it was piloted by angels or astronauts, it is unlikely that even he could say.

What Hampton saw, as a religious visionary, is lost to him. What he foresaw, as a postwar artist, we may interpret. It was the age of space—not the Cape Canaveral and the Apollo Program, but that decade of apocalypse that became the 1960s. He was a prophet of cultural Armageddon. By his death in 1964, he had seen the march of Martin Luther King on Washington, men in space, the murder of John Kennedy, the birth of rock 'n' roll, and the threat of nuclear holocaust.

He was a prophet of nuclear angst. Returning to Washington in 1945, a veteran of the armed forces that had bombed Hiroshima, he had taken up work on his *Throne*. Consider what nuclear war must have meant to a fundamentalist like Hampton. The day of judgment was at hand, and Hampton's task was to construct an early warning system, a holy ark that might alert the unrepentant and whisk away the faithful. That he used bureaucratese of official Washington—and of the United Nations, that pledged to bind up the hemisphere's wounds—to catalogue *The Throne*'s parts and cross-file its mysteries, is no surprise. That he worked in the materials of his "disposable" society, the jelly glasses and kitchen foil of an Ozzie 'n' Harriet economy, may have been intentionally ironic. The final result is as evocative of that hyper-productive malaise that was the postwar mindset as the work of more intellectual artists.

Hampton was a street artist, like Robert Rauschenberg or Richard Stankiewicz, in that he worked with junk objects that, in their reassemblage, screamed the contradictions of urban life: its richness and decay, its inspiration and despair. *The Throne* is trash worshiped as riches.

Hampton's archetypal metropolis may have been the "shining city" of Revelation, but Washington was his close second. To the rural black, it was the land of opportunity. Abraham Lincoln sat upon a great white throne, and there was employment for many. By the end of Hampton's life, Washington's richness and his own poverty must have appeared the bleakest of contradictions. Seventh Street and the "monumental" style of James Hampton were eons removed from the lushness of the Mall. Yet the street wisdom of his vision was prophetic. In four years the Seventh Street corridor would lie gutted by 1968's riots, victim of a sparser apocalypse. Hampton's Throne was both a warning and vehicle for escape.

There are those who believe *The Throne* should be more accessible to poor residents. Alice Denney, if she'd acquired it, would have displayed Hampton's vision in a storefront on G Street. Something about its police badge glitter, its Hells Angels flutter and Teutonic strut, demands a more visible forum. She had wanted to tow it on a float in Lyndon B. Johnson's inaugural, as a representative piece of Washington art.

That Hampton was a spokesman for black Washington is not lost on those who do visit the museum to view *The Throne*. Some feel the hieroglyphics to be Egyptian in spirit, reflective of Hampton's awareness of his African heritage. Others sense the irony of his use of urban materials. In everyone is a respectful awe.

"Few people know it's here," a guard said recently. "I bring in friends, and kids on Sunday. Others would come if they knew. The man was strange. But this was his vision of things. It's like a flower or a letter someone left behind."

Outside, on Gallery Place, a street singer ululates in the canyons like the ghost of Hampton's father. Bright kiosks lie about the concrete like beached spacecraft. The music is the gospel of the spheres, scarcely audible in Gallery 3-D. There, a George Segal figure stands at the curtain of a tenement window and stares. She is white as milkglass, a moon-maid sentinel without mufti. A stranger approaches, glancing left to cheerful paintings, then right to something her eye has not prepared her for. It is an explosion of light. It perches there, vibrant, filling one whole room....

The Washington Post Magazine, 1981

Prince of the City:
Donald E. Graham

Don Graham bobs nervously on second, the bright red of his softball jersey darting against the summer green of West Potomac Park. *The Washington Post*, inscribed in Old English typeface across his chest, lies in contrast to the fatigues and ragtag T-shirts of this evening's opponent—the DC Department of Corrections. Perhaps because he once was a cop himself, or because he is late for a *Post* board of directors dinner at his mother's house in Georgetown, Graham has not buckled down. He's normally a big hitter. But he's one for three in this semi-final lunge toward the championship. His team, Advertising, has not failed him though. It leads, nine to two. Still the young publisher is fidgety. "Call seven-thirty for me," he's said, and each trip to the bench has sputtered, "What time is it now?" But at eight-fifteen he stands doggedly at second, the Washington monument behind him.

The Ad boys are trading publisher's-heir stories. They swill Heinekens between turns at bat and laugh about Don, long before he succeeded his mother Katharine as publisher of the *Post*—taking her place as the second-most important person in Washington, after the President, and chief of what many consider to be the most politically-influential paper in America—when in a touch football game he played blocking back against a rough squad from the *Post* mailers' union, and "almost had his head ripped off."

"They couldn't wait to take a shot at the publisher's son," an Ad boy explains. "Don hung in the whole game, and they beat the living shit out of him."

The Ad boys love Don Graham. For he's a hard case. He rounds third now, looking as if he'll charge straight into the opposing catcher. A fly ball retires the side, and Graham jogs easily toward his teammates. A MOOSE, WYOMING roping cap offsets his *Post* jersey, and though his mother may have his head tonight, his grin is that of a truant fourteen-year-old.

"What time is it?" he inquires. Then retakes the field.

The Ad boys are burly fellows, some of them ex-pro athletes, or sons of pros; they're beer drinkers and grabassers, friendly guys who range, in background, from blue collar to middle management. Graham is obviously not one of them. A teetotaling Harvard alumnus, Phi Beta Kappa, Magna Cum Laude, president of the *Crimson*, the grandson of tycoons, heir to a great media fortune, and a man whom James Reston predicted "will be the most distinguished publisher of his own generation in this century," he looks finely bred. And late.

The Ad team clinches it against Corrections, and in a flash Graham is tearing off his bright sweat gear and pulling on a conservative suit behind his car. Somewhere in Georgetown, his mother sips a cocktail and makes small talk with guests. Here a weary Corrections outfielder, oblivious to the setting sun, crumples an empty Stroh's and accosts what's left of Advertising

"No wonder you guys won," he snorts, "you're drinking Heinekens."

Graham glances back wistfully, then is off in a roar.

"DON'S ALWAYS HAD this passionate insanity about baseball," Kay Graham remembers. But she'd as well substitute newspapers, for when he was a boy they were equally around him. They were his heritage. Kay's father, Eugene Meyer, had bought the *Washington Post* in 1933 at a bankruptcy sale, and had brought it to respectability, if not profitability, by 1945 when Don was born. Don's father, Phil Graham, had been offered the paper after his marriage to Kay in 1940, but did not accept publishership until his discharge from the army in 1945. Don's earliest recollection of the *Post,* he says, is "going to the pre-1950s, E Street building to watch President Truman's inaugural parade in 1949. That building was right on Pennsylvania Avenue, so you had this fabulous view of parades. Those bands and soldiers and everything made a big impression on a four-year-old."

As they did on Phil Graham, fascinated by pomp and circumstance all his life. He'd been a bright, New Deal fledgling, the protégé of Justice Frankfurter, for whom he clerked, and a man with a future in Washington. His ambitions were political—he wished to return to Florida where he'd grown up, and run for the Senate—and he'd taken his time to accept Meyer's offer. Kay Graham, though interested in journalism, had been passed over by her father—because she was a woman, and because her father preferred Phil. Don was the second of four children born to Phil and Kay, the first boy. He was the heir apparent. From the beginning his actions hinted an awareness of his destiny. He taught himself to read from the *Post.* "The batting averages of the Nats were about the first thing," Kay recalls, "when he was three. Somebody on the team was named 'Cryhovsky' which he could read before he could read 'cat.'" And he composed his own paper in his room. The *Post* then was a distant third in circulation to the dominant *Evening Star* and in deep financial straits. Don would be nine before the *Post* bought out its morning competition, making it economically secure and causing Eugene Meyer to remark that "the real significance of this event is that it makes the paper safe for Donny."

THAT FIRST MORNING, in 1954, after the *Post* merged with the *Times-Herald*, four full pages of comics appeared in the paper. These were more comics than were offered anywhere in America, and they had an impact upon Don's St. Albans School classmates, of which I was one. Yesterday he'd been another bright, yet terribly-shy kid in class. Today he owned *Dick Tracy*, *Li'l Abner*, and the others. He seemed to walk a little taller, even strut. And his classmates regarded him differently; with a kind of awe. The comics were evidence that stakes had changed, that the *Post* and Donny were to be taken seriously. "Until I was nine," Don remembers, "my dad was publisher of the third-largest paper in Washington. I was not burdened by notoriety." Subsequently, he was afforded a near-celebrity status that markedly affected his demeanor. He'd always been nervous, "Like a flea on a hot griddle," says John Davis, assistant headmaster during those years. But he became more nervous. The mantle of notoriety weighed upon him. And it drove him to cover—toward a life of camouflaged enthusiasms and needs. He wanted more than anything to remain one of the boys. Yet he wished to prove himself, to excel on his own terms.

He was one of the brightest students in a class many feel to be the brightest St. Albans has produced. He had its quickest mind and a near-photographic memory. He was unaffected, but extremely sensitive. And he was driven, particularly after the *Herald* merger. Work always had been easy for him, but I remember an unmonitored study period during that first year of the *Post's* ascension where—the majority of his classmates crazed with playful fidgeting—Don worked obsessively, his hands clamped over his ears.

John Davis thinks his mother was the strongest force upon him. "This is not a criticism of Kay," Davis says, "but John Knox wrote a book in the sixteenth century called *A Monstrous Regiment of Women*—about the female rulers of the time: Mary Queen of Scots, Elizabeth, and Catherine de Medici, all of them very strong ladies. They affect the oldest son most. Don's brothers, at St. Albans, were much more relaxed than he."

But Kay Graham then was a 1950's housewife, bundled in the bleachers or chauffeuring footballers in carpools. Phil, by contrast, was unforgettable, dynamic, obviously a star. Even to a kid he stood out, his face a lantern signaling, "What's this—what's so damn serious?"

He was funny, as are all the Grahams. "We were encouraged to express wit," recalls Steve Graham, the younger of Don's two brothers, "instead of emotion." For wit was Phil Graham's forte, helping to bedrock him as a prime mover and in Washington the most influential publisher of his day—a man who talked John Kennedy into picking Lyndon Johnson as running mate, who conceived much of what would become Johnson's Great Society, and who used his paper as a fulcrum, as a force for change. But after 1957, he was a desperately ill man, a manic-depressive alternating giddy highs with paralyzing lows. And though he more than anyone made the *Post* a success, he railed against his role as Meyer's son-in-law, against the paper as a tainted gift (its publisher before Meyer had destroyed himself with booze and drugs), and what he saw as a missed career in politics.

Don suffered because of these conflicts—"My father's long silences," Steve Graham remembers, "then dinner with Jack Kennedy or Lyndon Johnson, where you had to compete to be noticed and there was this tremendous pressure to excel, particularly on Don because of primogeniture"—but also because he bridged several worlds at school. He was a brain, but too much of an athlete to run comfortably with the brains. And he was younger, "a year younger and two years smarter," someone quipped, having skipped a grade—making him not quite mature enough to run with the jocks. By his senior year, he was editor of the school paper and "Best All Around Athlete." Much of his insecurity had fallen away. But not all, for he had another distinction: his family were "in trade," that is, business. And therefore not readily embraced by Washington society. In addition, the Meyers were Jewish and Kay Graham, in her 1997 memoir, would speak of the anti-Semitism she encountered growing up. Some of that lingered into the 1950s. The Meyers were of political Washington, as was Phil Graham. And they were tycoons. The *Star* was owned and staffed by an old Washington family—the Kauffmans, and in part, the Noyes. The *Star* was Washington's establishment paper, conservative, entrenched with an advertising base that was the solidest in the nation. "We liked the *Star*," Davis says. Phil Graham, born in South Dakota and raised in semi-frontier circumstances in Florida's Everglades, was—like his friend Jack Kennedy—representative of a new breed. The *Post* was liberal, "extremely liberal in those days," Davis recalls, and Don bore the brunt of that at school.

St. Albans was the private, Episcopalian school of old Washington families, and in the tradition of stiff upper lip. Reluctantly it catered to the city's political sons. But by the 1950s, the growing meritocracy could not be ignored; and no longer did St. Albans wish to ignore it. In Don's class, or surrounding it, were Restons, Smathers, Symingtons, a Jonathon Agronsky, a Dave Marriott, a Brit Hume, a Jack Smith, an Al Gore, a Cliff Case, a son of Eisenhower's Defense Secretary, and numerous others.

"Donny behaved much as many of our political boys do," Davis says. "Cautious, don't say anything that can be quoted. Very cool, covering everything. Otherwise it all goes home. Somebody might say, 'Do you know what Donny Graham told me?' And the Washington gossip mill picks it up."

He was yoked to duty and the often-conflicting drive toward an invisible brand of excellence. He took much frustration out in athletics, in wrestling, and a fierce game of tennis. But he rose with his classmates, at commencement in 1962, to sing the school hymn: *Men of the future, stand...*

"I don't know why he hasn't jumped out of a window," Steve Graham says.

Now, in July of 1984, Don Graham stands in the mailroom of the *Washington Post*, still edgy, still strained, but determinedly addressing five hundred employees at the Eugene Meyer Awards—instigated in 1983 to celebrate the fiftieth anniversary of Meyer's purchase of the paper.

"We're holding this party here," he jokes, "because so many of you have asked, 'What does the mailroom look like?'"

In fact, the mailroom was chosen for reasons of space. And its factory-like gloom is masked this evening by Astroturf and bright partitions, so that the event has been transformed from drab, corporate duty to cocktails in the garden.

"In a way," Don continues, "the mailroom is a wonderfully appropriate place to hold this party, because it is the essence of this place and what this award is all about—that everyone is very, very busy."

Certainly Don is, and by any yardstick, an extremely successful publisher. Yet he looks young—handsome as a TV anchorman—with red in his cheeks that electrifies with excitement or embarrassment. As the *Post*'s boss, he's raised its income, since taking the helm in 1979, from $35.4 to $78.8 million, increased its daily penetration to 56 percent of local households, highest in the nation (the *New York Times* boasts 31 percent), and has helped nudge the *Post* Corporation's operating revenues from $593.3 to over $900 million. He speaks of tonight's award as exemplifying "the journalistic and business values of Eugene Meyer." Checks go to an engraver, to an ad salesman (advertising being the *Post*'s richest department, setting records in 1983 for a staggering 104 million ad lines, and building papers so fat "they're breaking little newsboys' arms"), and to Herblock of editorial, each of whom has served nearly forty years.

There's obeisance to tradition here. Meyer's legacy is a weighty one at the *Post*. And Don remembers him fondly as "shy and gentle with children, a man who loved baseball, cigars, gin rummy, and who lived in a wonderful but improbable world of enormous houses." He'd been an internationally known financier who set up Allied Chemical, helped with the financing of World War I, cashed in his chips before the crash, was chairman of the Federal Reserve Board, worked as a dollar-a-year-man in four administrations, and wanted, for the *Post*, international clout. The son of immigrant Jewish parents, like Kay he'd been the target of anti-Semitism in Washington (the *Herald*'s Cissy Patterson sent him an elegantly-wrapped pound of raw flesh after losing to him in a business caper—the Shylock allusion unmistakable), but had persevered because he wanted a voice. He wanted a paper for the public good, "a modern, international paper," that was both independent and self-sufficient. And he considered himself a public servant.

His wife, Agnes, had been an author and the grandest of Washington's salon hostesses, after the intellectual style— she was the intimate of Thomas Mann, Paul Claudel, Edward Steichen, and others. Don remembers Agnes and her salon, but colleagues think that if he emulates any relative it is Eugene Meyer.

"That's the model in Don Graham's head," says William Greider, formerly of the *Post* but now a political columnist for *Rolling Stone*. "A hardheaded and successful businessman, super competent, reasonably aggressive, but honorable."

Tonight, the emphasis in Don's remarks is on business and circulation. Even cartoonist Herblock is chided for causing "Richard M. Nixon to cancel his subscription four times." Don's speech is funny, and Kay Graham—though presenting the awards—remains in the background. This is Don's party, an R&B group plays to the largely-black workforce, as editorial staff mingle and Don smiles through his shyness to clasp many a hand.

Employees mumble praise for his speech. "It was Don at his best." And veteran reporter Murrey Marder notes that "for the first time Don seemed to be speaking completely on his own—and with an extraordinary degree of confidence. This speech had a real, 'I'm in charge' tone."

The *Post* is not the first paper of which Don's had charge. His last year at Harvard, he ran the *Crimson*—an independent daily, staffed by students, that traditionally never makes a cent. Under Don's presidency it cleared $27,000 profit. "Which was a lot," his *Crimson* mates recall. His success surprised no one. Despite the notoriety of his father, who after the purchase of *Newsweek* and a *Time* cover story was well known, Don labored to prove himself—having joined the *Crimson* nearly against his father's advice.

Kay says that "Don always had an absolute passion for newspapers, to the point where my husband asked him not to go out for the *Crimson* right away. 'Because,' he said to Don, 'you have never known anything but newspapers, and you really should not have that narrow an experience—why don't you wait a while?' So he waited two months."

He'd been lonely, but the *Crimson* filled that void. And it introduced him to a slim, blonde freshman at Radcliffe named Mary Wissler, who eventually would become his wife.

"The first time I wrote anything for the paper," Don says, "Mary was the night editor. Harvard became enjoyable largely because of Mary and the *Crimson*."

What followed was something like respite for Graham—and splendor in the grass. His first date with Mary was an overnight jaunt with Andy Beyer (now the *Post*'s racing columnist) and his girl, to the Finger Lakes racetrack near Syracuse. "They said if we won," Mary remembers, "we'd stay in a fancy hotel—if not, a fleabag. We stayed in a fleabag." Don was gambling then—he'd loosened up that much—but his big interest was Mary, whom he dated intermittently at first, driving far in search of traveling rock 'n' roll shows, of which he was a fan. He knew black music; he blared Chuck Jackson and the Motown groups incessantly, stopped in New York for Murray the K's Christmas Show at the Brooklyn Fox, and would leave his sister Lally's wedding early to catch James Brown and the Famous Flames. He reviewed plays and movies for the *Crimson*, and befriended Timothy Mayer, now a successful director and playwright. Together they sought out the East Coast's hottest theater, and talked late, in Cambridge diners, of plays, movies, and literature. Don was tall like his father, but muscular and physically intimidating. "All the *Crimson* women were in love with him," says Marty Levine, a *Crimson* editor.

Don was so high on this existence that friends like Tim Mayer were thinking he might shuck his inheritance and follow "a more contemplative life" than newspapering, "where you got a chance to read and do a little writing— or perhaps choose something more engagé." Don was "high on weariness," Mayer remembers, on Mary, on correcting late-night page proofs, on Harvard's and the *Crimson*'s grueling pace. Then, on August 3, 1963, Phil Graham put a shotgun to his head and pulled the trigger.

Don was working as a summer intern for James Reston at the time. His father had been on leave from a private psychiatric hospital, and depressed. In recent years he had drunk heavily, flaunted a series of public romances, stormed against Meyer, Kay, and the children, calling them kikes and bemoaning his lot as son-in-law. He'd seemed to be progressing under treatment, but his psychiatrists concede it was a terrible mistake to release him that weekend.

When Don speaks of his father's illness, his voice drops to a whisper. He won't talk of it much, "I can't," he says. "He—was just a hell of a guy. I have that funny picture of him there, with a towel wrapped around him by somebody's swimming pool, because it's one of the few photographs I've seen of him where he looks as smiling and relaxed and funny as I remember him. And he was funny. He was—a very busy man. But I can remember lots of important times in my life when he was there. You took it for granted at the time, as kids do, but he took a lot of trouble to be there, as good parents do."

Don was eighteen when his father died. The experience steeled him.

"It's the kind of thing that focuses the mind, doesn't it?" Reston observes.

Don's *Crimson* friends say that they first noticed his remoteness after his father's suicide—and that a shell appeared. Four months later, Jack Kennedy was assassinated and Don was doubly crushed. "I believed in the guy pretty strongly," he says, and with characteristic understatement admits that the fall of 1963 was "rough." There was a good bit of anti-Kennedy sentiment at the plutocratic Harvard. But Jack Kennedy had been Phil's friend, and on the business board of the *Crimson*. When asked what responsibility Don felt then to succeed his father at the *Post* he says, "I don't know. It was not zero." On the day of Phil's funeral, his mother had reaffirmed to *Post* associates that "There is another generation coming, and we intend to turn the paper over to them, "

Tim Mayer recalls that "It was as if Don picked up the fallen sword, and went back to battle with it."

He toughened, earned the nickname "Mountbatten," and seemed determined to carry on both the *Post*'s and Jack Kennedy's burdens.

But to side with the *Post* was not necessarily to side with Phil Graham. Despite his grief, a Victorian aspect of Don's character emerged, down on drink, down on womanizing, and noticeably conservative. He majored in English History and Literature, writing his thesis on Thomas Babington Macaulay, a historian and author who'd enjoyed a strong career in Parliament. A favorite class became "The Age of Johnson." And friends like Marty Levine, his managing editor on the *Crimson*, noticed "a sense of duty that got in the way of a human response." One of Phil Graham's last public acts had been

to intervene in the New York newspaper strike of 1962—
on the side of the printers, or labor—and one of Don's
last acts as president of the *Crimson* was to intervene in
the Boston newspaper strike of 1965, by publishing a
scab paper, the Boston *Crimson*, in a nonunion shop.

"He saw it as a public service," Levine remembers,
"and the press run was tiny—a few tens of thousands of
issues—lasting eight or ten days. But it was Don's idea,
and he carried everyone with him." He was ecstatic at his
success, and Tim Mayer recalls, the first night, that "Don
waited until the presses were actually rolling, and saw that
there would be a daily, urban newspaper—complete with
the number—and he went outside into the darkness, by
himself, and having been nothing but crisp and efficient in
front of everybody else, quite literally clicked his heels."

It's a back o' town landscape out H Street Northeast,
less *Road Warrior* than when Graham patrolled here
as a DC cop after the 1968 riots, but still mottled
with debris-strewn lots and shuttered businesses—the
hogmaw carryouts and voodoo shops, the juke joints
and storefront churches, the sidewalk evangelists, the
row houses with corn in their tiny backyards, reminding
that this is a Washington of the deep South, a capital the
tourists never see. Ninety percent black and impoverished,
it's a high-crime neighborhood as far from his parents' in
Georgetown as one can get.

"Working here," Don says, "was the best education I
ever had, and the one I think back on most." The radio in
Inspector Max Krupa's car never stops squawking.

"Over there," Krupa says, "is where a guy bit the
breasts off a woman, stabbed and dumped her in a yard."

"And over that way," Graham says, "I found a body by
the river one morning, Dead from exposure. Probably a
drunk. There's the old Ko-Ko Club, which was so tough a
judge said once that in his court just being within a block
of it constituted disorderly conduct."

"I was surprised," Kay Graham says, reflecting on Don's

eighteen months with the police, "and a little distressed, I was looking forward to getting him in here at the *Post*. I thought maybe he should go to business or law school. And proposed those things to him. But he said, 'I want to do something that will teach me about the city.' And I said, 'Well how about being a reporter?' When he decided on the police corps it did not enchant me. I thought that after a year walking around in Vietnam with a gun, we might give that up. And get cracking."

Don had enlisted in the army after graduating from Harvard, and friends think it was Vietnam that turned him toward the police, and ultimately sharpened the *Post*'s focus on Washington's inner city. He'd avoided the army officer's corps, "to get it over with, to serve two years instead of three," but also to dodge notoriety. "Please don't tell them who my mother is," Herb Denton remembers Don asking, during their tour together in Vietnam. Denton, a reporter on the foreign desk of the *Post* and a *Crimson* mate of Graham's, is one of his closest friends—coincidentally a Southerner and black, Denton recalls that "our tour was right after Truman Capote's party for Kay, and Don was struggling to stay just Pfc. Donald E. Graham. His mother's friends, like Joe Alsop and Ted Kennedy, kept flying in though, asking to meet with him. And that blew his cover. Don has spent his life trying to prove himself worthy. It's a terrible burden for an American boy to be born into such wealth, such notoriety."

Graham enlisted, "because I was going to be drafted, and I had no intention of going to graduate school," but also because he felt it his duty to serve. At Harvard he'd been right of center on Vietnam—his *Crimson* mates gave him a live hawk at his farewell dinner as president—and editorially was a hardliner against withdrawal. "The talk then was of enclave strategies," he recalls, "of hope for a negotiated solution." What had been Kennedy's war was now Johnson's (Graham could remember JFK arriving magisterially at their house to meet with Phil before the election), and Johnson was very much Phil Graham's man. Don's world as a boy had been that of the Best and the Brightest. He knew Kennedy, McNamara, Mac Bundy, and the rest. They were guests at his parents' table; occasionally he'd surprise classmates in a St. Albans debate, by saying, "No, that's wrong. Last Night at dinner Mr. Stephenson said—" So that his awakening to the nightmare of Vietnam was especially traumatic.

"My view of the war changed totally the day I got there," Graham says. Much of what he'd read about the war failed to jibe—troubling because Graham's mentors, the Walter Lippmans, the Joe Alsops, the Scotty Restons, and others of Washington's premier columnists, were his parents' Georgetown friends. Johnson seemed, from Vietnam, "like a very bad wartime leader," and Graham came to feel "not supportive and not warmly" toward his father's colleague. Graham's assignment was that of an Information Specialist with the 1st Air Cavalry, writing hometowner releases for newspapers around America, and editing the division paper and magazine. (He was sent the *Washington Post* by the paper throughout his tour.) And he was both flack and a war correspondent in uniform, an anomaly, subject to censorship and the whims of his superiors—who once they realized his identity tried to keep him from combat. He threw in, defiantly, with that new breed of reporter making rounds in Vietnam, men like Michael Herr, Dana Stone, Jack Laurence, and Ward Just, who weren't afraid to tell it like it was.

"I spent a lot of time as a photographer," Graham remembers, "and my job, often, was to escort correspondents. Or to spend four or five days with an infantry platoon or company, either on a firebase or in the field, and write about it."

What he wrote about was the infantry, the grunts, a large percentage of whom were black, and a population with which Graham had had little contact—outside rock 'n' roll. His last night before Vietnam, he went "to see Janis Joplin and Otis Redding at the Fillmore West," he remembers. "It gave you a sense of what you were fighting for." The black grunts were rock 'n' roll, and he came to admire them enormously. "In Vietnam," he wrote, "there is the infantry, and there is everyone else." He followed them through An Khe, Bong Son, Chu Lai, and to Hue for the Air Cav's relief of Khe Sanh. He had a helicopter shot out from under him and was nearly killed. He saw "blacks and whites risking their lives for one another, and relationships among people of different races in those infantry platoons I've never seen anywhere else." And he felt deep respect "for the conscripts, the draftees, who did 90 percent of the fighting."

Graham had serious disillusionments about the war—about the US government's duplicity, and the press's failure to see. He expressed his views to correspondents passing through, and afterward cornered Secretary of State William Rogers for a half-hour piece of his mind. "He listened politely," Graham recalls. And Don's break with official policy was yet another break with his father's world.

"I remain very uncomfortable about what I thought and did at the time, in Vietnam. And I have enormous admiration for the people who conscientiously went to jail or refused draft service. It was a highly principled position."

He'd traveled a ways from the Harvard senior who'd snidely published, in *The Atlantic Monthly*, an article about the draft called, "Taking a McNamara Fellowship."

"I came back from Vietnam terribly saddened, and changed," Graham says. "And I was firmly convinced that I wanted to go work for the *Washington Post*—that a clear description of what went on in the world was one of the most useful things you can do. In college there's the tendency to think, 'will I be like Shakespeare, will I be like Tolstoy?' In the army you come to grips with the reality of what most of life is like. I realized that being anywhere around the *Post* was a dream come true."

Still there were potholes. By 1968, when Don returned

from Vietnam, Kay Graham had succeeded as head of the *Post* beyond anyone's wildest dreams. "It's the most amazing damn story," Don admits. At Phil Graham's suicide, Kay had had the Corporation dropped into her lap. With no business experience and with a few years to her credit as a reporter, she took over the family company. By 1968, she already was being spoken of as America's most influential corporate woman. And the widow who had wrung her hands waiting for Don to finish Harvard so that he might take over the *Post* was having second thoughts. She wanted him in the company—not as publisher but as a reporter, or a business trainee.

Don, who had trained dutifully at the *Crimson* and every summer during college at news desks from the *Winston-Salem Journal* to the *New York Times*, was being shunted aside. He called the cops.

"Actually," he remembers, "I got a call from them. Johnson had just ordered a thousand men added to the force, and the police were desperate for people."

Nevertheless, it was a difficult step. To be a white cop in 1968 was to be a pig. Or the man. And it was dangerous. Kay Graham thought of stopping him. "Our police reporter, Al Lewis, said, 'I can stop it, don't worry.' But I said no, it's what he wants to do, let's not stand in his way."

It was an odd step, and something of a vet reaction to coming home. But Don was pulling against the *Post*'s leash. Though recruited, he predated those Ivy League cops who discovered, about 1970, they could obtain both draft deferments and decent-paying, poverty-program experience by joining the police, The force was only 18 percent black when Graham joined. He befriended black officers, and was resented by his white peers in the segregated precinct house. "When Don was first introduced at roll call," Max Krupo says, "the lieutenant announced, 'this is Donald Graham, who graduated from Harvard.' Everybody was immediately suspicious. 'What's he doing here? He's writing a book. Be careful what you say.' And it didn't take long to realize who his mother was."

The reasons for Don's service are enormously complicated. Family intervention was a large portion of the patrolman's work, and he's said that, "plenty of times during a day you are asked to come into someone's life at a critical point, when by doing the job well you can make a substantial difference to them." His father's suicide and alcoholism factor into that, and his own veteran's reluctance to relinquish a firearm, coupled with that awful mandate of the suicide's child to brush against death, must have added to the burden. Yet he found police work "surprisingly enjoyable." And Tim Mayer says that "I have a feeling Don really liked being a cop."

And though he was rebelling against Kay and his heritage, the *Post* was never far from mind.

As it's not this afternoon. He and Inspector Krupo are old Sunday partners, having been rookies together—each volunteering for service in this, the former ninth precinct. Krupo has stuck with the force. "I wish I had a whole section like Don working for me now," he concedes. Graham, his brown eyes darting, patrician accent, but full sideburns and longish patrolman's hair, seems less a cop today than a grownup playing one. He converses easily with Krupo; this is a tour Graham makes periodically. He writes about the police, speaks at heroes' banquets honoring the fallen, and stays in touch with the street. It's part of his philosophy of publishing: metropolitan news is the backbone of the *Post*, and the *Post* must cover the city. The city is 75 percent black. To cover Washington, to write of it accurately and fairly, one must know Washington. And Graham's his own reporter. That's why he walks to appointments whenever possible, gets his hair cut in an old, black-run barbershop, and to an extent it's why he became a cop.

"I don't know any other publisher who has studied the underside of his community as extensively as Don did through that program," says Tom Johnson, publisher of the *Los Angeles Times*.

His mother concedes that Don changed more after his police service than after Vietnam. "He'd become more secure, or adult." And Ben Bradlee, who'd encouraged him to join, says, "There's something romantic about it—someone who knows he's going to be a leader of a community, starting out walking the streets of that community before walking into a job that has been there since before he was born. There's a whole lot of publishers who wouldn't have the balls to do it."

THE CAMERAS of *Entertainment Tonight* dart menacingly toward Joan Mondale as Graham, in a "Bob Forehead for President" tie and dark suit, shields the candidate's wife from Barbara Howar's frontal assault. He looks supremely annoyed, "My mother is really much better at this sort of thing than I am," he says, painfully, Then turns toward Pat Moynihan, who's still gloating over Mario Cuomo's keynote address and what many in San Francisco are calling "a New York convention." This is *Post/Newsweek*'s quadrennial bash, and that it's hosted by Kay Graham means that it's very much a Washington party. Here at Levi Plaza are Walter Cronkite, Warren Beatty, Gloria Steinem, James Brooks, George Lucas, Jerry Brown, Ralph Nader, Art Buchwald, Clay Felker, Tom Brokaw, George Will, Sam Donaldson, and every media celebrity worth his or her salt in San Francisco this week. It's a full house and tonight's coveted invitation. As cocktail music plays, eight hundred of the Democratic anointed stand cheek to jowl, packing in the rich food and top shelf booze, ad nauseum, ad Georgetown and the refined taste of a Georgetown hostess.

"Kay sure knows how to throw a party," someone croaks. And, "If Kay Graham can't roust them out, no one can."

This is the Post Corporation of international renown, still basking in Watergate, in Kay's and Ben Bradlee's reputations.

141

But there's a ghost lurking, the ghost of Phillip L. Graham.

"We had dinner the other night," Bradlee rasps in his sandpapery voice, "and were talking about how we're going to a convention in California, and it was twenty-four years ago that Phil 'went to a convention in California,' and was engaged in the kingmaking process that helped make the vice president. The idea of doing anything similar makes Don laugh."

But he's not laughing here. He's tense and a bit guarded. Though fascinated with politics and politicians, Phil's kind of meddling is not his style. The ghosts of Jack Kennedy and Lyndon Johnson are present, too. As are those of old responsibilities. Eugene Meyer had been born in California, and on a walk with me through San Francisco—a town so redolent with the rebellious history of the sixties—Don, oddly, has spoken of the old San Francisco families, and of their responsibility in building up the city. And as apologists of every persuasion wheeled and dealed at Moscone Center, Don asked a newsboy, "How's the *L.A. Times* selling?" And applauded *USA Today*'s front page interview, "Ferraro's Mom!" as the best headline of the day,

"Kingmaking is not my job," Don says. "I'm very romantic about what newspapers can do if they're good, and good papers can make a difference in the world because they tell an important story well." A registered Independent, because "it's both appropriate and how I feel," Graham moves easily through this crowd, telling stories and greeting everyone by name, but he does not join his mother and Bradlee in the Corporation's receiving line, and the questions he asks are those of a reporter: what's happening at the convention, who's doing what. "I'm here to see how good our political coverage stacks up," he says, "and I'll tell you it's a lot of fun to watch our national staff go to work." It's the sort of remark a politician would make. Celebrities spot him, say hello, make their pitch. Don's having none of it. At the *New York*

Times luncheon tomorrow, dour by this party's standard, New York City mayor Ed Koch will walk across the room to pump Don's hand. But here, Don looks exasperated. As Kay fawns over Warren Beatty, and Beatty fawns back, Don mutters, "I haven't had anything to eat and I'm very tired."

He was tired in 1970, after eighteen months as a ghetto police officer, but not quite ready to enter the *Post*. Kay threw a party for him and his police buddies at her house in Georgetown—and of course her friends were invited. "It was classically *Upstairs, Downstairs*," recalls Nixon staffer Frank Gannon, "with Joe Alsop mingling among the patrolmen." Max Krupo had a long talk with Don at Kay's party, about the force, and about Don's service.

"He regretted leaving," Krupo says, "but he had other things he wanted to do. That esprit de corps, though, that comes about from life and death situations on the force, is hard to give up."

"Mary had graduated from law school," Don recalls, "so we took four or five months and traveled, to Europe and to Kenya where we had college friends." She and Don had been married during his army service. They'd worried through Vietnam together, the police, and now they would tackle the *Post*.

In January of 1971, he went to work at the paper, as a city reporter. He can't remember how he felt at the time. "You come into the organization, though, and you are the publisher's son. One very lucky thing starting out is that, when people hear the publisher's son is coming to work there, it's almost impossible to be as bad as they expect you to be."

No one expected incompetence from Don, but there was a reservation of judgment. And skepticism. "The basic, universal instinct is to sneer at the young heir," says Meg Greenfield, then deputy editor of the editorial page, "often with reason. But Don worked hard around this building, and earned people's respect and friendship."

"He started in news," Kay says, "which I questioned at

the time. I asked if he shouldn't start in business, because he'd had news experience. But he made a definitive argument for starting in editorial, because he said that he didn't know how a big city room worked, and unless he knew that he wouldn't know how production should relate to it."

But it was more tugging at his mother's leash—perhaps intuitively struggling against future plans—and Don went for the fun rather than the ultimate responsibility.

This was Ben Bradlee's newsroom, after all, where Vince Lombardi was God, "creative tension" the dogma, and where machismo ruled. Don covered a police beat, reviewed Joseph Wambaugh's novels, wrote a series on alcoholism, and covered the May Day antiwar riots (as a cop he'd housed college friends during demonstrations, they off each morning to rail against the establishment, he off in uniform to hold them in line). By all accounts he was a good reporter, but Kay was antsy to move him along. And there was unexpected competition from Bradlee.

"Then," she recalls, "after he'd gone through the various city-room positions, and I was preparing to start him in business, Ben offered him the sports editorship of the paper. Without, as usual, discussing it with me. I really was furious. Ben had a problem to solve, which was that he needed to make a transition in sports. It solved Ben's problem, but not mine. And, I mean, it would have been like cruelty to animals to say, 'no you can't do that'— since it combined both Don's passions, sports and editing. I said, 'okay, but you really have to go in and out and replace yourself within a year.' And he did."

But during that year, he had a glass partition torn down that isolated sportswriters from the rest of the city room, hired and fired staff, improved the section's design, moved city reporters through sports for a diversity of experience, and ran a contest to locate a new horse racing handicapper.

George Solomon, the *Post*'s current sports editor and a reporter under Don, says that "He created an atmosphere that we've tried to carry on—that lends itself to a lot of creativity, enthusiasm, and enterprise."

Don liked being sports editor, and canonizes it in his memory as "that one glorious year." But one year it would be, as Kay had other plans for him—during a period she would call "War," and that would prove the darkest hours of the *Washington Post*.

BELLS OF THE MOVING presses ring, while the huge offset and letterpress machines rock about like trains in a switching yard, emitting a roar and then a fine mist of ink and paper fiber, as Don Graham cuts through on his night rounds of the *Post*. Black and Vietnamese press operators (some of them women) labor in dark coveralls, carrying long knives at their belts. The operators are muscular and extremely physical. There's a certain amount of restrained roughhousing here. Graham struts by in his rolling cop's gait, greeting each employee by name. It was here that Phil Graham shot craps with the pressmen and had his chauffeur set up drinks, warning, "Don't get too drunk fellas, we've got a paper to get out." And it was here, in 1975, that an all-white pressmen's union smashed and burned the presses, beat a foreman, rioted, and began a strike against the *Post* that lasted well into 1976. Before it was over, they would hang Kay Graham in effigy and brandish a placard reading, "Phil Shot the Wrong Graham."

Don looks exhausted. It's a long day at the paper that begins at six-thirty, every day, and tonight will extend until one. He's drawn, and various employees ask if he's lost weight. Some special dates approach: the tenth anniversary of Nixon's resignation, the third anniversary of the *Star*'s demise, and the twentieth anniversary of his father's suicide. All occur within a five-day stretch. Don will retreat, with his wife and family, to Kay's house on Martha's Vineyard for the weekend of his father's death. But tonight he spends time at the *Post*—his other family.

"There are a lot of workmen still here," Bradlee says,

"particularly in the factory part, who've worked for the Grahams most of their lives. It requires an understanding of that to understand Don—he's very into that."

Over the couch in Den's office is a print given to him by the Vietnamese press operators. It means a lot, and though some employees criticize Den's interest in the factory as "the plantation-owner side" of his personality, the Vietnamese know they wouldn't be at the *Post* if not for Don. Not in the old, segregated press room. He jokes with the Vietnamese, and with the tough, black pressmen, inquiring after their families. He knows everyone's job, and seemingly the names of everyone's spouse. What they don't know is that he and others of management are trained to run the presses and perform their jobs at the first hint of a walkout.

As they were in 1975. The *Washington Post* strike is a case taught at Harvard business school. It has had far-reaching effects upon the security of unions, both at the *Post* and at other papers. And it's had its effect on Don. When it occurred, Kay had just promoted him to assistant general manager of the *Post*—number two man in charge of production. The background to the strike is immensely complicated. But the *Post* had been suffering financially in the early seventies, and after it went public as a corporation—to save on inheritance taxes for Don, and to insure his control of the paper—Kay was being seen by Wall Street as a publisher soft on unions, the "little lady" on board, afraid to cut back. That attitude (which infuriated her), coupled to a recession and severe difficulties in the pressroom, caused her to hire a professional labor negotiator and to shoot doggedly for a high, yearly rise in profits. The *Post* was being milked by its pressmen's union (guilty of featherbedding, slowdowns, and opposed to any modernization of the antiquated, hot-type technology), and both Don and Kay realized they were coming close to losing control of their operation. The pressroom was chaos—a fen of drinking, racism, and inefficiency. And it was nomadic, 70 percent of its membership having no rooted loyalty to the *Post*. Still they were a work force, the grunts at the paper, and Don was torn when it became his job to run the pressroom without them.

"It was a sad thing to go through," he says, "because of the violent hostility between the paper and the people who worked here. But we had no choice about what to do."

That was the obvious, public stance. Privately, Don had to choose between the company (of which he was a principal shareholder) and organized labor. He went with the company.

It was a pivotal moment, violent and divisive for the paper, equally divisive for Don, He lost twenty pounds and showed anxiety only through a kind of efficiency-mania. He was under terrific pressure. "We were just damn mad," he concedes now, but cannot remember much else of how he felt or what he did at the time. Events were a blur. Most of management worked two jobs—running the presses, selling ads or classified at night. Don slept in his office and worked nights as a paper handler, performing the dirtiest and most demanding physical labor. Management had been trained to take a strike by the Southern Production Program, Inc. of Oklahoma City, a "scab school" to union members. And it seemed as if Don had been prepped further by Kay for this particular operation. Employees remember it as a "Vietnam-style operation," complete with helicopters landing on the *Post*'s roof to fly copy to sympathetic newspapers for printing. But there was a strange gaiety to it as well—tuxedoed waiters served refreshments to executives in the pressroom, and colleagues recall that, rather than show anxiety, Don "just glowed, it was like combat duty and he was a commander in battle." Of course, it was not the first time he had put out a paper during a strike. The ghost of the *Boston Crimson* joined that of Phil Graham, rattling craps on the pressroom floor.

Practically everyone cheered the elimination of the

pressmen's union—the pressmen were seen as having "ripped the social contract" in their smashing of the presses—but the swiftness with which they were dealt with, and a vacuum of organized labor in the new pressroom, shot a chill through the *Post*'s unions. Don himself toughened. The Newspaper Guild, which had crossed picket lines during the strike and helped insure publication, was treated to extended settlements of their contracts, and became embittered. Don's position was that the unions did not adequately represent his employees, and that he could better insure their welfare. He set out to prove this, in the pressroom, by establishing college programs, paid for by the *Post* at Rochester Institute of Technology, and by improving work conditions. But he was torn between wanting everyone to admire him as a regular guy, and duty. Or what Robert Kaiser of the *Post*'s Outlook section calls, "a remarkable, filial sense of obligation, an enormous obligation to Kay," and an "unusually intense son/mother relationship."

On January 10, 1979, when Don took over from her as publisher, he'd been general manager of the paper for two years—and had completed an eight-year apprenticeship that took him through every department of the *Post*, and to its subsidiary, *Newsweek*. "I suspect Don was ready before I was ready," Kay says. But for his wait, he received control of the largest portion of *Post* stock short of his mother's—and a far larger chunk than any of his siblings. That portion in 1984 translated to over $300 million in class A and class B holdings. One could not help but wonder if it was worth it. Or whether he'd ever felt he had a choice. His brothers and sisters, who'd complain of their share, became multi-millionaires without lifting a finger.

"Better him than me," Steve Graham says, of Don's publishership.

Don stood alone with Kay that first afternoon, at an emotional ceremony at the *Post*, and said, "Today, as in the rest of my life, my mother has given me everything but an easy act to follow."

IT'S THE TENTH anniversary of Watergate, and Carl Bernstein, long departed from the paper, ducks into Bob Woodward's office to meet him for a drink. "Aren't they shooting you with rays?" Bernstein asks, indicating Woodward's proximity to the Soviet embassy.

"Actually," Woodward says, "my penis fell off last week."

In the fifth-floor newsroom, a five o'clock mania has struck. Deadlines loom and the celebrated news team of David Broder, Jules Witcover, Haynes Johnson, Lou Cannon, Murrey Marder, and others—hustles to file. Bradlee is on vacation, but his presence hovers—that of an elegantly demanding chimera. This is the *Post* of international clout, "the most competitive newsroom in the business," says media critic Ben Bagdikian, which every foreign dignitary (including royalty) and the highest domestic officials court and visit regularly—for breakfast and luncheon meetings, usually hosted by Don. Although the *Post* and its subsidiary, the *International Herald Tribune*, are key targets, "Kay and Don are whom these people are coming to see," Marder notes.

The *Post*'s clout is so great in 1984, that Soviet leader Konstantin Chernenko will grant the paper his first interview to a foreign journalist—and make points to Dusko Doder of the *Post*'s Moscow bureau he hesitates to make directly to President Reagan or his administration.

Don has lunched with David Stockman of OMB, at the Executive Office Building today, But now he's on the subway home. This host to prime ministers and kings, a force in *Post* editorial decisions, boss of Benjamin C. Bradlee, and heir to a $900 million corporation, rides the Metro. It's his style. Colleagues tell of stumbling upon him at a bus stop, or in the bowels of Washington's underground, hunched in a drab overcoat and watch cap like a character from Dostoyevsky. It cheers him to be offered a ride, and he'll accept—for he'd never think to blow a sawbuck on a taxi, or to relinquish the isolation that cloaks him irrevocably at the *Post*, and that he flaunts like a badge. He'll always be the publisher's son. And on night rounds of the plant, or alone at dawn in the vastness of the deserted *Post*, where he sips coffee and pores over the morning's paper, Phil Graham's predicament of whether to accept or reject what's offered must always be with him.

He spends much time at Glen Welby, Phil's country estate near Middleburg—practically every weekend during summer. It was at Glen Welby that Phil shot himself, and to which Don hurried from Washington as his father's body lay in a downstairs bathroom. Don has a garden at Glen Welby, where he works for hours alone, weeding, hoeing. "He started gardening as something to do with the kids," Mary Graham says, "but has gone astray. There's no child out there."

And his siblings have run far. Bill Graham is an investor in California, Steve an off-Broadway producer, Lally an author and social figure in New York. She's been heard to remark, "Rupert Murdoch did it right. He's leaving one paper to a son, one to a daughter." But she doesn't want the *Post*, any more than Steve or Bill. There can be just one worker-drone. Let the butterflies play, while Don assures the company's fortune for generations to come.

The *Post* is Don's home, he cannot speak of himself or his drives exclusive of it. But ironically it's his concern for its safety that has isolated him most fiercely within the organization. Specifically, his fealty to the bottom line. The recent Newspaper Guild contracts are a case in point. "When I received the Eugene Meyer Award last year," says Murray Marder, "the *Post* was in a very tense position. People would see Don in the newsroom and try to pass behind him. Relations were extraordinarily strained."

It was not Don's stinginess, friends observe, but his belief that employees should be rewarded for exemplary service, and not haphazardly across the board. "He couldn't understand why people didn't see what he was doing for them," they say. "That high pay tracks for key employees and higher average salaries were better than a higher minimum for everyone. He was stymied." Finally, he relented and a negotiated settlement was reached. But it had taken three years. The nation's top reporters, pride and joy of the *Post*, the stuff of Pulitzers, Watergate, and the future, went that long without a contract.

This year the mood's vastly improved, And tonight, in the newsroom, it's kinetic, positively electric. There's little of the Grahams here, this is Bradlee's world, touched with his brashness, his flare. Reporters charge about, conferences assemble, discharge, reassemble. The next day's news is taking shape. Len Downie marshals his troops, in Bradlee's absence, hears arguments, makes quick decisions. The Raytheon terminals hum. Telephones jangle. How different this is from the carpeted torpor of Don's business floor. How seductive this must be to him— he who's spent his life in news, learned to read from news, who composed his own newspaper as a toddler, and who has sacrificed so much.

When Don came here to publish, "He walked into a situation with wall-to-wall land mines," says Meg Greenfield, now editor of the editorial page and a *Newsweek* columnist. Not only was his predecessor still in residence, she was his mother, as chairman of the board, his boss and as Kay Graham, the most powerful woman in America. "That's kind of hard." And thanks to *All the President's Men*, Bradlee was the world's most famous newspaper editor, and Bob Woodward its most famous reporter.

But a tremendous calm settled over Don. What had been fate all these years was now fact—Don was publisher— and he slipped into a kind of worried quietude.

Even his mother's dirty work failed to rattle him. "There were some changes that I thought had to be made," Kay says of the period surrounding Don's succession, "and that if they were going to be made, should be made by him." She won't say what, but one certainly was the removal of

Phil Geylin as editorial page editor, and the replacement of him with his deputy, Meg Greenfield. Greenfield is a close friend of Kay Graham—important, as Robert Kaiser notes, "for Kay in particular having a real friend isn't easy"—and she is a strong and competent thinker. But she may indicate a more conservative direction of the *Post* under Don's tenure. It's felt that he's a more conservative publisher than either his mother or father, but considering his sacrifices, how could he be anything else? "Relentlessly middle American," is what he's called, like his new managing editor, Leonard Downie. Yet Bradlee notes that "Katharine is more conservative now than she was." William Greider says, "It's part institutional. *Post* editorial positions have always been more conservative than its reputation. They're closer to the establishment view of things." Others feel that Don is "extremely conservative, and afraid he'll screw the *Post* up." Greenfield admits that Graham is a hardliner on defense within editorial conferences, and Woodward—who heads the paper's Swat Team of investigative reporters—observes that Don's efforts have been "to calm down the paper editorially. He counts to ten, asks more questions. He's uncomfortable with stories like Watergate. That's why it's important to have Bradlee around. Don's a hands-on, but not an ass-on publisher. He never sits on you. I've disagreed with him on controversial stories, but we've always run them."

Production at the *Post*—or business—has been that stratum of the paper in which Don's made his largest contribution. It is, of course, where Kay wanted him. But it's also been that area open to him for improvement. Though he appointed Greenfield and Downie, his widest ranging appointments have been in business. The Newspaper Guild contends this is his *bête noire*. But others feel that production, or the day-to-day business of getting out the paper, is what Don's best at. He likes the way things work. And worrying over the mechanics of publishing obfuscates worry over what must be his deeper concerns. There's a well of entropy in Graham, of anger, and despite his memory for facts and faces, he cannot remember his feelings at many important junctures in his life. "It's funny," he says, "how hard I find that to do." Thus he hurls himself at adversity.

His first large test at the *Post* was the pressmen's strike, but the second was that of The *Star*. In 1978, when Don was general manager, Time-Life bought the failing paper and pledged $85 million to make it competitive with the dominant *Post*. "We were really scared," Don admits. But by 1981, *Time* threw in the towel and the *Star* was crushed. Don had effected what his family had worked toward for decades. The *Post* long had been the established paper of Washington, but Don took the *Star*'s scalp. Eugene Meyer's dream had been realized, as had Phil Graham's. The *Post* truly was the establishment now; the old monarch was dead.

Don assimilated both the *Star*'s physical plant and the core of its staff (to say nothing of its readership and advertising), effecting a merger as significant as Phil's with the Times-Herald, and paid not a penny for it.

The *Post* reaches 65 percent of adults in Washington daily and 80 percent on Sunday. It is the paper of record in the capital, reaching the breakfast tables of every congressman, White House advisor, Pentagon general, and State Department official. Still Don worries. Much to the consternation of associates who feel the battle for supremacy—and indeed survival—that Eugene Meyer began on the auction block in 1933 has been won, "Things are going very well for Don here," Ben Bradlee says, "The paper is making more money than it ever made when Katharine ran it. We reached our circulation penetration goal for 1990 last year, and we tease him about that. He's a worrier by nature. In fact, the noise of him clawing at the bottom of the barrel looking for something to worry about is deafening."

Despite the *Post*'s success and his own renown, Don

worries enough to shovel snow off the loading docks during blizzards, and spends a week each year riding the trucks with his delivery people. And despite what must be a fierce ambivalence, his closeness to his mother remains firm. He describes working with her as "one of the greatest pleasures of this job—I learn from her all the time." And despite all they've accomplished together, observers believe that his true era won't begin until Bradlee and Kay are retired.

"Are Bradlee, Downie, and the others your friends?" Don's asked one day at lunch. "Are you close to them?"

"Oh yeah," he says, looking wounded, "Sure." But his eyes widen.

The hottest debate in newspapering today concerns the jockeying for position to succeed the sixty-three-year-old Bradlee. The game of "who'll be my successor" is one he's played for years. And it feeds the gossip columns: will it be Shelby Coffey, will it be Downie, will it be Woodward, Bob Kaiser, or Jim Hoagland? But one name's never tossed in the hopper: that of Donald E. Graham.

"I wouldn't rule him out," Woodward says. "He can absorb and do more than anybody I've known. Maybe he'll say, 'I want to be editor of the paper.'"

But to do so, he'd need to go against what his family has planned for him since boyhood.

"Don's heart is in the city room," Bradlee says. "It's always been in the city room, and it was no accident that he started here. He likes it here. And you could make a case as to whether he wants to succeed Katharine as chairman of the board. I'd rather be editor. I've often wondered why he didn't take that job. Or why he doesn't take that job. I suggested it to him. I said, 'Don't you want it? It's the best job on the paper—a hell of a lot better than yours.' But he says no. That's always buffaloed me. If I owned this paper, I'm not sure I'd let some sonofabitch run it for me."

There's talk of Don and Bradlee switching positions—

or Bradlee, at least, moving upstairs. "This company has no corporate person entrusted with editorial responsibilities," Bradlee says, "and they've asked me about that. But it beats the shit out of me what I'll do."

Don admits news is his passion, but when asked whether he'll succeed Bradlee as editor, he brightens but replies, "Naah." Then more decisively, "Nope."

THESE PROBLEMS OF succession. Don is on his knees before his rambling, Tudor house in Cleveland Park, with his tie askew and suit pants scuffed, playing on the sidewalk at his son Will's fourth birthday party. Don is surrounded by children—but not too many, as it's Mary Graham's rule that your number of birthday guests may not exceed your age. So the Grahams' kids—Liza, eleven, Laura, seven, Molly, two, and Will—are joined by just four children from the neighborhood. Mary Graham has decorated the porch with bright balloons and crepe ribbons.

The older girls are inside, playing piano, and Mary—in her peacefully easy manner—chats with a neighbor over beer. She is a lawyer, on hold professionally until Molly is bigger. She watches Don and Will on the sidewalk. The boy is intent on a toy locomotive, and Don, on the concrete facing the street, is equally intent on his son.

It seems no accident that, like his parents, Don has chosen to have four children. He's said wistfully, "Fatherhood is just the biggest fact in your life." Friends speak of his eldest, Liza, possessing that same photographic memory as Don. But everyone's careful not to mention succession.

Mary is a scholar, and her daughters are bright, calm. For a moment here though, it's Don and his boy, isolated and playing nervously in yet another realm of females. The old house in Cleveland Park is redolent with history. In the foyer is Don's Washingtoniana library, with illustrated books of the city as it looked in his grandfather's day—the avenues hung with maples and tall elms. The Grahams' furniture is sparse downstairs, but late Victorian in style and obviously inherited. There is Eugene Meyer's humidor, now serving as a table beside a reading chair, The Meyers' books crowd the shelves: an elegantly bound sets of Emerson, Dickens, Dumas, and De Maupassant. The Grahams are part of a reading group, and reflected here is Don's fondness for Victorian novels, the happy family ones, with everyone reunited.

The books on his night table are revealing. There's Polybius's *Rise of the Roman Empire*, Crockett's *Victory Garden, The Memoirs of Hadrian, Samuel Johnson's Dictionary, In Search of Excellence, In the Path of God— Islam and Political Power, Further up the Organization*, and the children's books, *The Adventures of Lightfoot the Deer*, and *Little Bunny Follows His Nose*. The course of empire moves, tellingly, toward childhood.

A supper of baloney sandwiches, cheese 'n' crackers, and Seven-Up is served, that the kids peck at. Then Will's cake is brought, lavishly decorated with a frosted locomotive. The engine is red, as bright as Don's *Washington Post* softball jersey. The little boy huffs at his candles as Don tries for a photograph. Will, inexplicably, has a thing for locomotives, and Don indulges him—driving to freight crossings near Glen Welby for glimpses of trains.

Guests drift away, it is dusk now, and the girls can be heard from the library tinkling a piano. There, leather bound volumes rise about them to the ceiling, but here, playing on the sidewalk, Don and his son are of the city, existing in some odd, parallel dimension of childhood and ancestry.

The boy is distracted, edgy. Don kneels beside him. Will planes his toy locomotive furiously across the sidewalk— again, and then again. Don leans forward, and in that strained voice he uses to confront both past and future, says, "Will? Will?"

Postscript

In May of 1993, Don Graham succeeded his mother as Chairman of the Board of the Washington Post Company. He became chairman of the newspaper in September of 2000. In February of 2008, Katharine Graham's granddaughter and Don's niece, Katharine Weymouth, became publisher of the Washington Post. *In August of 2013, citing declining revenues, the Grahams sold the paper to Jeff Bezos of Amazon.com—ending eighty years of family ownership.*

Esquire, 1985

Postcard of a Hanging

My parents' house is a 250-year-old log cabin on a hillside overlooking the Potomac. It's a tranquil spot, the river eight miles west of Georgetown, wide and interspersed with wooded islands, and the Chesapeake & Ohio Canal flowing placidly below our yard. The azaleas that May were inflamed with red and pink blossoms, the dogwoods icy white. Our ancient terrier Nellie was sick and I was home to help decide her fate. Also, I admit, to enjoy a bit of springtime.

We'd nursed her late, so the knock at 6:00 a.m. was unwelcome. A middle-aged jogger told us that he'd discovered a body near the canal. He was panting, agitated. I pulled on sweats, we dialed 911, and walked down to await the police.

Seventy yards below our house, a man hung by his neck from a tree. He was partially suspended, his legs bent to his right along the ground, Pieta-style, but his neck stretched upward by a thick rope. "I came round the corner and *wham*," said the jogger. "I thought it was a prank. But there was absolutely no movement."

The dead man hung mid-path by a creek that flows beneath the canal to the river. He was in his forties, Caucasian, with black hair and a mustache. His arms hung by his sides straight to purplish hands, and his eyes were closed. A bottle of wine lay by a large flashlight and plastic food container. The rope was immaculately white.

An emergency team arrived, two fire fighters and several paramedics. The path that, later in the morning, hundreds of recreationists would use, was partially hidden by foliage. A young paramedic turned the corner, saw the hanged man, and exclaimed, "Oh!" covering her face. A police sergeant averted his gaze. "You sure did it to yourself, didn't you buddy," he said. Then taped off the scene.

I could not take my eyes from the corpse. A few feet from the canal, it dangled near buttercups and daisies, nesting mallards and geese with tiny goslings. In the dark the man had walked past our house, found a suitable tree and hanged himself, like a dog from a leash.

"I'm glad I didn't come by here last night," I muttered.

"I wish I had," the jogger said. "I might have saved him."

One rush hour in New York, I'd strolled to the East River and, while crossing a foot bridge above the FDR, heard a man ask a boy if he wouldn't mind holding his dog. There was a *thump* followed by a screeching of tires. The man had jumped then been hit by five cars before traffic could stop. The boy turned, stricken, and asked me, "What do I do with the dog?"

That memory had blurred with time. City dwellers are used to stepping around bodies—alive or dead. They are sadly anonymous and unremarkable. But this one was personal. It hung seventy yards from the house where I'd grown up, on a spot where I'd fished and swum since I was a boy, made love as a teenager, weekended as an adult, and would no doubt retire. I could not ignore it.

It is written that medieval Europeans drove a stake through the hearts of suicides, to thwart their afterlife as vampires, then buried them at a crossroads where the weight of footsteps would dampen their rage. In Africa, the trees from which suicides hang themselves are burned, to cleanse them of spirits. We are haunted by the suicide's anger, his lust for revenge. "If I've killed one man, I've killed two," Sylvia Plath wrote, before gassing herself. "There's a stake in your fat black heart."

Of all suicides, the hanged are most vengeful. This man's expression, despite the bruising of his features, seemed ambiguous. Yet his body language was unmistakable. "Fuck you buddy," it said, "you won't forget me, and that's how I want it."

No one yet had touched him. The jogger left his name, then joined other runners pounding the towpath. An older woman hiked by, her eyes averted. A man chasing a golden retriever bounded down the hill, was intercepted by police and led wide-eyed to a detour.

It was then I remembered our pooch, Nellie. I climbed the hill and was told that in the night she had crawled under my mother's bed and died. Took the same elevator as the hanged man, I thought. For a second, my heart rose with them. Then I went upstairs to ask, "What do I do with the dog."

The Washington Post, 1995

Sessions at the Gate

On Independence Day Eve, the only place in Washington where FBI Director and Mrs. William S. Sessions appeared safe from political fireworks was their own living room. It was extraordinarily quiet there. Director Sessions had left for Bureau headquarters; the heavy front door was locked and its alarm set behind him. The parlor, furnished with Georgian and Queen Anne reproductions, was cluttered by stacks of recent newspapers. A photograph of the Director and his daughter Sara, who dances with the San Francisco Ballet, rested on a table. It had been taken at headquarters. Sara wore satin slippers and posed *en attitude* by her father's side. Behind them a granite wall read: "The efforts of all," and "Law of the American people"—its epitaph clipped by the lens.

Elsewhere lay art books, an outdoorsman's calendar and snapshots of the Sessions's pets: a dog who died last winter, and an eighteen-year-old alley cat, still living. The house is a two-story brick colonial in what Alice Sessions calls "the mixed neighborhood" of Crestwood, DC. Windows were locked against the tropical heat, but one could see guards next door at the embassy of Niger hauling trash to curbside. Behind the Sessions's yard, forest acreage of Jay and Sharon Rockefeller's estate—with its round-the-clock security—stretched to Rock Creek Park. Alice Sessions's privacy fence, at the heart of a January twelfth Justice Department report on the Director's alleged ethics violations, stood in the humidity like an afterthought.

Mrs. Sessions was speaking on the phone to a friend in Texas. "How do you run the Bureau?" she asked. "Bill's waiting for the President to fire him. He thought it was going to come down Monday night. He went in and said, 'What do I do about my travel tickets?' Webb Hubbell said, 'You go right ahead, make your travel plans through July.'"

She listened a moment. "The *New York Times* editorial this morning is *terrible*. I can't imagine somebody with Howell Raines's mentality and knowledge doing something like that. But Bill is not going to step out after all of this." She paused. "He didn't stand and defend himself, because he didn't want to weaken the Bureau... is that weak leadership he's given them? The agents are calling and writing him and saying 'Stand in there for us.' They're all scared to death to do it publicly." Another pause. "There's a difference between resigning and being fired! By resigning he'd say, 'I can't do this job anymore.' He's not saying that. He's said, 'Free my hands and let me do the job I've done so well up to now.' This is what he's at the office doing right now. He's not frightened for his job, he's frightened for the Bureau."

Mrs. Sessions rang off. She's a short woman of sixty-two, with graying brown hair and exceptionally blue eyes. Her daughter's grace is in her cheekbones. She wore a denim blouse and skirt, lavender half-glasses, a pewter necklace and hammered metal earrings. "I was a costume designer for years," she said. "My degrees are in Historical Costuming and Theater." She frowned. "You know, I do a lot of reading in *Julius Caesar* these days."

She gestured toward the Justice Department's 161-page, "Office of Professional Responsibility" report, in a plastic binder on the coffee table.

"That's what so ludicrous about this. I make my own clothes, we've never had a housekeeper, and in San Antonio Bill wouldn't hire one because of the green card thing. I had a woman who helped me one day a week in Waco, years ago, when the boys were little. That's how we've always lived."

There are numerous accusations in the report: that Sessions used Bureau aircraft to attend social events, transported firewood in his armor-plated limousine, abused spousal travel privileges, participated in a sham arrangement to evade income taxes on his home-to-work commute, gave rides to non-Bureau personnel in his limousine, and blocked an investigation into allegations that he received a sweetheart deal on his home mortgage. But a full thirty-six pages are spent on The Fence: a six-foot-tall, wooden barricade that OPR claims was improperly billed to the government.

"When I read that report at three o'clock in the morning," Mrs. Sessions said, "I got up out of bed and I thought, 'The one thing that's evident is that nobody ever saw the fence. They've gone through all of these gyrations with these professional people in charge of world security. And they've been going on about a fence they've never seen.' That's when I said, 'The next person who calls me about the fence is going to get a tour.'"

On cue, she disarmed the front door and walked through the yard to a high iron gate enclosing their drive. A white brick house with six white columns stood next door. She tapped out a security code and the gate swung open with a metallic sigh.

The fence was Deputy Director Floyd Clarke's idea, Mrs. Sessions asserted. "I was told that the only thing Mr. Clarke would approve was a twenty-four-hour detail for us, and an eight-foot-tall iron fence that ran all the way around the property and clear to the street, and across the front yard, with these gates, and all down the side. Now how would that look here in this neighborhood?"

At several meetings, including one on April 13, 1990, which she attended, number-two executive Clarke discussed the fence's design. The OPR report quotes him saying, "I made a series of recommendations to upgrade the security at the Director's residence, which included the installation of an iron fence...Mrs. Sessions voiced her objections...I explained that a privacy fence would allow an individual or individuals to conceal themselves...and, therefore, could create a security threat to the Director... inasmuch as such a fence would not enhance the security of the residence, it would be inappropriate for the Government to pay for its construction."

Sessions submitted his voucher and the government paid $10,000 for the wooden fence, as opposed to the $97,000 estimated for the iron. "But I've never had a privacy fence," Mrs. Sessions declared. "They told me that I *had* to have a fence. So I said 'Fine.'"

When William Sessions left the April 13 meeting, Clarke and others advised her to choose the iron. "Then Weldon Kennedy jumped me about being an embarrassment to the FBI. He said I needed to be more careful, to watch the ladies I had lunch with." Afterward, "I felt that I had been intimidated," mostly by Clarke. "I said to the Director, 'Bill, that guy is a real sonofagun. He's trouble. He's rude, he's impudent, he's disrespectful.'"

SESSIONS HAD PROMOTED Floyd Clarke to the Deputy Directorship (creating that office to accommodate him) in 1989, causing hurt feelings on executive row and fears that the Hoover era, when number-two man Clyde Tolson orchestrated hits, might return. "Sessions felt," a former exec told me, "that rather than a triumvirate of divergent opinions, which he was getting from the three Deputy Assistants, he needed somebody that he had explicit confidence in. That was Floyd." By most reports, Clarke today is running the FBI; should Sessions go, he'd most likely be named Acting Director until a successor is confirmed. Already Clarke's changed his badge number to "Two"—an unprecedented act of bureaucratic hubris, as only the Director's "One" is other than randomly selected.

"Floyd's like a court dwarf," said Special Agent Damon Taylor, a twenty-year veteran of the New York office, who's worked with Clarke. "The good thing about being a dwarf is that you're close to the prince. The bad thing is that you're *not* the prince."

According to sources, Clarke is at the heart of a cabal that William Sessions would later tell me is a "group—whoever they are, however large or small, directed by whomever—that seeks to oust the Director." Though he will not finger his Deputy, Mrs. Sessions—whom he's well aware speaks to reporters—has. "Floyd Clarke is orchestrating Bill's demise," she told *Texas Monthly* in May, after informing *Washingtonian* in March that the Director's enemies include Clarke, former Attorney General William Barr, and Special Agent Ron McCall, the former head of Sessions's security detail.

"This is vicious," she said. "The word 'perfidy' comes to mind." Clarke, FBI spokespersons told me, would not comment on such allegations, the change in his badge number, or any aspect of the Sessions dilemma.

Some agents discount Alice's charges—"I've never heard Clarke say anything about the Director other than positive things," retired Assistant Director Tom Sheer said. And Jules Bonavolanta, a former Supervisor of Organized Crime Investigations at headquarters, told me: "Floyd Clarke has always been the type of guy whose primary interest has been the good of the Bureau. I don't think his agenda would be to try to oust the Director." But another source insisted that, "What Floyd's committed is bureaucratic regicide. And it's very sad, because the Bureau is based on loyalty."

SESSIONS'S DEBUT HAD been shaky. As Reagan's fourth choice to replace William Webster, he had fainted in the aisle of a commercial airliner en route to his swearing-in, and had vomited blood. Sessions was diagnosed with a peptic ulcer which took a month to stabilize. During that time he returned to San Antonio, where he'd served as chief judge for the western district of Texas. He owned a reputation there for toughness and a humorless proclivity for rules. His father was a Disciples of Christ minister who'd written a Boy Scouts handbook. Sessions had grown up in Kansas City; he was Midwestern to the core. He owned none of Webster's patrician charm, and refusing to train with Bureau firearms, showed himself not to be a man of weaponry. Worse, in the male-dominated FBI, he took his wife's counsel—to a degree considered a violation of Bureau protocol. Sessions issued her a pass to headquarters which allowed underground parking and unfettered access to the executive floor. This infuriated some veterans. "It's the old Hoover maxim that only *your* picture is on your credentials," one said, "not your wife's or your children's or your dog's."

Jokes circulated throughout headquarters that Alice was the most influential Bureau wife since Hoover aide, Clyde Tolson.

Sessions had arrived at a sensitive moment. New allegations of old Bureau offenses—racist hiring and promotional practices, and domestic spying on political groups—surfaced, and the new Director handled them in a surprisingly liberal fashion. Coretta Scott King and Andrew Young endorsed him. The Bureau's old guard was miffed. "We don't need a kinder, gentler FBI," an agent told *Washingtonian*. Worse, Sessions ordered the Bureau to investigate CIA's and Justice's roles in Iraqgate.

For what some special agents saw as a caving in to political pressure, the Director earned his nickname, "Con-Sessions."

THE WEEK PRECEDING Independence Day had been a strange one in the Capital. President Clinton was under fire for waffling on Sessions's dismissal, as directives were issued to agents from the Bureau's seventh floor not to discuss his predicament with outsiders. Rumors surfaced that Judge Louis Freeh, a leading contender for Sessions's job, was being vetted by the Bureau. ("As a prosecutor, Freeh worked very closely with Floyd Clarke," Mrs. Sessions noted.) Clinton fled to Japan, leaving Press Secretary Dee Dee Myers to announce that no action would be taken before his return. And a bevy of Sessions's colleagues, loyal and otherwise, descended upon Washington as if to witness the execution.

William Baker, former Assistant Director of the FBI's Criminal Investigative Division, and now a senior investigator for the motion picture industry, brought his California tan and rumpled sport clothes to town for company business and a visit with Bureau cronies. Baker had worked with Sessions for nearly four years. He told me, over breakfast at the Hay-Adams, that he'd found the Director "wide but not very deep...he was everywhere gladhanding, and in doing so, it was my observation that he might not have focused on some of the key issues as intensely as was required. There was a detachment that I never thought I could penetrate successfully." Baker remains close to Floyd Clarke, whom he called "one of the most loyal people to the Director's position, and therefore to anyone who is sitting in that position, that [the Bureau] could have." Clarke brought Baker back to the FBI from CIA in 1987. And when Sessions did not promote him to Associate Deputy Director of Investigations in 1991, Baker quit.

At lunch Thursday, in a noisy Capitol Hill restaurant called the Pawnshop, Kenneth P. Walton—former Deputy Associate Director in the Criminal Investigative Division, reporting directly to Clarke—tried to clarify things. Sessions had raised eyebrows, Walton confirmed, by pushing hard for minority hiring, and for remaining aloof from the execs' old boy network. "An institutional bureaucracy like the FBI," Walton said, "is unable to handle a personality or a professional aberration. So they do one of two things: either break his will, or shuttle him off someplace where he's out of sight out of mind."

During the past three years, Clarke's loyalty to the Director has faded. By reliable accounts, Clarke was liaison between Justice and the Bureau for the damning OPR reports. But author Ron Kessler, whose forthcoming book about the FBI already has caused waves, argues that Clarke's disloyalty came not soon enough.

"Floyd actually was loyal to a fault to Sessions," he said, at his house in Potomac, Maryland. "Because he was aware of some of these abuses, as were other FBI people at that level, and never blew the whistle." It was Kessler's ten-page letter, submitted to the Bureau's Office of Public Affairs on June 24, 1992, that first outlined Sessions's ethics violations. It was from this and a second letter, signed "A Concerned Citizen," that Bureau and Justice Department investigations followed.

According to Alice Sessions, Kessler was Clarke's dupe. His subordinates were "Kessler's big sources," she said. "In fact, all of that stuff you saw in that letter come from [security chief] Ron McCall." Kessler denied this: "I wish the people Mrs. Sessions cites had come to me and handed the story to me on a silver platter. The fact is...the story was developed through interviews with dozens of people, and old fashioned digging."

"Nobody [but Kessler] has interviewed Ron McCall," Mrs. Sessions added. "McCall was the main complainant against Judge Sessions. His name was redacted [in the report], because he was in charge of our security, and as you probably read, he was the one that I found in the bedroom. He had twenty-five keys to our house, which he passed out to his security detail."

The Director subsequently reassigned McCall, and Mrs. Sessions had the house swept for bugs, not finding any. Yet, "If a study were done on Mr. McCall," she contended, "it would blow this thing wide open—along with his relationship with Mr. Clarke." Special Agent McCall was unavailable for comment.

One source at the supervisory level told me, "I remember when Floyd was Deputy Assistant Director in Charge of Organized Crime. People would tell me that every time they went in, this guy McCall was sitting there. In the morning, in the evening. It was uncomfortable for them, because he had no business even knowing what was going on. Yet Floyd would have him there like a permanent fixture."

Another veteran supervisor admitted, "Floyd has a history of turning on people."

CLARKE HAS MOVED upward through Bureau ranks, despite a degree that, Agent Taylor quipped, is allegedly "from Al's Accounting School." Clarke's official résumé does not specify his degree, only that he graduated from George Washington University. He joined the Bureau in 1964. From there he took assignments around the country, but has spent most of his career at headquarters—an unusual circumstance. He was appointed Special Agent in Charge of the Kansas City office in 1980, but came under fire for improper use of Bureau aircraft, and for employing Bureau pilots to teach him flying. "His wife ratted him out to the Bureau," an agent told me, "for having an affair with an Assistant United States Attorney." Agent Taylor reported that "His wife had him followed by a private investigator out there, where he was well-known as sort of a sexual Ulysses." David Hayes of the *Kansas City Star*, who covered Clarke from 1980 through 1982, and who wrote a scathing January 29, 1993 piece on Clarke's history, confirmed this.

"There was one ethics violation, and maybe two," Hayes said. "The pilot who taught him was basically forced to resign. Then I heard this really fascinating tale that Clarke had flown through Kansas City, maybe in '83 or '84, with a load of hijacked alcohol that had been seized. He picked up a couple of people and ended up in Nevada, partying. Supposedly there was some investigation about that which got quashed." A Bureau spokesperson would comment only that Clarke had been investigated for the flying lessons, and that "no disciplinary action was taken." Hayes said he "talked to about eight different people who verified" the unauthorized flying lessons, "including a couple of the pilots."

Clarke became the subject of a detailed investigation by OPR and "was given a Pasadena" or pass, Agent Taylor lamented, "for the same sort of infractions as the Director." Clarke returned to headquarters in 1982.

SESSIONS HAS HIS ALLIES, and Clarke his, but the most distressing reality of their feud is that it comes at a perilous moment for the country. As Alice Sessions concluded her tour, Director Sessions was meeting with executives at headquarters, "Pulling together the response to the arrest of Sheik Rahman," he told me later. "Because you know, the Islamic group spokesman over in Egypt apparently said, 'We will now begin terrorist activities directed at people both in Egypt and American citizens and Americans in America.'" Sessions also was testing his power base. (Clarke skipped the meeting.) "I need to have control of the Bureau in order to be able to carry out policy and direction," Sessions said. "And when there is the constant attack in the media, and the uncertainty, it's very difficult to do."

That morning the *New York Times* called for the Director's resignation: "Facing the challenge of a new tide of terrorism, the FBI needs effective leadership." The *Times* went on to suggest that Sessions's motives for not quitting were in part "to keep Floyd Clarke, his career deputy, from becoming Acting Director...but it will be easier to establish strong leadership in the FBI with an acting director than with one who is headed out the door."

Asked about the *Times*' editorial coverage, Sessions told me, "The thing I find unfortunate in all of that kind of reporting, including Mr. [David] Johnston's, is that it is from an anonymity that cannot be pierced." He likened his situation to "guerrilla warfare," complaining that "the media finds nothing, nothing at all imperiling about taking the Director out. I find it extremely imperiling. I think there is a shallowness about the approach of the *New York Times* to a great institution of law enforcement like the FBI. And I don't think they comprehend—as brilliant as their editorial writers may be—the seriousness of politicizing the Bureau. It's almost as if they are casual about it. I do not attach the word 'animus' to what they did. But I think 'shallow' is probably the word for the *New York Times* editorial policy. And I think it's not worthy of that newspaper. They are on an agenda. I don't know what it is, I don't know who they're with. But it's obvious they have some sort of agenda."

ACCORDING TO KEN WALTON, Sessions's and other Directors' media troubles are nothing compared with the executive bickering at FBI HQ. "Those guys on the seventh floor are constantly throwing javelins at each other. At that level in the Bureau they make the Kremlin in 1938 look like a bunch of rank amateurs."

Walton is a fifty-four-year-old ex-Marine with a blond pompadour, deep tan and canyon-like creases in his forehead. At the Pawnshop he wore a green double-breasted suit with an NYCPD Medal of Honor ribbon in its lapel, a striped shirt with highboy collar and monogrammed cuffs, and two gold FBI rings. He retired in 1989, but currently is investigating ATF's role in the Waco standoff for the House Appropriations Committee. Walton's Bureau sources are current. One told him, three hours before our luncheon, that Sessions was in the process of removing pictures from his walls. "Either he's leaving or bringing in an interior decorator," Walton said.

The conversation drifted to power brokers within the FBI. Of the Associate Deputy Directors they include "Walden Kennedy," Walton said. "Then there's Doug Gow, who was a First Office Agent with me in Denver, a nice enough guy but no brain surgeon. And there's Buck in Dallas."

Oliver "Buck" Revell, a former Associate Deputy Director at headquarters, is now Special Agent in Charge of the Dallas field office. He was a rival of Clarke's for the Deputy Directorship, and has been outspoken against Sessions: "If he cannot show our new president that he has conducted himself in an ethical and honorable fashion," he told the *Times*, "he should resign for the good of the Bureau and our country."

Revell, among others during this critical time, has been accused of ordering sensitive investigations without headquarters authorization. He did so last summer, when Ross Perot complained to the Dallas office that George Bush was bugging his campaign organization. Revell ruffled feathers when he asked John Connally's family for permission to exhume the Governor's body in search of Kennedy assassination bullet-fragments.

"You can narrow the Bureau's problems to two names," Agent Taylor told me. "Buck and Floyd."

Revell "bailed out of headquarters," Walton said, "when he was not selected as Deputy Director. Floyd was a protégé of Buck's. And that was more than he could tolerate. He's not as smooth as Floyd, and I think, had a tendency to tell Sessions he was full of shit. But Buck's a very bright guy. He's just absolutely, totally arrogant. He has a deep-seated love affair with himself." Walton hesitated. "Floyd is a very intense, very straight, very bright guy. But he's cold as a fish."

Revell may be "languishing in Elba," Agent Taylor put it, but as Alice Sessions told me later, "Hope springs eternal in Buck's breast."

TWO MONTHS AFTER the OPR report was leaked, Curt Gentry, author of 1992's *J. Edgar Hoover: The Man and the Secrets,* sent Director Sessions a six-page, single-spaced letter marked "Personal and Confidential." He asserted that, since Hoover's death, Bureau insiders, "Hooverites," have manipulated the downfall of subsequent Directors—tapping and bugging them, manipulating their security details—for the simple reason that each Director had been chosen from outside Bureau ranks. Gentry, who has studied the Bureau since 1975, advised Sessions that "On taking office, you listened to the wrong people. [You] reinstituted the policy of a single deputy, again putting all the power in the hands of one man, who by the very nature of his solitary position commands the loyalty of those under him. You failed to recognize...that you were also dealing with a palace revolt, the attempt of a small cabal, numbering probably no more than a half dozen senior officials, to recapture control of the Bureau."

Sessions accepts this thesis. "I am very concerned about politicization in the Bureau," he told me, "externally and internally. The Bureau must not be returned to whatever it was. If the President chooses to replace me, he has doomed the Bureau, at least for the foreseeable future, [and its Directorship] to being a four-year appointment. Because every President will see and know that he can safely do the same thing. [That's when] the fabled good old boy network goes back to work...taking care of their friends, and advances that have been made in terms of broadening the participation of all of the [minority] groups in the FBI will be imperiled. What was the Bureau known as ten years ago? It was predominately white male. Now there are twelve-hundred-and-eight females. The point is, if you allow [politicization] to happen, those advances in taking and making the Bureau a more diverse organization are dead in the water."

There's agreement with Sessions's prediction. "One of the things that would make a lot of agents look at Clarke and Company," a veteran told me, "and say 'we're on their side,' has to do with all this bending over backwards for the minorities, females and so forth, in lieu of everybody else. They generally don't like it."

But, he said, "the Director doesn't really have any day-to-day impact on an agent in the street." Another source agreed, adding, "Guys in the trenches don't have a lot of sympathy for the Director...they know if they did the same thing, they'd be sitting thirty days on the bench, and maybe even terminated."

"What kind of misdeeds or unethical practices are we talking about here?" a federal manager asked. "This is a city where former White House Chief of Staff John Sununu was flying to his dental appointments on the taxpayers' dime. The charges against Sessions seem pathetic."

Finishing his chili, Ken Walton mused about the FBI's contemporary role. "A similar job to being an FBI agent is probably being a Fuller Brush salesman. Because you've got to sell yourself and your own credibility. Agents on the street are going out all over America and are trying to conduct investigations, saying 'I'm with the FBI.' Some of the people come back and say, 'oh you're with the FBI, your Director is accused of ethics violations. Take a hike.'"

The sort of leadership the Director provides, critics maintain, is eccentric and flaky. And that's another reason Clarke wants him removed. Yet Sessions told me, "The suggestion that I may be eccentric or out of touch or that I am not capable of running the Bureau—that's nonsense."

Walton sipped his coffee. "About a year before I left, I was at a meeting up there with Sessions, Buck Revell, Floyd Clarke, and a bunch of other guys, and the discussion was one of these 'we got ten million dollars that we've got to use or lose, what are we going to do with it?' One of these fiscal year things. We finally conclude we're going to buy ten-millimeter guns for the agents. Sessions says, 'Well, in my dual role as Director of the FBI and Supervisor with Responsibility for DEA, we'll buy the guns and give them to DEA.' I look at Floyd Clarke and he's absolutely pale. I look at Buck Revell and he's red. Neither one of them are saying anything. So I said, 'Director, why would we do that?' He said, 'Oh Ken, these DEA agents are out there every day making arrests and buying dope.' The only conclusion you could have was that he had no idea what we did for a living." The Bureau has been investigating narcotics violations since the early eighties.

"He always had CNN on. There was another meeting

that had been going for some time, and he just suddenly says something like 'That's what they do with those green vases.' He's watching some story about the discovery of Egyptian vases in Israel."

Sessions told me, "CNN happens to be on the spot better than anybody else in the world. You may recall that there were four different times when Saddam Hussein made remarks about encouraging those people around the world who cared about Iraq to take the war to the aggressors. Now, if you're in the counter-terrorism business, how do you interpret that? I'll tell you how I interpreted it...it's a threat. What do you do with it? Well, first of all, you've got to know about it."

Agents relate tales of Sessions, at a concert in headquarters' courtyard, introducing the Beach Boys then ripping off his jacket, exposing a bright Hawaiian shirt. Others cite instances of his singing Brylcreem's "A little dab'll do ya," to illustrate a point. Charming idiosyncrasies or dangerously eccentric ones?

"In fairness," Walton said, "Director Webster in briefings—especially if it was an organized crime briefing—would fall asleep. I always concluded that it was the alliteration of vowels: 'Fat Tony Salerno, Mattie Ianniello, Frank Costello.' As soon as you'd stop he'd wake up."

Despite headquarters problems, the World Trade Center investigation and others proceed apace...though forty-thousand workers at 26 Federal Plaza, which houses the FBI's Manhattan office, were evacuated in a major gaffe, after nitroglycerin was discovered mistakenly stored in Evidence.

"The morale is so bad," Walton exclaimed, "it raises the question of 'how long can that exceptionally high efficiency rate go on? Is it running on fumes?'"

"I don't think there's a malaise," Director Sessions countered. "I look at the term 'drifting.' And I say to myself, 'good Lord, look at what we're doing. Look at the phenomenal things!'"

Some responsibility for Sessions's "arrogance," said Walton, "has to go to the institution of the Bureau. The elevators on the seventh floor, the ones closest to the Director's office, are programmed so there is always an elevator available. There's a car in the garage with the engine running and the door open, with people who anticipate your every personal and professional wish. In a very short period of time, you expect it. Then you demand it."

ALICE SESSIONS CLOSED the gate. "That's my squirrel feeder," she said, pointing toward a peculiar adornment to the privacy fence. The feeder consisted of a slim dowel placed vertically on a platform, before a tiny wooden chair. "I put the ear of corn right there, and the little squirrel has learned to sit up here and eat it." She turned. "Now, may I tell you if there was a sweetheart deal with our mortgage at all, it came in a sack of corn for my squirrels from Joe Albritton's farm land." Albritton is CEO of Riggs Corporation and Riggs Bank, where the Sessions have their mortgage.

Mrs. Sessions has a rebuttal to each of OPR's charges, as does the Director. Both say Attorney General Janet Reno has not fully examined OPR's charges. "But she has such a full plate," Alice said. She insists that the Director's only fault was that he trusted his advisors. "You've got to take what people give you," she exclaimed. "If he has one sin, he believes. And he trusted."

Settled inside on a sofa, she looked drawn and older. "It's enough to make you question human nature," she whispered, tears welling. "Rousseau had this ideal conception of humanity, as to its perfectibility. So did Hegel, whose thinking led to Marx. But then there was Nietzsche." She sat perfectly still. "I nearly had my faith shaken, but I was taught stewardship—that you have responsibility for what comes into your sphere. That's my core." She smiled grimly. "So I'm dealing with all those third grade girls on the seventh floor."

I laughed as she glanced toward the photograph of her daughter, Sara, and the Director. "The Bureau is like living with a bunch of third grade girls," she said. "I didn't *understand* third grade girls until I had a daughter who was in third grade. And they almost killed her that year—psychologically. I spent all that year and all fourth grade putting her back together. And let me tell you, she's a magnificent human being."

She rubbed her eyes. "We're fine. But we're not going back to Texas. Absolutely not. We're going to stay right here in Washington. We have some very loyal friends, and Bill has some nice jobs that he can go to." She walked to the window. "The people in this neighborhood couldn't have been nicer. In fact, somebody's having a little get-together tonight. They said, 'We want you to come and let you know how supportive your neighbors are.' Tomorrow we'll watch the fireworks from the Canadian embassy roof, like always."

She turned. "But listen, it's damn tiring... psychologically, emotionally. I'll tell you the hardest part of this. The hardest part is that they have gotten hold of a man who is a judge to his toes. He is legal, he is ethical, and he's a gentleman." She glanced up. "For Bill to look at someone he trusted, and know that man betrayed him, may kill him."

Mrs. Sessions escorted me to my car. The next morning, July fourth, I'd speak by telephone with the Director. He'd sound angry, but focused and resolved. At some point during that forty-five minute conversation, he'd speak of international repression and the Bureau's efforts to combat it, in a manner strangely parallel to his own situation.

"Do you remember that Saturday morning in June, 1989, when we looked and saw that column of tanks coming into Tiananmen square? And do you remember one fellow walked out with satchels in his hand and confronted that column of tanks? And they stopped! He set his satchel down and climbed up on the lower tier of tank and talked to a guy inside of the tank. Climbed up on the top and did it, climbed back down on the lower and did it. And got off. I thought, 'They are going to kill him. They can't let him live. Here's one man stopping a column of tanks.'"

I thanked Mrs. Sessions and left. Driving off, I turned and saw her walk back to check the gate.

The Village Voice, 1993

Postscript

This piece was assigned by Tina Brown for The New Yorker, *then killed because of the immediacy of Sessions's dismissal by President Clinton on July 19, 1993. Clarke was named Acting Director after Louis Freeh was nominated for the directorship, in a Rose Garden ceremony on July 20th. Freeh was confirmed and served as Director of the FBI from September, 1993 to June, 2001, when he resigned amid criticism of his leadership of the bureau.*

Gunkholing the Chesapeake

Cap'n Otis steered the yacht *Euphrasy* across the mouth of the Potomac, a pony of Stroh's locked in one fist, the wheel of the twenty-eight-foot Spirit in the other. It was the *Euphrasy*'s shakedown cruise. Spanking new and elegant—the pride of an interior designer from San Francisco—she lay in stark contrast to the man who sailed her: Cap'n Otis, in his frayed doubleknits, plaid shirt, torn sneakers, one brown and one black sock, vinyl belt, and baby-blue tennis hat. A half-proud, razor-toothed grin showed from beneath the wide brim of his cap.

"Go small, go simple, and go now," he said.

One hundred miles from Washington, we were headed for the open Chesapeake. Our immediate objective was Tangier Island, thirty-five miles southwest. But close-hauled and beating against the wind, we'd not make it tonight. So we lay back and watched the shore drift by: the dark blue of its nearest trees, the lighter, then lightest blue of its most distant tree line. In October, the shore would be a fierce yellow and red. Today, in early May, it was shrouded with haze. Cap'n Otis dodged crab pots and pound nets, studying Point Lookout for a shift in weather. Here the river was ten miles wide and primer-gray. Basically, we were *in* the bay. The 800,000 waterfowl that make the Chesapeake their winter home had moved along, leaving the region to ospreys, ibis, herons, eagles, and egrets. The Intracoastal Waterway, which cuts straight through the heart of the bay, would soon be dotted with migrating yachtsmen, but they mean little to the bay's ecological rhythms. The 18,000 watermen who make their living as independent fishermen—laying trotlines, hauling crab pots, sail- or power-dredging for oysters—mean more, for they are frontiersmen, professional trappers. They are an endangered species, as precariously pitted against the modern age as against nature and the seasons. But to the balance of aquatic life they are all equally small potatoes.

Chesapeake means "great shellfish bay," and it is America's (and Washington's) most productive fishery. Legitimate activity has sustained many waterman, but up until the 1950s machinegun fire was heard across oyster beds on the Maryland-Virginia line, and oyster pirating was a lucrative sideline. As were punt-gunning for waterfowl and rum-running during Prohibition.

"Now the worst are smuggling dope," Cap'n Otis said.

Descended from Virginia watermen, Otis Douglas should know. His physiognomy is a catalog of the Chesapeake: hawk-like features beneath a crude shock of flyaway hair. Chesapeake watermen are eccentric and stubbornly anti-agrarian. They'd become watermen, in part, because they hadn't owned land. Cap'n Otis flaunts the region's contradictions. His mother's family were Carters, plantation-bred, his father's without heraldry, seeded along the bay. It addition to being a licensed charter captain, Cap'n Otis teaches sailing and writing and practices Buddhism.

We flipped through charts as a lunch of chicken and iced Chablis was served—by Martin Tilley, the *Euphrasy*'s owner—and prepared to round Smith Point for the open bay. The point holds confusing tides and tricky currents, as is the case wherever rivers meet the bay. Shallow for much of its 200-mile length, the Chesapeake is notorious for its sandbars and mud banks. Captain John Smith ran aground in 1607 at Stingray Point, seventeen miles south, and was stung by a ray. He nearly died. He'd explored the Chesapeake that year and was the region's first cartographer. In his journal he'd precisely noted the bay's perils: its waterspouts in summer, its squalls descending with hurricane force in a matter of minutes; its mosquitoes and jellyfish, which make cruising a tropical adventure from June through September; and its large waves buoyed by wind on shallow water. But he also charted its pleasures: its forty-odd rivers and hundreds of tributaries, which in satellite photos cause the estuary to resemble a mammoth respiratory system; its stiff breezes in spring and fall; its plentiful shellfish; and its astonishing number of snug harbors. It is the Chesapeake's harbors that make the region a yachtsman's paradise.

"You can get lost for a whole summer out here," Cap'n Otis said, "never anchor twice in the same spot." Gunkholing is its name—leaving the bay at night to wind along narrow creeks in search of open moorings where no other yacht would lay.

That is exactly what we're to do. Cap'n Otis would pilot us to the center of the Chesapeake, and from there we would explore the remote lower bay, a sort of coastal frontier museum. Otis knows the area well enough to navigate through it while spinning his yarns like a boson's mate and taking his first rum before noon.

With the breeze in our teeth, Tangier was out of reach tonight. So Cap'n Otis tacked blithely before Smith Point lighthouse, sailing for the Little Wicomico River. A narrow and swift channel marked its entrance, with shoal banks at several removes. The trick was to fix a spot halfway between Smith Point lighthouse and a specific black-and-white marker, and from there cruise at 310 degrees to deep water. Cap'n Otis studied the fathometer—the *Euphrasy* drew three feet six inches—but there was the *whump* of hull meeting sandbar, and we were aground. A crab boat sped by in the channel, its pilot waving contemptuously. Cap'n Otis reversed under power and within seconds had freed us.

"You haven't sailed the Chesapeake until you've run aground," he muttered. We powered hesitantly upstream despite readings of five to four to three point eight feet. Then we were clear in six and could relax sufficiently to watch the forest slip by. We moored at Sunnybank, Virginia, deserted but for boat sheds of pewter clapboard, a cable ferry, duck blinds, and screech owls hooting from the shoreline.

"DADDY WAS A POUND-NET fisherman and a blasting contractor," Otis said. "He played football for the Philadelphia Eagles, taught physical fitness, and coached teams across the country. I was eighteen before I discovered a pattern to his activities, other than an attraction to high explosives and remote places."

Still beating against the wind, we were trailing six inches of hooked surgical tubing from sixty yards of twenty-pound monofilament, hoping to raise a fish. Otis had been cataloging his family, all of whom seemed to have fished these waters. The previous week, a yachtsman had caught a forty-two-pound rockfish here, but the Pepsi can we were using for rod and reel would make landing such a creature dubious. We approached Tangier Sound, a region that during the nineteenth century had been as infamous as the Comstock for savage entrepreneurs. It has shipped some 125-million pounds of oysters yearly, and shanghaiing, slavery, and murder had been common within the fleet. Otis's own grandfather had impressed "shippies" into service, paying them at season's end in cash—more generously, at least, than other captains, who paid them off with the boom.

Now we were in the main part of the bay, some fifteen miles from the Virginia coast, and the spires of Tangier

Island were on the horizon. Tangier's 850 inhabitants compose the densest concentration of watermen left on the Chesapeake. The oyster rush has dwindled since the 1930s, but Tangier Sound still produces more hard- and soft-shell crabs than any place on Earth. Two and a half miles long and less than a mile wide, Tangier is in the heart of the Chesapeake Bay. Ferries connect it to the mainland.

Cap'n Otis, with his uncle, helped drill the first artesian wells there in the early 1970s. "He always thought it was his wells that kept the whole place from drifting away." As we motored toward the crab docks, Cap'n Otis noted various landmarks: the tall steeple of the Methodist church; the white clapboard houses surrounding it, gravestones in their front yards; and a series of canals that crisscrossed the island. Then we were in a logjam of crab boats: drake-tailed or round-sterned power launches with names like *Joansy* or *Ginny Lee*, their decks piled with crab pots; barcats, shallow-draft launches of considerable width that are used in summer to scrape for peeler and soft crabs; and the ubiquitous skiffs, some of which were variations on classic Chesapeake sailing craft, others of modern whaler design. Across the sound at Deal Island, Maryland—where it is illegal to power-dredge for shellfish—reside the last of the skipjack fleet. The boats are named for the bluefish, which skip across the waves in mad pursuit of bait, and they constitute America's last sail-powered fishing fleet. On Tangier Island, Virginia, it's legal to power-dredge for shellfish, so the graceful old skipjacks are never seen.

Tangier held the air of a foreign country, and, indeed, John Smith had purportedly named the island for the north coast of Africa. We docked beside a crab boat rinsed as clean as its squirming cargo and stepped onto an oyster-shell lane. The island seemed to be cemented by oyster shells—though not permanently, as twenty-five feet are lost yearly to the remorseless bay. Two boys approached and mouthed something nearly unintelligible, in a kind of Cornish brogue that turned about on itself with extravagant "oys" and "teys."

"Eight dollars," Cap'n Otis translated, "slip fee." Master Tilley paid the hustlers off.

There are no cars on Tangier, as there are no roads to speak of: just a narrow path that winds for perhaps half a mile between white clapboard houses, small domino parlors and general stores. Bicycles and motorbikes raced past white picket fences.

Supper was at Hilda Crockett's Chesapeake House, a meal that consisted of crab cakes and all the clam fritters, coleslaw, beets, corn pudding, fresh rolls, potato salad, peas, iced tea, and pound cake you could eat. Afterward we explored the town. It was Saturday night, and the population was restless. The more adventurous had ferried to Crisfield, Maryland, 14 miles across the bay. But those left behind passed one another relentlessly in a procession that continued into the small hours.

The wind came up and by morning was rattling the rigging at twenty to twenty-five knots. I slipped by the deserted crab docks and hiked across the island to the marsh-grass flats. To the north, hunting blinds were visible—blinds where fall gunners would await long phalanxes of duck and geese. This morning, purple-winged swallows darted beneath the elevated footbridges. Rusted crab dredges lay in the shallow guts. A small boy in an overlarge skiff decelerated from twenty knots to zero for an eggshell mooring. There were no insects, and the wind blew stiff from the northeast. An old man stood scraping a boat in a field of forsythia. I asked him how the winter had gone.

"Came fast after Christmas," he said. "Bay froze solid and the ferry couldn't run. But I had fuel. And a freezer full of fish. Wasn't no matter to me."

Outside the clapboard church, watermen and their families clustered. Bright sun kicked off the stained-glass windows as formally dressed women bicycled up and the mahogany faces of crabbers showed mushroom-white above the eyebrows. A preacher ululated in Tangier's strange tongue. It might have been the seventeenth century.

"YOU'RE DEALING WITH isolation and loneliness," Cap'n Otis said, "but also with competence and the world."

We were running before the wind at hull speed, in three-foot seas, with the storm jib puffing before thirty-knot gusts. I'd asked Otis about his religion—the Crazy Wisdom school of Tibetan Buddhism—which under the conditions seemed not inappropriate.

"It's while sailing that I feel the Buddhism really kick into gear," he said.

One could hardly argue. Leaving Tangier, Cap'n Otis had absolved himself of whatever laxity he'd displayed in running aground. The twenty-four-knot gale had threatened to pin us against a crab dock, but Otis had expertly brought the bow around had powered toward open water. Once out in the main channel, he'd bounced like a tyke in a yellow safety harness, making hull speed with just a storm jib. Now we were on a sleigh ride, heeled over and belly-flopping at the widest point in the bay— some thirty miles between shores. It was deep water. We were at sea. The sun was a gray dime behind its cloud cover. The wind was cold. Several wrecks marked the US Navy's practice range, where on a clear day bombers chipped away at the rusted hulks. Cap'n Otis steered past the *San Marcos* wreck, and a thirty-foot piece of superstructure bobbed to starboard—too close for comfort.

"Big fish near these wrecks," Cap'n Otis said, "many large bucks."

It was blackjack, songwriting, and horse-racing tips that occupied us as we settled into the twenty-mile romp to Deltaville. Cap'n Otis entertained us with tales of his granddad, who'd owned a lumber schooner that he'd sail to Baltimore each year, then return via the Susquehanna Flats for hunting "with ducks hung from every inch of rigging." The old man had owned a fish plant at Reedville and was infamous for "fishing Cape Hatteras before anybody else," retreating from storm-driven seas with caulking beaten from his hulls.

I'd had something of a Chesapeake heritage. My father's family had lived by the Potomac's mouth near St. Mary's City in 1640, as English Catholics fleeing the Reformation. The Thompsons moved upriver to Washington around 1855, and my family to Cabin John, three miles northwest, on the Potomac, in 1951. Before that we had summered on the Patuxent, by the Chesapeake, and saltwater sunsets, blue crabs and skipjacks on the horizon were among my fondest memories.

The air blew warmer now. We'd abandoned our plan to sail up the bay long the storied Oxford-St. Michaels-Annapolis loop (where docks had parking meters, eighteenth-century mansions marked the creek banks, and the sensation was one of cruising through an antique shop) because the wind blew in absolutely the wrong direction, and because we'd tasted a lower bay we'd rather savor.

"Follow the wind," Cap'n Otis said. "North one day, southwest the next, spend *years* and never cross the same trotlines."

It was the open-endedness of this kind of cruising that had lured our host, Martin Tilley, to the Chesapeake. There were thousands like him, transplanted westerners and mid-westerners who had thrown in the towel and retired to a life along the bay.

"How long have you been out?" was a standard question.

"Oh, seven months."

And that meant *cruising*, not lying moored in home port.

It was too rough for lunch, so we guzzled beer and swatted whitecaps, watching the bay turn from silver to pewter to deep green as the cloud cover parted. Ospreys rested in buoys and markers, flapping to feed their young. Gulls fussed. A tanker churned north. The *Euphrasy* beat a true course, but it was a tremendous effort to maintain one's balance. Cap'n Otis rode the wheel.

A FULL MOON shone across a harbor as romantic, to our minds, as that at St. Tropez. Dozier's Dockyard lay surrounded by white frame houses and tall poplars that shivered in the moonlight. We were bone-tired from our bucking-horse ride. Master Tilley poured coffee as we recovered from a Deltaville supper of crab cakes and pork barbecue. There'd been a sign over the bar that read UNATTENDED CHILDREN WILL BE SOLD AS SLAVES, and the bathrooms were marked SOOKS AND JIMMIES. That was crab slang for ladies and gents.

There were yachts from all about—from Delaware, Massachusetts, and South Carolina. Deltaville is a center for Chesapeake boat building. Any number of boatyards are scattered about the small peninsula that separates the Rappahannock and Piankatank rivers. Earlier, we'd visited Paul Mooney, a thirty-year-old boatbuilder from Detroit, who made steel yachts with hulls so true they were smooth as fiberglass. Mooney had been in Deltaville six years. He specialized in the Departure 35, a cutter-rigged yacht of five-foot draft, ideal for either blue water or the Chesapeake. Mooney was adamant about steel. "Fiberglass breaks down, wood rots, but steel lasts," he'd said. Mooney had built a forty-foot catamaran when he was a teenager, a craft that one can barely imagine in a Detroit backyard.

"The perfect boat for sailing the Chesapeake is of sharpie, or modified-sharpie design," Cap'n Otis said, nuzzling his coffee. There were no hull-shattering rocks in the bay. But to cross sandbars and grass flats—the epitome of Chesapeake gunkholing—one wanted the shallowest draft. Log sailing canoes had been developed by the early watermen, to tong for oysters in the flats. Strikingly graceful, many had been restored as sport craft and were raced yearly in the upper bay. A pungy with a New York port of call lay moored not far from us tonight.

Her spars were varnished and her hull painted white. She, too, had been converted for sport. The pungy was a reduced version of the Baltimore clipper and an ancestor of those bugeyes and skipjacks that later inherited the bay.

Moored next to us tonight was a weathered sloop with a self-steering vane astern and a variety of gear, including a Moped, lashed to her deck. Her captain came topside and introduced himself. "How long you been out?" someone asked.

"Twelve years, two in the bay."

It was Bill Moeller, co-author with his wife, Jan, of *Living Aboard*, a standard of the cruising genre. Moeller was in Deltaville to have his boat's hull sandblasted. Cap'n Otis handed him a beer, and we traded stories for a time. The Moellers were writing a second book, titled *Simplify*.

"You're selling dreams when you write about sailing," Moeller said. "It's *the* escape."

"Yeah, there's something about being a bum that appeals to me," Cap'n Otis said. "But on a yacht you never really are."

The important thing was to keep moving. Tonight we were secure, but tomorrow we'd test Stingray Point and explore the Plankatank, close-reaching through its mouth to Wilton Creek. There we'd wind through the shallows to an anchorage of particular isolation and beauty—one with an Adirondacks feel to its steep hills, thick with hardwoods that were soft green in early spring and with water clear as a mountain lake. Next morning we'd backtrack to the Rappahannock, tacking slowly and finally motoring to Urbanna, the *Euphrasy*'s home port. Urbanna is a seventeenth century town and something of a museum piece, its Victorian architecture unmatched along the bay. There we'd evaluate the *Euphrasy*'s shakedown, anticipating highest marks.

If spirit and wind moved us, we'd sail across the bay to Virginia's Eastern Shore for a tour of its desolate, marsh-grass coves before mosquito season. That might take a month. By then we'd be primed for Crisfield, Maryland, the oyster and hard-crab capital that during the 1880s rivaled Tombstone for its lawlessness and in the 1980s continues to marry a Wild West insolence to Chesapeake bravura. Then a visit to the skipjack fleet at Wenona before fulfilling our original pact to explore Topsider country— the most proper Tred Avon, Choptank, and Severn rivers. Perhaps at Annapolis we'd have had enough. But there would be Baltimore farther north and the charm of her big-city harbor, with the beautiful old saloons at Fells Point and row houses from Dickens's London.

Maybe then we'd finally turn south, exploring a hundred fresh ports before Labor Day and Crisfield's incomparable Hard Crab Derby. There, blue crabs representing every state in the Union would compete in a weirdly orchestrated footrace. And Miss Crustacean, Miss Skipjack, and Miss Delmarva Poultry Princess would parade in open cars. By October, the waterfowl would be migrating, Canada geese by the thousand darkening the sky. On November 1, the skipjacks would begin their winter's dredging, and that would be special to see—

"Go now!" Cap'n Otis said, from his mantle of ocher lantern light. "Just pack it and go!"

Outside, 1983

NEW YORK

Living Alone

In October 1965 my uncle died as he had lived, alone, in a society of single people. That society was Manhattan: the city. He was found rather quickly by friends, the same friends who had moved him, weeks earlier, to a smaller, more comfortable apartment. My uncle had a faulty heart. He had chosen to live alone but he was not lonely. His friends saw to that. He had been a successful writer and television producer, an actor and musician. He was a world traveler. Most of his life had been spent happily around show business. His friends were show people; they were painters or composers. His friends were his closest family. The only sad part about my uncle's having died alone was that he did it at fifty-three.

Many of us have bachelor uncles or maiden aunts who served as models of independence throughout our childhoods. Recollections of them are anti-familial; we were encouraged by parents to think of such relatives as sad. At the very least, strange. They were strange, in that they chose to go it alone in an era when the American nuclear family meant everything: stability, prosperity, a future.

The sort of life my uncle led, post-World War II, could not be considered odd today. He eschewed family for career, suburbia for the city, "responsibility" for romance. He was responsible foremost to himself, though the varied circle of friends he maintained looked out for one another. His life would be judged as sensible today; self-aware, ambitious, open to improvisation and change.

I REMEMBER MY UNCLE at the piano: a baby grand in my grandparents' apartment, a New York apartment crowded with show people. Always a party. I see my uncle in a smart tie, myself seated beside him in bandanna and cowboy boots. I am six years old. I stare at my uncle's hands, how they knead chords from the keyboard in baker's dozens. I hear his voice over the party din, "—crush on you, sweetie-pie, mornin', noon and night time, hear me sigh—" see his back arched straight, head swung high. "Play 'Ragg-Mopp'," I plead. His fingers rollout the boogie-woogie and we chant it together. The party laughs. I stand on the radiator beside the piano and belt "There's No Business Like Show Business." I sing it precisely as I've heard my uncle, parroting his every embellishment. "—No people like show people, they smile when they are low—" The party is captivated. They clap and stomp appreciation. I find myself the center of adulation. Such talent. So mature. I run to my parents, ecstatic in the glow of successful performance. I see the anger in my father's eyes.

WHY DO WE LIVE alone? Why have so many drifted from marriage toward a solitude only the city can appease? Why, like our estranged relatives, do we seldom feel lonely? Ask friends. Ask family. Ask yourself. Then dip further back to that past which shaped your answers.

NOBODY COULD PLAY the piano like Billy Nichols. Nobody could enliven a party like he, sing a song, or interpret a part. He was handsome. He was charming. He'd go all the way. He had a sister, five years younger, who could knock your eye out. She'd already transfixed my father.

By the time my uncle dropped out of Georgetown Foreign Service School in 1934 and caught *The Senator* for New York, show business was in his blood. My parents and he had attended Western High together, but my uncle was a Midwesterner who had spent his formative years in Indiana. His and my mother's father was an aggressive businessman, archetypal in the decade of *Main Street* and *Babbitt*. Grandfather migrated to Washington during the 1920s. In search of richer pavement, he would migrate to New York. Somewhere between Indiana and Georgetown, my uncle discovered show business and became a local legend.

Though the 1920s had seen the infancy of a sexual revolution, conceived in wartime and whelped on draughts of bootleg hooch, no one lived alone. The automobile lent privacy to premarital couplings which theretofore relied on cramped buggy space. But the notion of a young person setting up house, alone, was unheard of. This was the Depression. One lived with one's parents. The traditional means for escaping one's hereditary family was to establish a family of one's own. The twenties suggested broader opportunities for sexual experimentation, but those opportunities had yet to acquire cachet. The dreamiest tradition of erotic fulfillment to most middle-Americans was joining the tent-show circuit: showbiz, or running away with the circus. The circus inevitably wound up in the city, and that, to small-town romantics, was the land of Oz.

New York during the 1930s was not quite Dorothy's emerald city, but it was the Great White Way. It was the seat of Eros for Depression America, the most sophisticated of carnivals, where one might dissolve familial authority to the anonymity of a private bliss. You could have some fun.

MY UNCLE DID NOT immediately live alone, but moved from his parents' apartment in relative haste. Much to my grandfather's dismay. A career in show business was not the course of growth Midwestern fathers saw as promising during the Great Depression. My grandfather hit the ceiling. That his daughter had dropped out of high school her senior year, was modeling, carousing with theater people and artists, generally immersing herself in the sophistication of thirties New York, did not bother. That his son would forsake a career in foreign service, take up with vaudeville, as most theater was considered then, and move to an apartment in Greenwich Village, proved too much. He laid down the law.

My uncle responded by landing parts in a variety of off-Broadway productions. He studied hard with the best of the New York companies. He worked with Theatre Union and Group Theatre, appearing onstage with John Garfield, Cornel Wilde, Dame May Whitty, Walter Slezak, Vincent Price, and Judith Anderson. He studied dance with Martha Graham, acting technique and makeup with the Moscow Art Theatre, speech at the Neighborhood Playhouse. He performed on radio and recorded full-length plays for the blind. He supported himself with a variety of jobs, pounding the piano in saloons around New York. My grandfather, gradually, was won over.

I doubt that my father was. To live in Washington, at home in an attic room and struggle first through college, then medical school while maintaining a slew of part-time jobs, must have raised New York in his imagination to staggering heights. Washington's city life was decidedly small town. New York was the fun. And the sex. Though my father respected Billy Nichols's talent, he must have been furious at the society to which he introduced my mother. It was frustrating enough to court her odd weekends in New York, fighting eight hours' traffic each way, excruciating to imagine the world of Eros to which she was exposed, nightly, in his absence.

My parents were married in New York City. I was conceived in the St. Regis in December of 1943, and born the following September. My father, a Lieutenant Commander in the Navy, shipped out for the Pacific. For a time I lived with my mother on Riverview Terrace—in a house owned by the writer and art patron John Becker and his wife, Virginia. The Beckers loaned their house, during their travels, as an artists' collective. Tales survive of Aaron Copland composing as I crawled at his feet beneath the piano, of Max Ernst gushing over my childish sketches, and of Boris Karloff tickling my toes to make me walk. John Cage's ex-wife, Xenia, took me under her wing. Later she carted me to museums and oversaw my obsession with art. If I remember anything from that period, it was rooms lighted with music, bright paintings and laughter. The men were off at war.

THEY WOULD RETURN to a different America, each with different experiences of that main event that had irrevocably altered American life. My father returned a hero, shaken, resigned more fiercely to the stability of family life. My uncle returned a veteran, disappointed that his single opportunity for combat had been thwarted by rheumatic fever. I retreated with my father to the parochialism of Washington. My mother joined us, longing for New York. My uncle thrashed around, reaching for a toehold on the ladder of success. We discovered television.

The nation discovered television. I recall that first Philco and the small gray world it unveiled one Christmas morning on Columbia Road. Its reception was the fuzziness of death, or oblivion. I perceived it as awesomely captivating, yet seductive in a way that previewed some dark future. Not until we moved to suburbia did television affirm its harshest grip, but by then I was grateful for company and the compromises of TV's slickest assault.

America divided. Suburbia yanked the familially oriented from city center as the cities boomed with postwar wealth, attracting legions of combat-weathered rurals to the mysteries therein. A large proportion of these immigrants were black—they could not afford or were restricted from suburbia. But another portion was the conscientiously single. They were drawn to great founts of energy geysering from World War II, the eroticism, carnality and carnivalism left from victory celebrations.

There was never any question that my uncle would leave the city. He had made his move. Dorothy's Midwest was a decade behind. Showbiz was a one-way ticket out of the heartland, yet this strange new medium of television heralded a return. Not geographically, but electronically. There still existed in America that imperative to spread the gospel of brighter futures. My uncle would never resettle in Indiana, but his good news might—that news of an urban frontier, wilder, freer, and achingly longed for by millions of Americans such as he. My uncle got into television.

I often wonder what part my situation played in his decision. I was his only nephew. I was talented, what's more, interested in the vagaries of a creative life. I loved the city. Like a generation of contemporaries I had been shuttled to suburbia at an age, and during an era, when the city had riches to offer. Suburbia was evolving as a Midwest of the spirit, a desperate over-compensation for lean years that sought to erase memories of Depression and the horror of war with hermetic isolation. We became hermits. The entropy of city life proved too scary for our familially shell-shocked. A decade of Depression trailed by five years of war had sufficed. Our families numbed themselves with possessions. Who could blame them? That they retreated to a midland yokelism that belied the cosmopolitanism gleaned from world war was an irony less troubling to them than to us. Thank God for radios in family cars, and the ultimate possession, TV.

In an age of regression that saw the tail end of American isolationism—heir to rugged individualism—resuscitated in suburbia, Communism (read: community) was the dirtiest word in the English language, nuclear extinction a daily threat, and the dollar omnipotent, television reached out. Radio injected us with the spirit of rock 'n' roll. Television gave us theater. Raucous, irreverent, vaudevillian in its ludicrousness, fifties television was absurdity on review. We took TV seriously in that it mirrored our lives. Grownups were fools: *Father* rarely knew best. Suburbia was racist and condescending: *Beulah, The Life of Riley.* Suburbia quartered the perceptually stunned, where an adolescent quip might enliven the day: *Ozzie and Harriet.* Release surfaced in the guise of seltzer-squirting Clarabells, transvestitish Milton Berles, and heavily armed cowpokes. If Clarabell reappeared as a sixties' Yippie, Berle as a seventies' drag queen, and the Lone Ranger as an outlaw Weatherman, it was no surprise. TV was our strictest teacher.

It was our hope. Television not only nurtured rebelliousness but suggested possibilities exclusive of the nuclear family for sustenance. Lash La Rue, the Cisco Kid, Hopalong Cassidy, Matt Dillon, and Yancey Derringer never bothered with wife and kids. They had lives that were action packed, idealistic; they sought comfort in sidekicks. Even cop heroes such as Broderick Crawford and Jack Webb were loners. Their shows were Hollywood productions, descended from thirties movies, more determinedly mythic than their New York counterparts. They enjoined the distance of film. New York came at you live and it was by that intimacy we saw escape from suburbia.

Sid Caesar was the circus come to town, and you could follow. Ed Sullivan was a carnival on Main Street, and you could join. Steve Allen was a pie in the face on Broadway that you could heave. Jackie Gleason was a bus you could hijack. Philadelphia's Dick Clark was a record hop you could crash. Mort Sahl and Lenny Bruce were street-corner hipsters you could berate. TV was sexy, dangerous, and iconoclastic, like the city. It spelled excitement, a hint of which has been recaptured in past years by *Saturday Night Live.* Steve Allen was live in New

York, with cream pies and alligators. We were suffocating in middle America.

MY UNCLE WORKED a while as production assistant on *We the People*, then became an idea man for *Your Hit Parade*. Eventually he became a producer, staying with the show seven years. *Your Hit Parade* was a strange item. It interwove a fifties obsession with ratings (read: status) to popular music and our old pal, vaudeville. Popular music, fast encompassing rock 'n' roll, was the sound of the city. Vaudeville was city theater. It was my uncle's job to marry vaudeville and popular music in weekly skits that dramatized the hits comically, or with romance. A ludicrous task. Nine skits a week needed staging, seven hits and two standards. My uncle wrote them all. This was a period that saw tunes such as "The Ballad of Davy Crockett" and "Doggie in the Window" hanging on for twenty weeks. How many skits could anyone imagine for such self-dramatized pap? How many different ways could Dorothy Collins or Snooky Lanson croon to a beagle pooch? Or stroll before the Alamo? When "Hound Dog" hit the charts in 1956, it nearly broke my uncle's back. He could barely face the horror of five months' more dog skits.

Still, the show had a wackiness to it that intrigued, and that wackiness spun across the airwaves. These were our songs the grownups were fumbling with—we couldn't help but smirk. I remember begging my uncle to make Snooky Lanson sing "Green Door" like rock 'n' roll, rather than some Crosby retake on the cutting room floor. My uncle, who nurtured a deep love for the roots of rock, merely laughed. Though the compromises hurt. He knew he was lubricating an orifice through which a heavier message might be injected. Foreplay took time.

The New York sexiness of lush production numbers appearing weekly on *Your Hit Parade* was compounded incredibly once viewed live. Other kids had family TVs. I had family on TV. I recall blue-lighted rehearsal halls at NBC, heron-limbed dancers in tights and slit gowns sailing through crowded studio elevators. Casts pulling together, teams of individual talent pooling resources for the common weal. After work they dispersed, living alone but not lonely. And so erotically. The sexiness of TV was not diminished by studio familiarity, but increased when street language and innuendo were heard to drip from famous lips. An eroticism of family percolated backstage that proved supremely attractive to a pre-adolescent... one still young enough to be awed by a private skit from Kukla, Fran and Ollie, enchanted by the dark glamour of Gisele McKensie.

My uncle kept an apartment near Times Square that overlooked Forty-Fifth Street and the stage door to Steve Allen's show, where all manner of elephants, blue kangaroos, and kaleidoscopic weirdoes milled. Times Square, then as now, was a nut haven. It was a theater district that, with the intrusion of TV, quickly puckered toward a pornographic ghetto. All of New York's erotic and neurotic deviance centered there, or so it seemed, and TV slapped the mind-set into focus. Theater during the 1930s had implied sophisticated opening nights, evening gowns and late suppers at El Morocco. TV, fast co-opting Times Square, hawked manic participation. You were part of the show. And it was sleaze. Steve Allen might coat you in Jell-O, Ed Sullivan goad you to scream like a banshee—you'd best be ready. Gentility dropped from the eroticism of Times Square like a stone gargoyle from a parapet.

My uncle met John Cage on Broadway one afternoon. He asked him, what's new?

Cage, busy composing "silent" pieces of several movements during which no intentional sounds were produced, glanced about and said, "Three sonatas!" beaming at the cacophony.

THROUGHOUT THE *Hit Parade* years, my uncle had written television adaptations of Shakespeare or Gilbert and Sullivan, for classic dramatic series such as *Hallmark Hall of Fame, Omnibus, DuPont Show the Month/Week, Project 20* and *The Bell Telephone Hour.* These shows aired my uncle's soberer side. At least one was chosen by the Museum of Modern Art for a festival of the decade's outstanding television, and most others are in the Museum of Broadcasting in New York. My uncle quit *Your Hit Parade* in 1957 and got into big money, working exclusively on specials with Rex Harrison, Dinah Shore, Joan Crawford, Ethel Merman, and Richard Rodgers. He wrote eight *Judy Garland Shows* for CBS. He invested wisely, building two houses on Fire Island and moving to a penthouse on Central Park West. He traveled, studied yoga, continued in modern dance. He played the hell out of his piano. He inched toward fulfillment as a musical scholar with the research and writing of "The History of American Musical Comedy" and "Those Ragtime Years" for *Project 20.* "The Ziegfeld Touch," "Music of the Thirties," "Chicago and All that Jazz," "Regards to George M. Cohan," and "Fads and Foibles" for *Dupont.* His intention was a careful orchestration of America's urban taste. His dedication was to himself, and to the new medium's vision of carnival life in the city. Like other pioneers in TV, he'd tickled our fancy with Vaudeville, to ambush our intellect with legitimate theater. And what theatricality implied: city life as salvation. It was dangerous and uncertain, but worth a gamble. My uncle lived alone, above Central Park, basking in this creative vision. One morning in 1962, while bird watching near the Ramble, he was beaten by street punks and left for dead.

My uncle never again played piano. He suffered aphasia his remaining years. It took months for his face to heal, and in the end his commitment cost him two life passions—music and language. On warm nights he could sit on his terrace watching the lights of Manhattan, and hear congas thumping from the Park accompanied by taxi horns and the odd ballyhoo.

AT MY UNCLE'S funeral, a cocktail gathering attended by a handful of close friends, I wore his best suit, danced in his shiniest shoes, and did everything but get up on the radiator to sing. I mugged lyrics to his records and told jokes in his style. I became my uncle in a way that cheered those present, but proved damaging to me. I drank a quantity of Scotch. The actress Lee Remick got us into Arthur, the chic discotheque of 1965, where my mother flirted with Bobby Kennedy and I danced with Ethel until even Bobby got worried and came looking. We wound up very late and very drunk at a bar on First Avenue where my uncle had played piano in the thirties. It was not mass at St. Patrick's or a funeral at St. John's, but our way of commemorating him.

My uncle had loved the sixties. Loved the Beatles and American rock 'n' roll, loved the new films such as *Whatever Happened to Baby Jane?* In their self-conscious grotesquerie, loved the absurdist theater of Pinter and Genet, loved most ecstatically the new theatricality rife in the streets of New York. We mined it together—I on leave from college, in town for weekends or the short vacation. We became friends. My passion for theatricality asserted itself; I was playing folk music in clubs up and down the East Coast. During a theater intermission in New York, I was approached by a girl who had seen me perform near Philadelphia, and asked if I wasn't who I was. My uncle loved that. He smiled and watched it happen. I was collecting fans; that's how it should be. I was the generation he'd worked to illuminate, and I was taking over.

Like the privileged majority of that generation, I was spending the sixties in school—enduring a barracks life of prolonged adolescence, stacked in dormitories atop peers until the communal lid might blow. Primed for catharsis by a decade of television, we sat frustrated four more years, eight for the ambitious, quartered together in approved housing but more alone than if on extended polar bivouac. We fought the penny wars of grades and sex, in a decade that encouraged sexual acrobatics but discouraged intimacy. The more erudite we became the more insistent was our drive toward independence. Modern education was teaching us to rely less on family than production; on a professionalism that substituted work for love, and that had conditioned us from grade school to view our friends as the enemy—in unspoken enmity, a state preparing us for a marketplace where no one was a friend. That most colleges were stuck in dreary little towns that, if not the Midwest, were so mid-American as to evoke nightmarish recollections of suburban isolation, was a message received. The urban potential for eroticism and individual eccentricity had been drilled into the countriest of us, through television, and the prospect of graduate study in more remote gulags of the American hinterland, enflamed our fiercest sensibilities. We had seen the elephant, in Lucius Beebe's phrase, and that elephant was the city. It played a Fender Telecaster, was slathered in grease paint, and blew peanut shells at the ringmaster.

Dissent fomented in universities but did not emerge in riotous dismay until students hit the street—then exploded transculturally. It was no accident that the great antiwar demonstrations of decade's turn were city events—transpiring in Chicago, New York, Washington, DC. Inner cities were occupied by invasion forces of half a million kids, enraged at an unjust war and incensed by a draft that stood as yet another post-graduate tour between themselves and release. A decade's sublimated theatricality arose in antiwar demonstrations that were, intentionally, immense concatenations of street theater, calculated to unstop emotions boiling since childhood. Vietnam was some extravaganza cast and directed by grownups, fated to bomb in New Haven. It was further exile. The antiwar movement cloned the righteous indignity of Hopalong Cassidy to the Dada hysteria of Clarabell. It considered Times Square to Lafayette Square a reasonable transition.

Grownups inhaled TV during the 1960s, mostly news, sprinting to catch up. We became what we'd ingested, excreting residue at demonstrations more involved with our collective sanity than the madness unfolding abroad. It was televised coverage for grownups, theater in the street for us. We discovered each other in downtown Chicago or federal Washington, and saw we weren't alone.

Vietnam divided our generation as it did the rest of America. We did not reunite until that conflict stood resolved. Vietnam was theater, but relied more on Hollywood and World War II imperatives than the post-modernist aesthetic of television. That cadre that served in Vietnam learned absurdity first hand, and derived a sense of community from having faced it. In fact, the late-sixties, early seventies experience for most middle-Americans was communal—whether through war, "dropping out," or dissent. Not until post-armistice did survivors begin trickling toward city-center, alone, with intentions of living alone, in the midst of a decade reverting toward family.

Our shell-shock proved no sterner than our parents' in its retreat toward stability. If the most riveting television of the 1960s had been *Colorsplash News*, the most intriguing of the 1970s was *All in the Family*: a sitcom formula old as *The Honeymooners* and straight from the 1950s. Dumb grownups grousing and, in *Family*'s case, hip kids (married now) desperate to cut the apron strings.

I returned home after college/antiwar and married a female Vietnam veteran, a three-tour second lieutenant in the nurse corps named Corinne Collins. Dubbed "the astro-niece" by friends—her uncle was astronaut Michael Collins, of Armstrong, Aldrin, and Collins—her father was a brigadier general and her grandfather had been Lightning Joe Collins, a World War II hero, Army Chief of Staff during Korea, and the first ambassador to Vietnam, under Eisenhower. But before war, we'd attended coming out parties together. In Cabin John, we settled into a gate house owned by my parents, chocked full of my uncle's furniture. I had no more sense of who I was than before I left. I thought I'd achieved some identity in college, through music and writing—and even through marriage. I thought I had a life with book contracts and friends who performed, but something was a sham. I'd pushed theatricality as far as I could. Every ideal I held came directly from show business, from television's or my uncle's view of the cosmos. I took one look at my uncle's furniture and felt a silent fury—fury at the lightness with which it had perched in his apartment above Central Park, fury at the weight I felt receiving it in Cabin John.

Throughout my marriage I refused to allow Corinne to move one piece. I felt trapped, more alone in wedlock and the maze of my uncle's leavings than ever. The night my marriage dissolved I thought quickly of those prison antiques, terror struck that I'd die alone. Not the happiest of emotions, but one that swelled my chest with resignation.

"WE SOUGHT HARLEM, *or something sacrosanct as Julie London*," Ken McCullough wrote in a poem to me. "*The uncle, then, was slight—but now is twenty hands and eighteen stone.*"

Television during the 1970s was a bachelor uncle we had to desert—a relative as troublesome to discard as our parents, whose influence was arguably as powerful. As marriages derailed, shooting parental dreams of tidy nuclear families into the draw, theatricality itself needed confronting. And suspending. It was time to drop the masks and scrub off the grease paint.

Television had provided community during the 1950s, street catharsis during the 1960s, and was nudging us toward a 1970's cult of self. The questions we began to ask truly dealt with living alone: Is there a world distinct from the mind's perception of it? Is there identity exclusive of media? Are we ever alone? We retreated from the catholicity of McLuhan's crime-lighted global village to monks' cells of the spirit.

It is ironic that Marshall McLuhan, guru to the sixties cult of pop, should have been superseded by Swami Muktanandas, Werner Erhardts, and Fritz Perls of the soul. For McLuhan, in his secularity, was a religious visionary. He saw TV as an all-engulfing medium, a sort of electronic mass that might rescue man from the isolationism of print to bathe him in spiritual community. Drama (read: theater) had evolved from religious ceremony—tragedy from Dionysian rites concerning life and death, comedy from those dealing with fertility, or sexuality. McLuhan, as if strung out on the eroticism of fifties TV, had blessed the wedding of sex and technology. He had prophesied that cities would become obsolete as work centers, but would flourish as Casbahs of sensuality—or pleasure. TV he saw as a more sensual medium than print, because it engaged not just the visual sense but the audio and tactile. Print was a medium that fragmented man's perceptions; it engaged just one sense. Print's introduction in the fifteenth century had plucked man from tribal bliss—specifically, the dark medievalism of Christian Europe—and fragmented him, resulting in all manner of sociological rifts, from nationalism to schizophrenia. Television was a religious medium, grounded in Dionysian revel and grim catharsis, that might heal.

The wedding of sex and technology, seen as easily in rock, space, film and war as in TV, was an idea that encapsulated the 1960s. After Vietnam's last apocalyptic shudder, we unplugged the TV, pulled out of the global village and confronted ourselves. This we did by meditation, yes, by a dropping of theatrical masks; also by a retreat to print, as if flying in the face of McLuhan's strictest admonition. Print was selfish. You read by yourself, to yourself. It fragmented you from community. I touched the being in spots where TV feared to tred.

A relinquishment of posture allowed novices to feel pain and pleasure in a manner discouraged by sixties hysteria. The seventies came to symbolize vulnerability as readily as they came to exploit it. The retreat to print seeded an industry: the loneliness business. One need walk into any bookstore to confront walls papered in self-improvement tracts; self-awareness, self-actuality. Psychiatrists raked in the cash. Psychiatry was a language-based therapy but a tongue's slip from its founder's obsession with literature. The book industry flourished. We pickled our psyches in print and, as if by decree, fragmented into medievalisms of the self.

I PROVED NO MORE immune than the next pilgrim. A writer, I threw myself feverishly into print, into isolation, seeking release through typescript as fanatically as I thought to instill it. I saw myself as point man, some avatar of the collective malaise who took Hemingway's dictum that "writing at its best is a lonely life...if [one] is a good enough writer, [one] must face eternity, or the lack of it, each day."

We were facing eternity, but self-awareness was slipping toward self-effacement. A fact most obvious in fashion. Where sixties clothing had flaunted primary colors and the audacity of position, seventies dress camouflaged armature in earth tones and fragile humility. Then, about 1978, hair shirts gave way to trimmer duds and costumes surfaced as they had a decade earlier—in 1968, the year Sixties saturated middle-America. We were re-evaluating theatricality.

My descent into print paralleled that of the culture's in a telling way. My first book, completed in 1969, concerned Bob Dylan—specifically, Dylan as theatrical pundit. My second, completed in 1976, concerned old saloons and a four-year-hegira across America, in escape from theatricality and in quest of the Great American Bar— that chapel of boozy meditation where TV did not exist, people talked to one another, and language was king. My third, completed in 1978, concerned the sixties—was a selfish and generational exposé of where we'd been. These books were in addendum to essays and stories charting a similar course. At the finish of my sixties book, and in subsequent pieces, I looked toward the city, as I had in the 1950s, for impetus to change.

I am thirty-five. All but two of my adult years have been spent alone. Living in exurbia, frustrated by print, all but fed up with self-examination, I have felt the pull toward city life stronger than since I was a child. What I imagine there is a society of single people, living alone but in community, caring for each other familially, erotically, but without the restrictions of conventional family. I imagine this because I see it happening generationally, and among friends.

I feel the pull back toward theater, epitomized by the city as Great White Way, with no trepidation at a return toward costume, toward dramatic posture. For the sublimated passions that hid beneath cloaks of war or antiwar, Bircher or Digger, boozer or Day-Glo doper, have largely been spent. Costumery today is not something lifted from TV, unconsciously aped in revolutionary garb, but conscious expression of considered position. Taken less seriously. People are moving toward the city to live alone and to love in community, because theater is fun— and indispensable to romantic possibility.

In its mid-thirties, our generation is moving singly into neighborhoods of peers in a way that our parents' generation is just beginning to—after spouses have died and retirement ghettos have beckoned. It has taken us half a lifetime to leave homes they still struggle to. Distraught as our generation may appear, we have weathered so much so fast that mid-life crises have passed by twenty-five and menopause has worked itself through by forty. Then it's the thrill of a downhill run, with minimal encumbrance.

Perhaps we will reach maturity—the emotional self-sufficiency that bedrocks living alone—faster for the tutelage of TV. No other generation has absorbed such a relentless flow of theater from a tender age, thereby assuming ritual and knowing unremitted catharsis:

extravagant expenditures of fear and pity upon a nonstop chorus line of scapegoats. TV was infantile psychodrama, electronic group therapy that guided us through changes and cemented our perceptions.

But TV was not enough. It sped up the process. During the sixties we acted out communally what we'd absorbed from televised theater. During the seventies we dipped behind masks, alone. During the eighties we'll re-emerge in communities of the self-sufficient, for a smoother buck and wing.

Apologists speak of the 1980s as an apocalyptic decade, politically and socially, but they fail to mention one fact: that the eighties will most likely see the death of our parents. Then we'll truly be alone. As the sixties saw the death of our parents' families, resulting in a decade of unprecedented growth, so will the eighties free us. A terrible and terrifying notion. But inevitable as change.

WE KILLED OFF THAT bachelor uncle, TV, in the 1970s, but as a generation we are conversant with resurrection—it might be pleasant to see the old boy back. An apostle of solidarity, he calls us to the fold each week on NBC when—from the studio where *Your Hit Parade* was broadcast— a celebrant shouts, "Live from New York, it's *Saturday Night*." Then icicles caress the spine. All the imagined eroticism of life alone, *live*, in the city, away from familial stares, brims in recollections of childhood. Except now we are grown.

Today, I don't refuse an occasional soft shoe. I'm not angry at my uncle for the changes he put me through. I see his life's work as messianic, the twinkle in his eye at the dawn of the sixties as benevolent. He understood theatricality as that cosmic two-step that might spring us from suburbia. The old message of absurdity learned at the knee of that gray Philco has proved a palatable aesthetic. It has knit us together. Like all spiritual illumination, we had to experience it ourselves—apart from the set. Each generation creates its own theater, discarding scripts of the former. We're still writing ours, but the casting call's out.

1980

How Sweet it Was:
Jackie Gleason

Jackie Gleason looks beautiful. He's seated in a tall director's chair with "The Great One" written across its back. He's draped in a maroon dressing gown, and his tiny dancer's feet shine in brightly polished slippers. A cigarette dangles from his left hand. He stares straight ahead. Presently his energy will fill the set as he improvises a scene with Richard Pryor in this, their new movie, *The Toy*, to be released by Columbia in December. But for the moment Gleason is quiet, an island of New York sophistication in a morass of California yahoos.

If character had a theme song, the strains of "Melancholy Serenade" would light Gleason like a Manhattan dawn. His mustache is perfectly trimmed. his hair tinted blond for the part. Smoke curls about it. He is tan and, for Gleason, moderately thin. He motions to his valet for another cigarette. As usual, Gleason is furious about waiting. Unlike his halcyon years in television, he has little control of his time on the movie set. And Jackie Gleason needs control. So he sits, a stone figure, aloof, brooding, alone with his thoughts.

The setting is the game room of a wealthy businessman in Baton Rouge, Louisiana. (Gleason plays the tycoon, who buys Pryor as a toy for his eleven-year-old son.) Here reality and fantasy overlap, for the company is shooting in the mansion of A. C. "Ace" Lewis, a Baton Rouge entrepreneur, reputedly the richest man in Louisiana. In fact, the set is Lewis's game room—temporarily garnished with big-game heads, a stuffed lion, and a pool table. But here Jackie Gleason is padrone. Exercising his prerogative, he rises nimbly from his chair, performs several trick shots on the pool table, then runs half a rack.

The crew is waiting for Richard Pryor. The crew has spent two weeks waiting for Richard Pryor, who has been hospitalized for exhaustion and is currently indisposed with an eye infection.

"An *eye* infection," Gleason mutters. "Has anybody seen it?"

Pryor's indisposition has been the butt of Gleason's sarcasm the past few days. Gleason, who, despite his sixty-six years, triple-bypass heart surgery, and a partially incapacitated leg, arm, and eye, has not missed a day on the set. Pryor is here this morning, and the company is eager to see the old and new masters mix.

Gleason picks up a shotgun he is to use in the scene. He works its breech. Director Richard Donner *(Inside Moves, Superman)* walks him through the action once and calls for Pryor. There is the sound of a door opening. Gleason whirls, shotgun in hand. Pryor slithers along the wall, mugging in mock terror.

"You saved my life," Gleason says. "I guess l owe you one."

"You owe me one?" Pryor says. "I owe you one," and on like that, in dialogue meaningless outside the context of the script, yet strangely significant. For both comedians *do* owe each other: Pryor for Gleason's mythic example, Gleason for the chance to work in a high-budget film with today's hottest star. Trading barbs with Richard Pryor will do Jackie Gleason's pocketbook no harm.

The two perform brilliantly. There are shades of Laurel and Hardy, Abbott and Costello, Gleason and Carney. As the scene finishes, the set erupts in laughter and director Donner turns, exclaiming, "Now *that's* comedy."

Gleason strides toward his trailer.

THAT'S COMEDY, BUT these days nothing seems terribly funny to Jackie Gleason. It's not that he's depressed; he's down with a case of having seen it all. Except for a six-year hiatus in the seventies, Gleason has, since 1931, worked nonstop in nearly every branch of show business. He has emceed talent shows, carnivals, and nightclubs; danced; performed in vaudeville, burlesque, Broadway theater, television comedy, and television drama; composed and conducted music; and, since 1941, acted in a succession of Hollywood films—sometimes two or three a year.

Jackie Gleason is *tired* of working. But there is something in his personality that won't let him quit. At least, not on the crest of a new wave of popularity. Fifties and sixties audiences remember Gleason for his blisteringly eccentric cast of television characters—Ralph Kramden of *The Honeymooners*, Reggie Van Gleason III, the Poor Soul, Joe the Bartender—and for movie roles like Minnesota Fats in *The Hustler* and Maish Rennick in *Requiem for a Heavyweight*. But to an emerging generation he is instantly recognizable as Sheriff Buford T. Justice from the phenomenally successful Burt Reynolds *Smokey and the Bandit* vehicles.

"Everybody had done a southern, redneck sheriff," Gleason says, "and it bothered me, when I read *Smokey*, that I couldn't think of how to do it different. Then I got the idea of the pencil mustache; then I got that accent. And I wrote every line I did, in both Smokeys."

When Gleason wraps *The Toy*, he will begin shooting the next *Smokey*. Counting *The Sting II*, to be released in February, it will be the third picture he has made this year.

"After this *Smokey*, no more comedies," Gleason mutters. "I've got some dramatic projects I'd like to do—

but maybe not even them."

For someone so impatient with movies, Gleason spends enough time working in them. And he surrounds himself with the accoutrements of movie stardom: a two million-dollar house in Lauderhill, Florida, a lavish wardrobe, a personal valet. Back in his trailer, after the game-room scene, Gleason perches in yet another director's chair, flicking ashes on the rug and crying, "Mel!" to Mel Pape, his functionary of many years; he demands Pape's assistance in the slightest task. Gleason seems to feed on the man's presence. He seems anxious about being alone.

When Gleason was nine, his father abandoned him. His mother died when he was sixteen; an older brother had died when he was two. As long as Gleason can pay a man to remain in his service, he will. Pape serves drinks, adjusts the air conditioner, and fetches cigarettes. Gleason smokes five or six packs a day. He may nip intermittently at light beer or Scotch during the afternoon. By his own admission, he is and always has been a world-class drinker. It was Orson Welles who, after an evening of tippling and reciting Shakespeare with Gleason, dubbed him "The Great One."

"I never missed a performance because of drinking," Gleason says. "I take only one or two when I'm working. Otherwise it throws off your timing. The coffee cup on *The Jackie Gleason Show*, that was always booze. One week we threw out a *Honeymooners* script several hours before the show, started drinking, and improvised the whole skit. But that was rare."

Today, author James Bacon and Marilyn Taylor, Gleason's third wife, are on the set. Bacon, a contemporary of Gleason's and the last of the old-time Hollywood columnists, is collaborating with Gleason on the star's autobiography. Their method of working is to pour the Scotch, turn on the tape recorder, and swap stories until one or the other quits. The stories are hilarious. They are by turns inflammatory, licentious, and crude, and they involve everyone of whom you've ever heard.

With only one reaction shot left this afternoon, Gleason is not holding back on the Scotch. He drinks it straight and without ice. Still, he seems morose about breaking training. Other days, he's confined himself to diet soda. "It's the boredom," he says to no one in particular. "That's the terrible thing about making pictures. You work two minutes, then wait for an hour. It's a pain in the ass. You pray for a long scene."

Boredom wasn't always a problem. During television's golden age, when Jackie Gleason was Mr. Saturday Night and had an eleven-million-dollar contract with CBS, he was producing two *Honeymooners* a week and was hopping. "We used to do an hour show, before a live audience, in an hour and fifteen minutes. The fifteen minutes was for set changes. In all those years, we only stopped the show once, when the backdrop collapsed, and we *had* to. I broke my leg onstage, and Carney went out to close the show. Fortunately, it was right near the end. I used to make mistakes, then come out and tell the audience—but never from within the scene. We did *The Honeymooners* in a theater, like a play. That was the first live sit-com; Skelton came afterwards, and so did Lucy."

Would Gleason consider a return to television?

"Every year they want me to come back and do a variety show. Too tough. You can't get the writing. And the writers got it easy now. All they have to do is show a broad's ass wiggling. Or give an inference that somebody's pregnant. The *easy* kind of writing. Nobody would want to try and write the stuff that I would do. 'Cause we had to have real scenes."

There is a knock at the trailer door. "Ten minutes," a script girl says.

"Ten minutes," Gleason laughs. "Ten minutes means forty-five." He calls for another drink.

THE CONTRADICTIONS OF Jackie Gleason's personality are the contradictions that have endeared him to the public as a star: an affection for lavishness juxtaposed with a propensity to blue-collar crudity; a skill at broad physical comedy combined with an indulgence in pathos and an ability to play tough dramatic scenes; a soft spot for romance, "lush strings and gorgeous dames," undercut by an intense loyalty to theatrical realism. It is theatrical realism that may be Gleason's principal contribution to television. In an era when television comedy was "all jokes—joke, joke, joke," Gleason personally created a cast of characters that he presented dramatically, and that he delineated as fiercely as any in the medium's history. Most were from his past, and many reflected parts of the Gleason personality.

"I knew a hundred guys like Ralph Kramden in Brooklyn," Gleason affirms. "And there were seven or eight Nortons on every block. Pop Dennehy, from 'Joe the Bartender,' lived downstairs from us when I was a kid. And the set for *The Honeymooners* was *exactly* our living and dining room—we had a different kind of stove, but that was it."

John O'Hara, in complimenting Gleason as an artist, compared Ralph Kramden to "a character we might be getting from Mr. Dickens if he were writing for TV." Certainly *The Honeymooners* set, and the way it vaulted Jackie Gleason from childhood destitution to adult stardom, is Dickensian. It was in that room that Gleason's parents argued, like Ralph and Alice Kramden. And it was to that room that Gleason's father returned, the last night Gleason saw him, to destroy every family photograph in which he appeared.

His father's disappearance was a pivotal moment in Gleason's life. The elder Gleason, a clerk for an insurance company, was a drinker who would vanish for entire weekends on binges. But he did introduce his son to Saturday vaudeville shows. The first time Gleason realized he wanted to be an actor he was a six-year-old seated in his father's lap "at a movie and an American Film five-act vaudeville show at the Halsey Theater. During the stage show I turned around, like the comedians, and faced the audience. I saw all the people laughing and I *knew* that life was for me."

After his father left, Gleason's mother worked as a change maker in the subway. Gleason finished grade school but dropped out of high school. From the time he was eleven, he had hustled pool in Brooklyn billiard parlors and gambled; he was always able to make a few cents. Gleason was venerated in the neighborhood for his skill at pool, his fancy dress, and his sense of humor.

"I was a riot in front of the candy store." Expressions like "How sweet it is" grew out of his shenanigans in the pool hall. "I was a riot up there, too." Gleason's first professional job in show business was emceeing the amateur shows at the old Halsey Theater.

When his mother died, he left Brooklyn for Manhattan. He took any work he could get. He was an exhibition diver in a water show and an emcee for a traveling carnival called "B. Ward Beam's International Congress of Daredevils."

"That was a terrible life. All you did was drink booze and eat eggs with ants in them." He worked for three years as an emcee and bouncer at Newark's Club Miami. His first big break was a two-year run at Manhattan's Club 18, on West Fifty-second Street. "That was one of the best nightclubs in the world," he recalls. "You couldn't do an act there. Couldn't tell jokes. You had to ad-lib. Every night it was packed with celebrities. We never did the same show twice."

It was there that Gleason honed his improvisational techniques, and it was there that Jack Warner saw him and offered him a one-year Hollywood contract that resulted in a string of bit parts in some less-than-memorable films: *Navy Blues* (1941), *All Through the Night* (1942), and *Larceny, Inc.* (1942). For Twentieth Century-Fox he did *Springtime in the Rockies* (1942) and *Orchestra Wives* (1942), with Glenn Miller. Gleason, it is claimed, was the only comedian who could ever make Miller laugh. And it was in Miller's band that Gleason met musician Bobby

Hackett, with whom he would later initiate a series of some forty albums of romantic music, featuring the Jackie Gleason Orchestra.

Although making movies had been a lifelong ambition for Gleason, live theater and nightclubs remained his first loves. During the forties, Gleason appeared in a number of Broadway shows, including *Keep Off the Grass* and *Follow the Girls,* and continued to work in clubs, most notably Slapsie Maxie's in Los Angeles, "the second-best nightclub in the world." It was from Slapsie Maxie's that Gleason was hired in 1950 for "a two-week engagement" as host of DuMont Television Network's *Cavalcade of Stars*, an engagement that stretched to two years and was the springboard for his extraordinary career in live television.

Before DuMont hired him, he had worked for twenty-six weeks during the 1949-50 season as Chester A. Riley in the first television version of *The Life of Riley*. But that NBC show was filmed and was not the best format for Gleason's talents.

Cavalcade was live, it was variety, and it was a showcase for all that Gleason had learned in nightclubs and burlesque. He demanded total control of the show, and got it.

Why take the risk of demanding total control at such an early stage in his television career? Because, Gleason says, he didn't care. "I was anxious to get back to Slapsie's, where all the fun was. I told the producer, 'You've only got me for two weeks. If I'm going to flop, I'll flop my own way. And if I'm a hit, I'm going to take all the credit.'"

Gleason composed his theme music ("Melancholy Serenade"), approved the writing, and began to create the characters that would make him famous: Charley the Loudmouth, Rudy the Repairman, Pedro the Mexican, Stanley R. Sogg, Reggie, and many others. With the exception of Reggie, most were blue-collar predecessors to the Archie Bunkers and Fred Sanfords of the seventies—and anomalous on television. "I knew I had to create characters," Gleason says, "because no personality is rich enough to last an hour—and because I always hated to tell jokes." Gleason's sketches worked, and his two weeks were extended. But it was not until the creation of *The Honeymooners* that his future in the medium was secured.

Much has been written about *The Honeymooners*: about Ralph Kramden as the perpetual loser, the quixotic dreamer, the get-rich-quick schemer; about the sympathetic magic between the three principals, Art Carney, Audrey Meadows, and Gleason. But not much has been said about the show's tone. Overall, it was one of anxiety. Like contemporary television, *The Honeymooners* was structured around tension: that of a household in disarray. The Kramdens argued incessantly, and though the ending was always happy—Ralph holding Alice in his arms, crooning, "Baby, you're the greatest"—there were constant threats of violence and desertion. "How would you like a knuckle sandwich?" or "Pack your bags, Alice!" or "You're going to the moon, Alice—bang, zoom, smash right to the moon!" The audiences sat wedded to this action, and of course laughed.

"It's not violence when it gets laughs," Gleason has said. The Kramdens' problems infected a generation, just as Gleason's instinct for situation comedy certainly influenced television through the years.

"Carroll O'Connor, when he was doing *All in the Family*, wrote me a letter," Gleason states. "It said, 'I know I'm doing all the things that you did.' I sent him a letter back and said, 'I *wish* I had done some of the things you're doing.'"

IN 1952, GLEASON left DuMont for CBS and *The Jackie Gleason Show*. Again he received total control over production. He took with him the June Taylor Dancers (Marilyn Taylor is June's sister) and the cast of *The Honeymooners*, plus as many extra beautiful women as he could squeeze into an hour. Gleason's shows, right through the late sixties, were some of the sexiest on television. It wasn't just the chorus girls kicking, but Gleason's "Glea Girls," who, to suggestive music, cooed, "And away we go."

"Sexy, yes," Gleason admits, "but always in good taste. It was a hell of a lot better having some gorgeous broad announce me than Jack Lescoulie."

In 1955, Gleason deeded the variety portion of his show to Tommy and Jimmy Dorsey—"Although I maintained control of production"—and concentrated on *The Honeymooners*. For the next year, he filmed thirty-nine episodes—then quit, claiming the quality of the material could not be kept up. "CBS wouldn't believe I'd walk out on an eleven-million dollar contract," Gleason says. But walk he did, taking a year off to compose music and consider the future.

Gleason continued in television, in various comedy formats, throughout the sixties (with *The Honeymooners* an intermittent feature), but began looking more toward Hollywood. "Any comedian who is a decent comedian is a good actor," Gleason said at the time, and set about to prove it. He won acclaim for his dramatic role in a 1958 television production of *The Time of Your Life*. He then returned to Broadway in *Take Me Along*, the musical version of O'Neill's *Ah, Wilderness!*, and won a Tony Award as outstanding actor in a musical. In 1961 he appeared in *The Hustler* as Minnesota Fats, a role that earned him an Academy Award nomination and with which he has become identified almost as closely as he has with Ralph Kramden.

For the first time, America saw Gleason's darker side—and loved it. To watch *The Hustler* today is to be shocked at how much Fats resembles Kramden. Yet Fats is a winner. He has character. And grace. There's even something religious about him. He presides over Ames Pool Hall, a place that Paul Newman, as "Fast Eddie" Felson says "looks like a church...a church of the good hustler." Gleason hustles in the picture—and off camera he took Newman for fifty dollars one afternoon, running ninety-six straight balls—but his overall image is that of a sensitive perfectionist, of one who may have spent an occasional night poring over Teilhard de Chardin or *Lives of the Saints*.

Which is exactly what Jackie Gleason was doing. Although he denies being religious ("My mother was; she was very religious"), he delayed getting a divorce from his first wife because of his Roman Catholicism. And he has counted among his friends Chardin and Fulton J. Sheen.

"I consulted Bishop Sheen about my divorce," Gleason says. "And I used to discuss penance with Chardin. He'd laugh sarcastically and say, 'You know, it's different on Fifth Avenue than on Tenth. There, people are ignorant and require more Hail Marys.'"

The darker Gleason roles are rife with penance. "Figure you owe me" is a recurrent phrase in *Requiem for a Heavyweight* (1962) and *The Hustler*. In both, Gleason translates the comedic realism with which he infused live television to a Brooklynesque film noir. Even in *Gigi* (1962), for which Gleason wrote the story and the music, he is the saddest of clowns. "I don't believe that crap about a comedian's talent coming from a well of loneliness," Gleason has said. But one need only glimpse those films to wonder.

As real-life morality plays, they were somber counterpoints to Gleason's well-publicized life during the sixties. He had a Fifth Avenue penthouse, show girls, Rolls Royces, and a mansion in the country that George Jessel described as "sort of a bar with a built-in house." An average day consisted of lunch at Toots Shor's with Joe DiMaggio, Whitey Ford, Mickey Mantle, Bob Considine, and Jimmy Cannon—"all good, funny people"— home for a nap, partying from six until two in the morning at Shor's, 21, El Morocco, or the Copacabana. The cabaret life was the reason Gleason eventually moved his operation to Florida. "I'd heard the jokes a hundred times, and I was sick of the routine."

But in the early sixties, he was Mr. Goodtime. When

Papa's Delicate Condition wrapped in 1962, Gleason hired a private train and invited everyone he knew to make the trip from Hollywood to New York. A Dixieland band was obtained; there were show girls, Gleason's favorite press, and nonstop booze and food. At every tank town in which the train stopped, Gleason was challenged by the local pool shark, and won. Gleason orchestrated a similar trip when he moved his television show to Miami in 1966, and private trains became part of the Gleason legend. "I never did like to fly," he explains.

Gleason continued to live high in Florida, sharing quarters with show girl Honey Merrill, playing golf on the course adjacent to his lavish new home, and spending nearly a quarter of a million dollars a week, then a record amount, to produce his show.

In 1971, Gleason obtained a divorce from his wife of thirty-five years; he remarried, divorced, and in 1975 married Marilyn Taylor. Gleason's CBS contract was terminated in 1970, allegedly because his variety format was not attracting younger viewers. (Excerpts from the sixties variety show have recently been syndicated for television in half-hour segments by Twentieth Century Fox.) CBS claimed the occasional *Honeymooners* skits were what the audiences had wanted more of—but Gleason had had enough.

Throughout the seventies, Gleason did do a few *Honeymooners* specials, on television and onstage in Atlantic City, but for him the show was basically finished. And in all the years Jackie Gleason had performed *The Honeymooners* in his family kitchen-living room, he'd heard not a word from his father. The one fan he cared about the most had never picked up the phone.

GLEASON'S STILL SIPPING Scotch. Outside, director Donner and cinematographer Laszlo Kovacs *(Easy Rider, Shampoo)* race miniature jet boats across Ace Lewis's private lake. Producer Phil Feldman *(The Wild Bunch, The Ballad of Cable Hogue)* is around, and somewhere lurk the reclusive Richard Pryor and his entourage. Pryor is reportedly under pressure from his group to ditch this Uncle Tom role.

"Of course, he and Gleason hate each other," one crew member claims.

There's no evidence to support that observation—in fact, each actor has praised the other— but a generational tension does exist. With Gleason around, it's very much Broadway versus bluejeans. Outside, new Hollywood cavorts. Inside, old Hollywood reminisces—outrageously.

"Slapsie Maxie Rosenbloom had the room next to mine," Gleason says. "He had these terrible hemorrhoids, you know. For the hell of it, I took some Tabasco and drilled a hole in several of his suppositories, wrapped the foil back just right, and put them in the jar. It took about three days for him to hit one. I stuck close, and one morning there was this 'Whoaoaoaoaoa!' you couldn't mistake."

James Bacon interjects a few tales about Errol Flynn, Forrest Tucker, and Trevor Howard—all equally bizarre— finishing with a respectful nod toward Bob Hope.

Gleason adds, "Hope appears on television so often because he doesn't want anybody to see his hair recede. He's fearless, that sonofabitch. He'll do a nightclub act with cards. He'll do a show anywhere and make it pay off. He takes a vacation to go fishing and tells jokes to the fish."

Gleason has his version of why *Citizen Kane* infuriated William Randolph Hearst. "Orson told me it wasn't the movie as a whole, so much as the fact that 'Rosebud' was Hearst's pet name for Marion Davies's pussy." And, says Gleason, "everyone thinks Ed Sullivan discovered Elvis, but I had him on my show before anybody. Someone brought in his picture, and I said, 'Holy shit, have you got anything where he makes noise?' They sent out and we got this record. I said, 'Nab him.' I had him for six weeks on 'Stage Show,' with Tommy and Jimmy Dorsey, and he got so good that Tommy and Jimmy were getting angry.

They were my friends, so I had to let Elvis go."

Gleason's thoughts have turned, mercifully, away from movies to his great pal, television. "The future is HBO," Gleason says. "As soon as people realize they can get quality by paying for it, they will. The networks will go. CBS wanted to give me Saturday night recently to put on any shows I wanted—from seven-thirty to eleven o'clock. I said, 'Why don't you get Sid Caesar, Milton Berle, myself, and we'll all do an hour? The old style. I *know* that would be a riot.' Well, they started to ask how much everybody wanted, and that was the end of that.

"Without these people, the variety show is a thing of the past," Gleason points out. "Comedians now are all monologists; they can't do sketches. And they're not great stars. You've got to *like* a comedian for him to last. I saw *Saturday Night Live* when Burt Reynolds was hosting, and everybody went into a vomitorium and threw up. Where do you go after that? And Richard Pryor—well, it's his time. People expect him to do the vulgar stuff, but I think he'd like to do a show without it. He's too good a comedian. We said 'fuck' in the old days, but we didn't say it on *The Honeymooners.*

"In pictures, you can play a villain. But in television, if they don't like you you're fighting an uphill battle. Then you *got* to tell jokes."

How great *was* the golden age of television?

"The same as the golden age of pictures. Terrific. That era's gone because there aren't any Gables, or Garbos, or those kinds of people left. Same in television. There aren't any more Berles, Caesars, Gleasons, or Skeltons. You've got to be able to do sketches and scenes. That's what *makes* television. As with the beginning of motion pictures, there were certain performers who clicked. Those guys made people buy sets and made television a great industry. Live television was it. There'll *never* be anything like that again. Today I watch sports, documentaries, and dramas on PBS. That's about all."

Did he have a philosophy of television comedy? "Yes.

We never did anything that couldn't have happened in real life. Reggie was the only extension of that. And anything he did, some nut like him would do. And whenever we were doing a scene, we never turned to the audience. That was the fourth wall. We did it exactly as you'd do a play."

Was realism important? "If there's no reality, you can't do comedy. Comedy comes off of reality."

Gleason takes a slug of Scotch, and unexpectedly there is laughter. Except that Jackie Gleason is not laughing. The Scotch has gone down the wrong pipe. He's choking. Someone slaps him on the back. Gleason heaves convulsively. His eyes water, mucus pours from his nose, and for a minute—despite his ruffled shirt and movie star accoutrements—Jackie Gleason is pathetic, a sick old man with a busted heart. Everyone looks concerned. There's an uneasy silence. Then from the depths of his convulsion, as if recalling the comedic traditions by which he, Jackie Gleason, has lived, he sputters: "I think I'm coming down with an eye infection."

American Film, 1982

Making it Nightly:
Tom Brokaw

Talking to a talking head is hardly talking at all.

It is 6:40 a.m. and co-host of the *Today* show, Jane Pauley, is applying makeup. Not in the set's makeup room, where she might, but to the rear of the set—behind the sunrise, amid thick black cables, ratballs, and Styrofoam cups that litter the floor. She is staring into a shaving mirror and applying mascara. There is a space of approximately two feet in which she can maneuver. Interviewing her here is curiously intimate, like catching her in the bathroom at home. We have been talking about her co-host Tom Brokaw—rather, talking around Tom Brokaw, as neither of us, at this hour, has the will to get into their celebrated spats, the fencing on air, etc. So we speak of Brokaw's dedication. We speak of his tremendous energy and how marvelous his new job will be as co-host of the *NBC Nightly News*, a post he will assume April 5. I don't ask what she thinks of Tom Brokaw, because I don't expect a candid answer. In scores of interviews, not one colleague has fired an unkind word in his direction. On the contrary, each has praised him as one would a fierce young politician who has unexpectedly wrested control of the party.

"On what level are we speaking?" they've asked, before proceeding to enumerate Brokaw's merits and relate the history of his grooming for this anchor slot: the documentaries, specials, and global-village news stints NBC has provided to increase his visibility. "How wonderful a talent," they've said. There's no reason to disbelieve them—Brokaw is a formidable talent — but their caution speaks to the cutthroat nature of the business.

If ever there was a herd instinct afoot, it is in the clutch and claw of network news. The competition is otherworldly. "Television does not reward the maverick journalist," ABC News correspondent Brit Hume has observed. As a company man, Tom Brokaw is unexcelled. He's spent sixteen years at NBC and last summer, with the expiration of his *Today* contract, he became the most sought-after newsman in television. He was offered multimillion-dollar deals from each of the networks but chose NBC out of loyalty and for the opportunity to work with Roger Mudd. Brokaw is one of the most valuable products in the medium. As co-anchor of the *Nightly News*, he wields considerable power in the selection of news and over those who present it.

This morning, Jane Pauley—who has worked with and come up against Brokaw—is notably silent. Doctoring herself in the tiny mirror, she passes time before air time, smiling, happy as any young politico would be to have come this far.

"Where's Tom?" somebody screams. "Two minutes!"

Brokaw hurries past and ducks into the makeup room. Jane Pauley takes her chair on the set. The *Today* show theme sounds as Brokaw hustles down the hall.

"Tom," the director shouts. "W-h-e-r-r-r-e's Tom?"

TOM BROKAW IS RUNNING. He has run ten blocks from his Park Avenue duplex to the Ninetieth Street entrance of Central Park, where he will run three miles before jogging home. He is dressed in a Lite-beer jacket and Adidas shorts and is much bigger, more muscular, than he appears on television. This is the second run of his day. It is one week since the assassination of Anwar Sadat, and Brokaw has been on the air six of the past seven mornings. On the day Sadat was shot, Brokaw did his usual two hours of *Today*, had approximately an hour off-camera, then did six hours of commentary with John Chancellor before flying directly to Cairo. There, he labored as NBCs chief correspondent for five days prior to Sadat's funeral, which he covered. On Sunday he flew back to New York, and on Monday morning he was back on *Today*. Tuesday he is resting—if running eight miles and logging several hours at the office may be called a rest.

"It helps to stay in shape," Brokaw mutters.

Duncan the Wonder Horse was a Brokaw nickname at *Today*, and in the five years he'd been with the show, everyone was in awe of his diligence. "It was like having a third and fourth producer," executive producer Steve Friedman has said. "Tom works eighteen, twenty hours straight. He never lets you down."

This afternoon, Brokaw has a cold. Tom Brokaw with a cold (to paraphrase Gay Talese) is like Bjorn Borg with a wrist sprain: something akin to travesty. The elegant baritone skips and flutters, a 45 at 33 rpm, and resonates an octave deeper than normal. Still, Brokaw runs. Below the reservoir a photographer is shooting a *Time* cover for a story on fitness in America, and Brokaw greets him by name. The president of the New York Road Runners' Club hails Brokaw. He stops to say hello. Acquaintances cluster. It's as if Brokaw knows everyone in the city of New York. That has been one of the great benefits of *Today*. He has met or interviewed thousands of successful people, and his contacts are now as broad-based as any television journalist's. If there's one thing that fascinates Tom Brokaw, it's successful people. Their names dot his conversation, he enjoys them as sources, as distant friends (no one gets too close to Tom Brokaw). And that fascination is as it should be, for as co-anchor of the *NBC Nightly News*, he's now simultaneously one of the most successful and influential people in America.

Some guess it's the money that drives Tom Brokaw— an estimated $1.5 million to $2 million-plus per year at *Nightly News*—but to anyone who knows him, the cash is insignificant in comparison to his insatiable curiosity. Tom Brokaw is a looker, a hearer, both professionally and privately. For an upcoming vacation, he plans to spend part of it cross-country skiing in Yellowstone Park, then fly with his family to the Middle East in hopes of interviewing Yasir Arafat. There's reward in such a vacation, and not a little control in $2 million a year. But then it will be back to work on several more documentaries for NBC. It's all part of a long campaign for prime visibility, but also for personal satisfaction. There's not much rest in Tom Brokaw's life. It's as if, at forty-one, with a fabulous career already behind him and the youngest anchorship of a network-news program ahead, time is running out.

WE CARE ABOUT OUR pitchmen, at some level comprehending that it is the broadcaster's personality that colors how we receive his message. And that it is his background that in large part contributes to the message we get. The network anchor is a classic, American problem-solving type. He works long hours researching each evening's newscast and it is his personality—one experts believe must "leap out of the screen at you," while communicating trust, comfort, respect and authority— that determines whether he will put the news across.

Potentially there's a credibility gap, and Tom Brokaw wasn't always the princely shaman one now sees five nights a week—a man Tom Snyder calls "Perfect," and others, "Charmed," and "An Eagle Scout who's won every merit badge." In the summer of 1960, he was just another rudderless sophomore, blown out of two universities from an overdose of "wine, women, and song," he says, slumped at home in his parents' house in Yankton, South Dakota, with no job, no prospects of one, and excessive time to watch television. Yankton, once the territorial capital of the Dakotas and home to the Yankton Sioux, is a western town seeped in a midwestern stolidity that can sheer off one's boot heels with boredom. Television constitutes an escape. Brokaw came out of high school as "sort of a hot-shot wizard," an exceptional student who ran his school newspaper, worked part-time at a radio station, and had good luck with girls and athletics. But that summer all that roused his interest was television. Specifically, "the whole long night of the 1960 convention."

In Tom Brokaw's seventh-floor office, overlooking the skating rink at Rockefeller Center, the conflicts between South Dakota anonymity and New York celebrity are manifest. Before his desk is a poster-size photo of a frontier gravestone marked CHRISTIAN SUNRISE, taken in the Missouri River bottom near Yankton. Behind is an equally large photo of the Flatiron Building in New York. Beneath his carefully tailored jacket is a cowboy belt with the buckle, MONTANA WILDERNESS ASSOCIATION, and around the office are smaller photos of himself and his wife, Meredith—backpacking, himself mountain climbing in the Tetons with Yvon Chouinard; western saloons and the rustic Americana; as well as a plaque that reads, THE NEW YORK YANKEES WELCOME TOM BROKAW, and a cap that says, TAKE THIS JOB AND SHOVE IT. Brokaw plucks a pen from an Orvis day pack, swivels, and for a moment seems lost in the skaters below.

Television broadcasters, almost exclusively, are emigrants from elsewhere in America. "There aren't a lot of Ivy League guys in this business," Paul Greenburg has said. Greenburg, for years executive producer of *CBS Evening News*, and now executive producer of *NBC Nightly News*, should know. Chet Huntley, Frank McGee, Eric Sevareid, Walter Cronkite, Dan Rather, and Harry Reasoner are from the West or Midwest, and Johnny Carson grew up fifty miles from Brokaw's Yankton.

These are men who wanted out. The fastest out for such heartlanders had been show business—or by midcentury, the communications media.

"Television was a window on the world," Brokaw says. "The *Today* show was the most important program in Yankton. I'd see that every morning when I was a boy. My mother would have it on. It was watched more than the *Nightly News,* and even now serves rural America as a kind of morning newspaper."

In person, the solidity of Brokaw's presence is commanding. His seriousness often has been deflected by the fripperies of *Today,* and by his movie-star looks. But he is thoroughly engaging. "One of the things I'd like people to remember, when I'm gone, is that Brokaw was a pretty good guy," he's said. It's difficult to find someone who doesn't like him.

"What's not to like?" a colleague has said.

Brokaw comes from hardworking stock. His grandparents were wiped out in the prairie dust bowl, picked up and started again. His father was "a resourceful construction worker" who followed jobs around Missouri, North and South Dakota, while Brokaw was growing up, and did exhibition roller skating on weekends to help pay the bills. His Irish-American mother had a strong political consciousness, instilled by her father, a fierce Roosevelt-Truman Democrat. Both of Brokaw's parents are alive, and he confesses he "talks to them" through his broadcasts—for they represent the mainstream America he wishes to reach.

Brokaw did so poorly in college, that spring of 1960, he thought it imprudent to return. "It was wheel spinning," he says, tapping a pen. He'd always been curious, had wanderlust, and "for as long as I can remember" wanted out of Yankton. "When I was ten I won a trip to Minneapolis and was exhilarated by the experience." He'd been a news fan, had watched Garroway and Murrow, cut classes for space shots, and though his major was political science, had become more attracted to journalism. "If television hadn't existed, I'd probably have been a newspaperman." But television was there. That summer of 1960, the Democratic convention with Huntley-Brinkley was "etched vividly" in his mind.

"Broadcasting had been a trick I could do," Brokaw says, "to make money." He'd worked for a couple of radio stations in Minnesota and South Dakota before landing his first television job in Sioux City, Iowa. "The cosmetics were right for TV," Brokaw says. "But I took one glance at the newsmen stuck there without formal education, and went back to school."

Politics already fascinated him. He spent the next two years taking a political science degree from the University of South Dakota. "I figured I'd wind up in law school. But on impulse I drove to Omaha and literally begged for a job at KMTV." He was hired, and "a very important time" in his life commenced.

"The newsroom was run by a man with old-fashioned journalism values, who pored over our copy and hammered our heads, and we covered the town like a newspaper would. Only we did it on television. I learned a great deal in two-and-a-half years. And it was happenstance that I ended up there."

Happenstance or no, these reportorial values served him well in Atlanta, where he moved in 1965 to become news editor and eleven o'clock anchor at WSB-TV.

"The South was in flames. It was the time of Selma. NBC couldn't get people to go there fast enough, so I'd be called by the New York desk in the middle of the night, saying, 'Can you go?' I'd give somebody twenty dollars to cover my show and be off to some small town in Georgia, and have rocks thrown at me or be led around by my necktie. WSB liked it because it got one of their guys on network television."

Like trench-coated correspondents of old—Murrow, Collingwood, Sevareid, Smith—Brokaw found war, or its domestic equivalent, a broadcaster's fastest ticket to recognition. There was a big story in Americus, Georgia:

"It was so dangerous a lot of people kept coming back. Our man said, 'Get me the hell out, they're shooting people. I don't want any part of it.' I said, 'Well, I'll go.' I went down and worked round the clock with a single cameraman. We whipped the ass of CBS's network correspondent. I'd never had a better time. At the end of that, the NBC guy in Los Angeles called and said, 'Who is he?' They flew me out to L.A. and said, 'Wouldn't you like to come work for the big company?' I said, 'No.'"

Six months later, he succumbed. NBC raised the stakes, offered a Sunday night program and "more money than I'd ever heard of," and in 1966, at twenty-five, Brokaw moved to KNBC-TV, Los Angeles—at a time when California was to become the hottest story in the nation.

He covered Watts, Berkeley, the antiwar movement throughout the state; he covered Reagan and reported incessantly—though his anchor responsibilities at KNBC did not demand it. "He took on the Los Angeles Police Department," ex-*Newsweek* bureau chief, Carl Fleming remembers, a sacred cow few journalists dared to offend.

"I lived in the vortex. California was an important story. I was the first television reporter I know of to have gone to Haight-Ashbury. I stumbled on it in my coat and tie, my trench-coat, and I was about the same age as many of the kids who were there. I couldn't believe it. I did a number of stories, and felt I was caught between two tides. I was fascinated by the Haight. There was a kind of daring to these kids that I didn't have in my soul. Even today, the closest I get to bohemianism is when I go backpacking in the summertime. I was so ambitious and so intent that I couldn't quite identify with the freedom of their behavior, and their absolute lack of discipline about where they wanted to go within the establishment. I was trying to fight my way up through it, and they were oblivious to it."

By the 1968 convention in Chicago, Brokaw would pass between the demonstrators and the National Guard, and feel "Like I was walking through the parted seas of

America."

The sixties story was Vietnam, and Brokaw longed to go. His wife, Meredith, with two small children, did not try to stop him. But KNBC did. Brokaw had become too hot a property to risk under fire. And his contacts within the antiwar movement at home were invaluable.

"Would I have served in Vietnam if drafted? I doubt it. But who knows. I had a brother who was a Marine sergeant. And my dearest friend was killed there. I'm kind of a traditionalist. But how do you know until that moment comes?"

Brokaw stayed in Los Angeles. But while doing delegation reporting at the 1972 conventions, he was spotted by John Chancellor and David Brinkley as an obvious comer. "John took me aside and said, 'It's time for you to grow up and leave that cushy job in California.' I said, 'Make me the right offer and I will.'" The right offer turned out to be the NBC White House correspondency, plus anchor desk of the Saturday *News*. And at thirty-three, Tom Brokaw debuted on the *Nightly News* in one of the most important assignments on television.

Brokaw's timing was perfect. It was the summer of Watergate, and the Nixon White House was the world's biggest story.

"It was a time when you were either a good reporter or you weren't," he says.

Brokaw had known both Bob Haldeman and Ron Ziegler in California. Ziegler had had the advertising account for KNBC and been an eager gofer for the Republican party. Haldeman had been UCLA alumni president and a member of the Board of Regents. "I used to get a fair amount of information from those guys," he recalls. "And when Nixon was elected, Haldeman sent an emissary to see me about working in the White House, which really startled me. I was not interested at all. But one of the reasons I became White House correspondent was that I already had a working relationship with those people as sources."

The move to Washington was not entirely smooth, however. Brokaw took a pay cut to leave Los Angeles, and he encountered substantial resentment from the Washington press establishment upon his arrival. "I was this kid from LA. doing the local news, who was coming to start out as White House correspondent." But Brokaw quickly established his credentials. At a news conference, the first question he asked Nixon was, "If you have no guilt and there remains this question of your guilt, wouldn't it be better for you to volunteer for the impeachment proceedings in the House so that this matter can be settled in a trial before the Senate?" Nixon said no, his eyes widening.

Dan Rather was then White House correspondent for CBS, and the competition that currently rages between Rather and Brokaw had its genesis there. "Dan was the point man in a lot of people's eyes." Brokaw remembers. "If anything, I leaned over backward in my reporting because of personal feelings toward Nixon—which were negative. I never tried to take cheap shots, which would have been very easy to do. The sympathy of the press corps would have been with you, and there was a constituency for that kind of thing that existed in the television audience, so that you could have become a kind of bargain hero to a lot of people. I always thought Nixon was going to win the case or lose it based on his own behavior."

Brokaw's prestige was so enhanced by his job as White House correspondent that in 1974, when Frank McGee died, he was approached by NBC and asked to take over as co-host of *Today*. He declined when it became clear that he would have to do commercials—a task he considered not in his best interest as a journalist. "Besides, I was interested in seeing out my assignment at the White House," he says. "But by 1976, I'd run that course, and NBC news was saying, 'We'd like you to do this because we want people to see you in broader terms—at some point in your life we think you'll be doing an anchor job.'"

NBC capitulated on Brokaw's refusal to do commercials (he has never done them) and raised his salary to a figure close to $500,000 a year.

In August of 1976, Tom Brokaw took over as host of *Today*. Not everyone thought it a great idea. *New Yorker* critic Michael Arlen said last year: "I thought the *Today* show was an unfortunate format for Brokaw, and my guess is that he thought so too. It was a career choice—a Faustian bargain with his employers—and he paid for it as a newsman."

At first, the theatricality of *Today*'s format nearly floored Brokaw. "I came right off the White House beat covering the resignation of the president of the United States, going with Gerald Ford to Vladivostok and China, and the next thing I knew I was talking to Dr. Art Ulene about fingernails. Or hammering Miss America on her values as a young woman in this age of feminism. I was a dreadful *Today* correspondent for a time."

But the *Today* show, like the White House assignment, was of inestimable importance to a would-be anchorman. Walter Cronkite, John Chancellor, Barbara Walters, and Harry Reasoner had all done morning shows: there was something about that "quick fix" in the morning that garnered intimacy with a television audience. There were very few shows that provided two hours of live daily exposure to ten million people. The contacts were unbeatable. And there was more latitude, a chance to accomplish more with the news. Brokaw pulled himself together.

"When I first took over *Today*, my mother called and said, 'I remember David Garroway taking his son on a tour of Washington, and it was the most wonderful thing, because we saw the Lincoln Memorial and we saw the White House.' She was sort of suggesting that would be a good thing for me to go back and do. I said, 'Television's changed. Since then, you've seen those buildings.'" When Dave Garroway did go to Washington, a lot of people in Yankton had never seen its special architecture live on camera, or filmed in quite that way. And that intimacy has been a strength of *Today.*"

It still is, says Brokaw. On his last morning on *Today,* he stared into the camera and said, "More than any other news program of which I'm aware, there's a personal bond between *here* and *out there,* and I have learned from all of you as well."

TODAY AND THE *Nightly News* have taken Brokaw full circle. Television was that ticket out of the heartland that, if one was successful, might lead one home again. Tom Brokaw may never resettle in South Dakota (he is co-owner of a twenty-four-hour country-music station in Rapid City), but his message will. And part of that message is a gospel of brighter futures, a willingness to take chances, sense of confidence in initiative and hard work that has been Brokaw's signature on *Today.*

"When and if the *Nightly News* goes to an hour, it will look more like the *Today* show, taking the best news aspects of *Today:* its interviews, live pickups, in-depth stories. Roger and I both will have a major role in deciding what goes on the air. There'll be regular features on the electronics revolution in this country, economics and science—and I don't mean Art Ulene on fingernails."

The telephone rings. "No," Tom mutters, "nope, hunh-uh, I don't think so." He says goodbye.

"That was Meredith, with about four invitations to tick off, saying 'we don't want to go to this, do we, or how about this?' We get invited places, obviously. But I find most great social occasions counterproductive. You don't learn very much. It's small talk, trivia, there's an awful lot of preening. The narcissism level is higher than I am comfortable with. So I just don't go out a lot. It only drains your energy, it doesn't add anything to your appreciation of what's going on, and certainly very little to your intellectual understanding. Occasionally there will be affairs which will be worth going to simply because you expect to have some fun—or more often in my case, because there's someone there I want to meet, there's someone I want to talk to that I can learn something from."

From a man whose access to every stratum of American society will increase, at *Nightly News,* from what it's been at *Today* to something hardly imagined, such dedication to self-improvement is sobering. It seems ascetic and bordering on compulsive.

When Brokaw speaks of his family, it is to weigh his affection for them against that he holds for his profession and for "the great outdoors." A small-town protectiveness cloaks his feelings about those he loves. "I really do care about my family," he says. He and Meredith have three daughters, ages sixteen, fourteen, and twelve. "I've been married a long time," he says, laughing.

Meredith Brokaw is a marathon runner and former Miss South Dakota. She is a slim brown-haired woman who owns a brace of toy stores, called Penny Whistle, which she started from scratch. The stores are successful. She has spoken of weekends in Connecticut the family spends together, vacations and crazy dinners concocted each evening by all five. Friends tend to view Brokaw and her as a golden couple. The two attended high school together in Yankton, but did not start dating until senior year at the University of South Dakota.

Meredith has winced at the recollection of that Miss America pageant of which she was part. "It's not what I would recommend for my daughters," she told me. And she has praised Brokaw's consideration during the long campaign of *Today.* "There were clocks all over our bedroom," she said. "Tom laid out his clothes the night before, dressed in the dark so as not to wake me, and went downstairs to exercise and have breakfast." Meredith's day begins at six with a three-to-four-mile run in Central Park, followed by breakfast with her daughters. Then off to the Upper East Side's Penny Whistle. She and Brokaw run together whenever they can—in fact were in training for the New York Marathon until he dropped out with an injury. They go out perhaps two evenings a week. Both love good food, patronizing inexpensive restaurants, as well as Lutèce. Brokaw admits to having few intimate friends, but he and Meredith are close to a number of people out West, visiting them for skiing and mountaineering. The New York social whirl accessible to a couple in their position is largely allowed to pass.

On Brokaw's desk, near his typewriter, dictionary, tapes of Willie Nelson and Joe Pass, tennis gear and political tomes, is a color snapshot of Peter Lisagor, then Washington bureau chief for the *Chicago Daily News*.

"I took that in the Crimea," Brokaw says. "Peter was a journalistic muse to me, a stabilizing force when I first came to Washington. He's dead now. but when we met, he was the dean of the Washington press corps and a conscience to many of us—including John Chancellor. He was a first-rate reporter. He could cut through the Washington bullshit better than anybody I ever saw. And he could cut through us, especially those of us on television. He'd see us across a room, all puffed up at some gathering where people surrounded us, wanting to know what we thought, and mouth 'Fuck you' with this crooked little smile. It always brought me back down to earth. I thought this picture would be a good thing for the desk. Since he couldn't say it anymore."

The bullshit ceases at *Nightly News* each morning when Brokaw picks up the phone and begins to draw on that reservoir of sources he's collected in twenty years of broadcasting. It's then that he begins to earn his salary, becoming more than a product or a pretty face. During the morning and early afternoon he will concentrate on two, maybe three stories, using every connection and wile to nail them down. About four, he, Roger Mudd (whose contacts are as good as anybody's in Washington), and executive producer Paul Greenberg will confer to decide what will make the air. Brokaw throws considerable weight in that decision. Paul Greenberg will have final say, but he has admitted, in recollection of his years with

Cronkite, that tangling with the star "is like wrestling a six-hundred-pound grizzly." It is here that the politics of network news is most suspect—and the public vulnerable. As news time approaches, and feeds come over lines from around the world, Greenberg, and to some extent Brokaw, will decide what America gets as news. It is an awesome responsibility. And one delegated to men and women the public has selected by no other ballot but their viewing habits. It is dangerous in the anchor seat, and Brokaw will become one of the most visible men in America.

As with politicians, Brokaw's drive toward celebrity stands at odds with a predilection for the safe passage of grass roots. Tom Brokaw is many things—the intimate of movie stars and statesmen, a two-million-dollar-a-year man who rides the subway, can dine comfortably with Henry Kissinger, yet entertain a friend from Montana who's hitchhiked in to run the New York marathon. He'd like to keep it that way.

Celebrity's easier in New York—a city "eternally entertaining" to the emigrant heartlander. And comfortably anonymous. "I ducked out last night just to go for a walk, and when you look down Park Avenue on an early fall night, and the air is crisp and the lights are on in the Helmsley Building, and you can just see the out-of-focus taillights...it's a really spectacular sight. I walked down Madison Avenue past all the shops. They were shooting a film in the Park, and I thought to myself, as I often do, that I never expected at this stage in my life to be living in New York—and to be as comfortable as I am."

It's late afternoon now, and soon Tom Brokaw may shuck his coat and tie, pull on an old pair of jeans, cowboy boots, and western shirt, and stroll with the ease of a visiting rancher. It's been rancher's hours he's kept these past years—hours that in part have isolated him from the populace. *Nightly News* has sprung Brokaw into the light of day. His desire for anonymity resonates with a desire for safety. There's something about Tom Brokaw that's too perfect, tinged with the charisma of 1960s politicos, too golden—vulnerable. We shake hands and there is a melancholy to his cheerfulness, a kind of resignation.

"You really want to know one of the things that worries me about my new job?" he says. "It will be even more impossible for me to be alone. In this whole big country there won't be any corner that the television signal doesn't reach. And that just reinforces the familiarity of Tom Brokaw. I'm not sure that's very good for me."

Rolling Stone, 1982

The Bassmaster

Guy De Blasio has a 200-year-old map of Manhattan he's bought from the Museum of Natural History or some such place, and it's spread out across the kitchen table of his apartment in an old Italian neighborhood of Greenwich Village. The map shows trout streams at Wall Street, spring creeks at Minetta Lane, and about thirty species of marine life in the Hudson and East Rivers. The river species include sturgeon, shrimp, shad, catfish, herring, tommycod, porgies, spot, blue-claw crab, the feisty bluefish, and striped bass. Since 1976, De Blasio has seen all but two of these species in Manhattan waters: the lobsters and sheepshead. With the exception of sturgeon, which he hooked, he's landed them all.

"I flash this map whenever somebody moans about the rivers being dead," De Blasio croaks. "Then I get out my log."

De Blasio's log—which contains the size, time, and lunar peculiarities of fish caught—is mouthed into a cheap Japanese tape recorder at pier side or in the backseats of taxicabs as he hurries around Manhattan seeking to mine

242

the vicissitudes of tide. His pursuit of prime incoming or outgoing water is no less hysterical than that of a subtropical flats guide, and probably more arcane. Behind skyscrapers in midtown Manhattan and from rat-infested piers, De Blasio has landed fourteen-pound bluefish, twenty-pound striped bass, and six- to eight-pound shad, in. numbers difficult to believe.

"My brother and I caught a thousand striped bass in 130 fishing days this year," De Blasio reports. "That's keeper-size, over sixteen inches."

What unlikely anglers the De Blasios are: Guy and his brother Bill, seated in this Thompson Street apartment a half-block from the Village's most startling parade of punk roisterers, junk thespians, transvestites, chic druggies, and professional hit-men. A postal worker and a part- time elevator operator, the De Blasios are legendary among street fishermen. They speak like characters from a Martin Scorsese film. Hooded in watch caps and bright windbreakers emblazoned with Penn reel and J. W. Lure badges, they are armored against more than the night. The angling they do is perilous: Guy has been thrown from a pier into the East River by street punks, and there is always the threat of gangs. Billy totes an axe handle when he fishes alone. Over his heart is a badge that proclaims, I'M A FENWICK MAN.

THE DE BLASIOS ARE masters of a type of fishing that has persisted quietly in Manhattan for centuries, but now, because of complex socio-ecological factors, flourishes. The rivers are cleaner, thanks to the Environmental Protection Agency's 1972 Clean Water Act. And people are hungrier, due to the economy. But there is no neat explanation of why tough street kids are abandoning tape decks and basketballs for fishing gear appropriate to Manhattan waters.

"The fishing's simply fabulous," *New York Post* fishing writer Ken Moran has offered. Street angling in New York is a phenomenon relegated largely to piers and bridge abutments—any place the urban angler might escape summer heat and unfold in something resembling a breeze. One such pier extends a hundred yards into the East River below Brooklyn Bridge, underscoring the bridge's Gothic arches with a carnival of activity, Latin to the extreme. To reach this pier one must cross a parking lot, sidle around a chain link fence, and wade through various junked armchairs, automobile parts, and elevator grates. Once braved, the pier is as close to the Caribbean as many Manhattanites get. It's a cherished access to the river, frequented by sunbathers, picnickers, lovers, and, not surprisingly, fishermen.

As traffic booms overhead, anglers work big surf rods, hooking fifteen-pound stripers in a body of water widely thought of as dead, but in fact clogged with migratory fish. "Play 'em light," an oldtimer coaches, as street kids jig with bloodworms filched from voodoo shops in Spanish Harlem or spoons rigged from strings of aluminum pop-tops. Aloof street punks hoot like Rotarians, joshing each other roughly, but afraid to grab bass wriggling and slapping about their feet.

"His tail, man," one simpers.

"Your ass, Ricco."

Taped music beats Latin rhythms against the traffic, a stiff breeze sings, and to the freshly initiated it is dreamier than an evening in old San Juan.

ALL GREAT AMERICAN cities were founded on water, and the history of urbanization has been, in large part, the Minkoiling of citizens against this elemental balm. Yet the piers and rivers of Manhattan offer street fishermen access to a kind of wilderness. And their sport, long considered aristocratic, here takes on an anarchic tinge. For the underclass folk who fish here, it is the classic invasion of wilderness to harvest game. And despite warnings and restrictions on consumption—one fish a week, none for pregnant women or children—there is evidence that poor families have been subsisting off river species for years.

Now middle-class anglers have joined, them, lured by reports of cleaner rivers and better fishing, and attracted by the staggering runs of striped bass publicized during the spring and fall. There are heartening tales of fly fishermen in *chest* waders stumbling over rocks off the East Eighties, taking bass two blocks from their apartment buildings; stories of gypsy bait mongers, old black men who cruise the piers in station wagons full to the scuppers with bloodworms, skimmer clams, sandworms, and lugs.

Still, this is frontier sport; scoffed at by the general public, and anglers share a camaraderie. How hip to take game species from urban waters thought to hold little more than "Hudson River whitefish" and suicidal dogs.

A trading post for street anglers is Spiegel's sporting goods, off Nassau Street in the downtown financial district. There, kids from Chinatown, Little Italy, and housing projects fronting the East River mix easily with Wall Street traders and others hooked on the local sport. Spiegel's is a hole-in-the-wall shop, but it is hung with every sort of tackle. John Lobber, Spiegel's fishing manager, will talk bait, tides, and lures to anyone. He will outfit the novice with a seven-foot Ugly Stik to get him casting, and 15-pound monofilament, jelly worms, and Trout Magic Tails to get him jigging. A copy of *Long Island Fisherman* will provide the tidal charts, and Lorber will rig a sturdy treble-hook on twenty feet of sixty-pound line so that the novice can haul his catch in.

"I don't fish the piers with less than three friends," Lorber advises. "It's too dangerous. Some fishermen pack a gun."

Lorber will differentiate for you the colors of a healthy striper (bright green along the back) from a poisoned one (tinged reddish). He will explain their feeding habits and tendency to forage near heated water around sewage drains. He will pinpoint hot spots, date the various runs, and philosophize about fishing. He might even sell you a rod fashioned by his own hands. And when street anglers are mentioned, he'll speak of Guy De Blasio.

THE FIRST THING ONE notices about De Blasio's apartment is a pair of huge Igloo coolers in the hall, then how amazingly tiny the place is. This is the apartment of a man on the run, no hearthside angler fingering Tonkin cane on a winter's eve. De Blasio fishes four nights a week from March through November and is not averse to wetting a line in a snowstorm. The apartment is thinly decorated but for his trophies, which include a sixty-five-pound striped bass taken outside New York Bay, and related souvenirs: photographs of tumultuous catches, Fenwick Master Fisherman awards, an occasional article composed for the *Long Island Fisherman*. The bass's great belly sags overhead, the fish the size of a teenager.

De Blasio's toddlers fidget in an interior nook as we talk fishing, Bill De Blasio having just detailed a two days' catch of 746 weakfish at Verrazano Narrows.

"We don't just catch fish," Guy says. "We take scale and gonad samples for the Conservation Department and work hard at our own expense for the future of these rivers. There's this story I may write called 'Fishing, What's That?' about a kid who finds a fishing rod and doesn't know what it is. I want my son to know about fishing, even growing up in New York."

De Blasio is thirty-four years old, and by all accounts has been obsessed with fishing most of his life. Raised in Greenwich Village, he was taught to fish by his grandfather, off the Fourteenth Street pier. From the first, he had an uncanny instinct for finding fish—to such a degree that Village psychics fingered him early for success. De Blasio's grandfather, a Neapolitan immigrant, was a dory fisherman out of Sheepshead Bay, and De Blasio became a deckhand at eleven, mating charter boats, hauling tar lines in dories, and working party boats.

"In the fifties when everybody else played stoop ball, I was fishing. In the sixties when everybody took drugs, I was still fishing."

Not until the 1970s did De Blasio abandon

professional fishing and take a job more traditionally geared to supporting a family. This land-based servitude, if anything, pushed him more forcefully toward angling. He was driven to prove that the Hudson River estuary is still one of the world's great fisheries, despite pollution. This he managed to do with astounding catches: fourteen striped bass over twenty pounds in midtown Manhattan, eight-to-ten-pound shad by the gross, a fourteen-and-a-half pound bluefish farther uptown, and evidence that tropical species such as triggerfish, jack crevalle, and albacore were frequenting the rivers. He caught fish for newsmen off midtown piers and proselytized at every opportunity for the health of the Hudson River.

"We have three conservation officers in the city of New York," De Blasio says. "Somebody had to help."

De Blasio will talk all night about conservation, but only with prodding will he divulge favorite fishing spots. Striped bass, the aristocrat of coastal gamefish, is why.

"Bass bring money, and money brings greed," De Blasio says. "The species is overfished. Approximately eight million stripers migrate around New York, and thanks to a ban on commercial fishing from the Battery north to Fort Edward, the Hudson is a last great haven. Still, people poach. Undersize bass with high PCB counts are being sold all the time to restaurants in Chinatown— mostly by street kids. Wouldn't take long for the big-money boys to move in."

De Blasio recommends these spots for sportfishing the island: beneath the Brooklyn Bridge, the rocks off East 86th Street, the seawall along FDR Drive, the lighthouse beneath George Washington Bridge, the 200th Street train trestle, 125th Street and the West Side Highway, the 69th and 34th Street piers in the Hudson, and various piers behind the World Trade Center.

"Watch that 34th Street pier, though, it's all busted up and crawling with rats."

If Manhattan's proposed Westway project—a freeway along the Hudson—is built, it will destroy the old piers and most of the fishing.

It's not just access for street fishermen, De Blasio says, "but a disturbance of ecological balance. Baitfish live around those rotten pilings, and gamefish are drawn there to feed. Dredging would disrupt things further."

BILLY HAS TO WORK the night shift, but Guy has agreed to hit a few piers—though it is late December and nineteen degrees. He rigs a couple of six-foot rods with twelve-pound Andy line, no leader, salty dog jigs with a lead head, and Penn 930 reels. "There may be one terribly confused fish out there," De Blasio says. "The big striper runs are spring and fall, but we caught bass in December last year. Of course it wasn't cold."

Even in Greenwich Village it is tough to hail a cab at midnight in December carrying fishing rods. Cabbies swerve around us, and pedestrians laugh. "All my life," De Blasio moans. "A cross to bear." Finally a driver stops, and we are winding through Little Italy, the financial district, to South Street and Brooklyn Bridge. The driver leaves us in a dark, empty parking lot fronting the East River and burns rubber getting out of there.

The joke is on him. Beneath the bridge the East River is lighted by a combination of full moon and cityscape, just this side of ethereal. A hundred yards into the river, the skyline is a child's diorama of illuminated bridges, skyscrapers, and neon crèches flashing from project windows. The World Trade Center stands to the west, Delphic as Easter Island. A moon tide muscles through at six to eight knots. Ducks sit on water broken by rotted bridge pilings and discarded hardware. Bait swirls in the eddies. The *Watchtower* thermometer across the channel reads 17 degrees.

We walk the length of the pier, jigging pilings where grass shrimp live, and suddenly we are fishing. This is a condition that has little to do with taking fish; it's a mixture of concentration, lassitude, and communion. I am *in* the East River, its waters are on my hands; I share an intimacy with Manhattan previously unexperienced. My lure is bumped, then bumped again probably the tide. De Blasio courses along the pier, silent, consulting some private oracle. He reels in, takes the lure in his mouth. "River's warm," he says, tenderly. "Could be fish." I cast toward a skyline orchestrated with sparkling architecture and understand why dreamers fish the mountains. The least bit disoriented, I'd think I was working the northern Rockies.

We hike past Peck Slip and the Paris Bar, open all night to serve Fulton Fish Market, and the South Street houses are something out of Melville. What piers remain in this nineteenth-century neighborhood are commandeered by tennis bubbles. Most are fenced.

"Money's got access to this river and they don't care anything for it," De Blasio says, furious. "People who love to fish can't hardly toss a cast."

We work another pier, the one De Blasio was thrown from, but nothing's hitting. We plug a few into the steam of a sewage outlet, and still no luck. "Too cold," he concedes. Our faces are purple in the artificial light, the wind a good sixteen knots.

"I used to watch *American Sportsman*," De Blasio says, puffing, "and there was always some guy fishing Hawaii or the Bahamas. I can't afford that, I'd think. This depresses me. I'm a lower-class guy who fishes what's available—fortunately, a lot. Cable TV may let me put together a fishing show. What I plan is to gear it to the poor fisherman. Tell him how, when, and where to catch fish. That's a dream. Another is to run a little boat station someday, where I rent skiffs, give information, have a big pot of coffee on the stove, and live in an atmosphere that's positive. People don't know what they've got around New York. They're laughing at us, and they're the ones who are fools."

We trudge through the deserted financial district, hunting a cab. One brakes, then another, each accelerating uptown at the sight of our fishing rods. It's like hitchhiking;

one must meditate on a ride. A cab spots us, takes the bait, slows and turns.

"Must be a fisherman," De Blasio grunts.

"How was that ice fishing?" the cabby says. "You guys crazy? Ain't nothing in that water but blind eels."

"Now wait a minute," De Blasio says, and trots out the rap.

"That right?" says the cabby "Bass? In these rivers? You know, I do a little blackfishing out of Peconic Bay, raise some fluke, and always come home with seafood in the cooler."

"Blackfishing's sweet," De Blasio says. "You use those green crabs for bait, or worms?"

"Crabs. Nothing beats crabs. We go out with six or seven guys, rent a boat...."

It is one-thirty on a December morning in the empty canyons of lower Manhattan, and two sport fishermen are cranking it up. I recline against the cracked leather seat, inhaling gelatinous air. Familiar landmarks pass.

"Twenty pounds," De Blasio is saying, "right there behind Korvette's."

"Korvette's?'" the cabby whistles. "No!"

Outside, 1981

Dandy Tom:
Wolfe at the Bonfire

It's raining in New York, on one of those spring nights when a light shower contains all the blessings the city might bestow. The white umbrella Tom Wolfe unfurls against this patter does little to conceal his glee at a stroll down Park Avenue—past those co-ops where apartments sell for four million dollars apiece and for which one must pay cash, showing a portfolio of thirty million dollars to even apply. Wolfe himself has shopped for such an apartment, but, he says, laughing, "anyone can shop." The homburg and spatted shoes he protects with this circus tent of an umbrella suggest a man who fritters his life away at Le Cirque or in private dinner parties overlooking Central Park. But this is a writer, a worker happy to see the publication of his first novel after three years of backbreaking effort. *The Bonfire of the Vanities* is a big book, 560 odd pages, with a first printing of 150,000. And Wolfe is a major author. Still he steps through the streets of Manhattan with some reserve. "New York feels very much like home now," he says hesitantly, and with a touch of irony. "But it took a long time for me to feel that way...like it was *my city*."

THERE'S AN ART DECO back bar at Benjamin's, with a wide, oval mirror set into its mahogany, so that polite Richmonders may check out their neighbors inconspicuously while that softest of Southern drawls—the Richmond drawl—wafts around them. Tom Wolfe is at lunch here, a few blocks from the neighborhood where he grew up. This is a conservative crowd, yet Wolfe sits beneath the pie plate ceiling in white slacks, white shoes, and a baby blue jacket with exaggerated lapels—oddly gangsterish in that Broadway elegance of his. Benjamin's is the sort of 1930's barroom that survives, in the South, only in its least reconstructed cities. And Richmond is that, the capital of the Confederacy and Dixie at its heart.

Wolfe is reminiscing about his boyhood. His face, often flinty, here is soft-edged, relaxed. "When I was nine, I started writing a biography of Napoleon," he says. "I read Emil Ludwig's *Napoleon*, and my work was rather heavily drawn from his. That being the only source I knew. He was small! And I was small, I was nine years old. It bothered me that the world was run by large people. I felt very small, and Napoleon was this little guy who, at one point, ran the world."

He sips his iced tea. "Mozart was a child prodigy, so he was small. Also, his first name was Wolfgang, and that had a resonance to it. I did an illustrated children's book about that time, about a musical genius who gives concerts to *tremendous* applause...."

Wolfe is in Virginia to accept Longwood College's John Dos Passos Prize for Literature—which he will hang next to his American Book and Columbia Journalism awards. "Then," he says, "I had a long fascination with sports writing. But I think that was bound up with my aspirations to be an athlete. That's who got applause in school! You can write your head off, and there's a handful of faculty members and one or two students who are interested in what you're doing. But the whole business of stardom in sports is so...."

Wolfe grapples for the proper word. Can this lionizer of the Right Stuff, champion of the New Journalism, explicator of Kesey's Pranksters and the Pump House Gang, scourge of Radical Chic, eradicator of the Painted Word and Bauhaus, deflator of the Me Generation, and a man who's just written his first novel on deadline—as Dickens, Zola, and Dostoevsky did—with a new chapter appearing every two weeks in *Rolling Stone* for over a year...can he still be worrying over applause from sports?

"I honestly thought that any minute I was going to make it in baseball. I went to a tryout camp for the New York Giants, and they told me in not all that polite a way, that I didn't have a chance. The denial is rampant."

Despite Wolfe's fame, despite the arrestingly gangsterish elegance of his dress, nobody here at Benjamin's appears to notice him. A tablemate remarks that Wolfe is one of a few serious authors never to have written about his childhood, and asks why.

"I don't know," he answers thoughtfully. "I probably need a psychologist to tell me." He glances up, appraising the room. "It's true, though. I've never written about Richmond." His eyes narrow. "Maybe I want a safe harbor to come back to."

ONE OF TOM WOLFE'S great themes is status—how individuals claw their way up the status pyramid through competition, or create personal status-spheres outside the boundaries of polite society—and no southern city possesses a less-penetrable Brahman caste than Richmond. It is a Victorian city of wide avenues, with as many monuments to war dead as trees. Marshall Fishwick, the Virginia historian and a professor of Wolfe's at Washington and Lee, calls it "the most haughty and self-inflated city in our area, and one which has never gotten over losing the Civil War."

Its hierarchies epitomize the ducal orders Wolfe has

lambasted viciously in his work. Yet its conservatism, ironically, is the seedbed for his vitriol against subjects as diverse as liberal fundraisers for the Black Panthers, and the big-city intellectualism of contemporary painters and architects.

It is safe to surmise that he was profoundly affected by his family's move in 1927 from the rural Shenandoah Valley to Richmond. Wolfe was born there in 1931. Though his parents were gentry, they were rural gentry. They were enlightened, Jeffersonian democrats who felt themselves above the fripperies of Richmond society.

"My father was the editor of *The Southern Planter*, a farm magazine," Wolfe says, as we drive toward Longwood College. His voice is full of Richmond, but his hands are thick as a plowboy's. "He was an agronomist and the director of a farmer's cooperative, but I always thought of him as a writer. He kept the novels of Thomas Wolfe on his bookshelf, and for years I thought he'd written them."

Thomas Wolfe Sr., a Cornell PhD and a professor at Virginia Tech, died in 1972. He had moved to Richmond to run the *Planter*, which was geared to the squirearchy and to the elitist philosophy of the agrarian South. Wolfe's mother is now ninety and living near his sister, Helen Evans, in North Carolina. "My mother's interests are artistic," Wolfe says fondly. She is remembered by one Richmond neighbor as "delightful...and a liberal Presbyterian lady of the intellectual variety." In her youth, she studied social work in New York and was accepted at medical school but did not attend. The family lived in the Sherwood Park section of Richmond, far from the fashionable west end: "We had professors living there, working people...everybody," Wolfe's sister remembers. Wolfe attended public schools until the seventh grade. But that year his parents enrolled him in St. Christopher's, an Episcopal prep school where boys were taught "math and manners, Latin and lineage," as one friend describes it.

There were nineteen sons of the conservative Richmond

elite in Wolfe's graduating class. Wolfe was still spending weekends and summers on his father's farm in the Shenandoah Valley; he was also actively Presbyterian, and "from the north side," remembers John Page Williams, his headmaster. "Not the part that was moving out to the country club." Perhaps from loneliness, Wolfe bragged to a Sunday-school teacher of the eight brothers and sisters he did not have. He was a sensitive boy, who studied tap and ballet, and who became an overachiever. He was an honors student, chairman of the student council, a fair athlete, and co-editor of the school paper, for which he wrote and illustrated "The Bullpen," a column already crackling with his style: "Different spectators have suggested motorcars, bicycles and rickshaws for keeping up with Coach Petey Jacobs's live five," he wrote of the basketball team.

Notice me, was the subtext of these early accomplishments. *Applaud.*

AT FIFTY-SEVEN TOM WOLFE has received more applause than any other literary journalist of his time. An author who has influenced his era, he's perhaps the best-known nonfictionist in America. As a humorist "he's the funniest fucking guy *standing,* when he's on," says novelist Thomas McGuane. As a phrasemaker Wolfe is nonpareil: "radical chic," "the right stuff," "the me generation," and other idiosyncratic designations have entered the language. McGuane calls him "our Thackeray. His style has been imitated so much that he has the burden of having to live it down."

It's surprising to hear Wolfe speak of writer's block and of the time he's had producing *The Bonfire of the Vanities:* "I remember something Red Smith said when someone asked him how he managed to turn out a column five days a week. 'There's nothing to it,' he said. 'You sit there at your typewriter and you think, and if that doesn't work, you open a vein.'"

For about six months Wolfe had sat there, "and

absolutely nothing was happening." Believing that pressure would be helpful—as it had been when he began *The Right Stuff* in *Rolling Stone*, he'd decided to compose his first draft on deadline, "to put myself in a vise and force it out." Publisher Jann Wenner jumped at the prospect of a Tom Wolfe novel appearing in twenty-nine consecutive issues of *Rolling Stone,* and offered a contract for close to $200,000. "No question," Wolfe quips, "that spurs you on." The public reaction to the *Rolling Stone* serialization was mixed. There was a rave from the ultraconservative *American Spectator*, but one major New York editor, a Wolfe fan, described it as "just dreck." Few of Wolfe's colleagues responded to the book. "I don't think they're reading it," he commented at the time.

In *The New Journalism* (1973), Wolfe declared that "the most important literature being written in America today is in nonfiction," and predicted that journalists "would wipe out the novel as literature's main event." But "the road has been built," he says now of literary nonfiction. "We're seeing what's traveling down it. Which is not as exciting as building the road.... And I didn't want to be in the position where at the end of my career I looked back and said to myself, 'Wonder what would have happened if I'd written a novel?'"

WOLFE FIRST DISCOVERED FICTION writing at Washington and Lee, a private university in Lexington, Virginia, where Lee served as president after the Civil War. "The kind of boy that goes there is the boy whose family still believes in the Confederacy...planter money from Mississippi, big money from the Delta, from Memphis, and Texas," says Marshall Fishwick, one of Wolfe's teachers at W&L. The tobacco executive Smith Bagley is a fellow alumnus, as is Herb Hunt, the oil billionaire. Hunt's father bought him the local Texaco station after Herb suffered a slight there as a student. Wolfe found he could compete against W&L's wealth and its adoration of athletics by writing about sports for the school paper—and by publishing short stories. He pitched for the varsity team, pledged a Richmond-boys' fraternity, and flouted the dress code "out of contrariness," he remembers, with styles that were both hyper-English and Hollywood tough-guy.

Wolfe used W&L as a laboratory to polish his innate good manners, for as his friend Clay Felker, now editor of *Manhattan, Inc.*, says, "Formal manners are a marvelous way of fending people off—without offending them."

George Foster conducted a fiction seminar once a week in an off-campus taproom called the Dutch Inn. "We would read our work aloud," Wolfe recalls, "and that could be brutal." He was disquieted by the credo that "the only valid subject matter was something you knew very personally within your own life." Or, as his classmate novelist William Hoffman put it, you had "to undress to write fiction." Two of Wolfe's stories appeared in *Shenandoah*, then a campus literary magazine. In one, "Shattered," a freshman football player dreams of "a wonderful someday hero worship by the whole university," but his hopes and a weak knee are smashed in the first game. "It has actually happened," he thinks, "these dumb goddamn people are gawking at your helplessness." In the second story, "The Ace of Spades is Black," a night Greyhound-bus ride of excruciating loneliness is described: "The bus was like a city: among all the people you're still alone, and the closer you get to them the farther you're really away...and you're in your own (world) and you can't get out of it."

He did get close to William Hoffman, a war veteran from the mining country of West Virginia, and even more of an outsider than Wolfe. The two became close friends. Hoffman found the younger writer full of contradictions. He'd confide about St. Christopher's, for example, that "I didn't really belong to that group...I didn't move with that crowd," and would talk about status "in practically every other sentence." Yet he persisted in his dreams of playing professional baseball—hardly a gentleman's occupation.

Hoffman remembers Wolfe's early stories as being "filled with fireworks and astonishing, huge detail... Tom had, from the very first, a real sense of the absurd. I hated to go to the movies with him. He'd see something ridiculous like Elizabeth Taylor in *Ivanhoe* and call out in the theater, 'You can't beat Hollywood!'"

Wolfe was galvanized, his senior year, by Marshall Fishwick, W&L's popular-culture guru. "He gave a course," Wolfe says, "which in effect was all of American Studies compressed into one year—American architecture, American art, theories in psychology, history, across the board."

"I tried to baptize the proletarian," Fishwick explains. "Tom immediately took the bait." Fishwick organized field trips to hear country music, taught his students how to rebuild old farmhouses, and even how to lay mortar. To Wolfe the course was an epiphany. His respect for his father's rural heritage increased. And he found he could use the discipline of sociology creatively, turning his sharp literary eye away from himself. "He saw through the facade of the small, elite college," Fishwick says, recalling Wolfe's student papers, "and demonstrated that everyone was of the same pattern."

Though Fishwick had persuaded Wolfe to pursue American studies at Yale (instead of a career in baseball), Wolfe continued to write fiction. "I was the sort of person who from a certain moment *knows* that he's going to write novels. You just know you're going to do it. But when that's going to happen is another question."

TONIGHT, SOME TWENTY-FIVE years later—as Wolfe accepts the Dos Passos Prize at Longwood College, it's his fiction that he's showcasing, rather than the journalism that made him famous.

"This award means a lot to me because the last of the Wolfes living in Virginia, Frances Roberdeau Wolfe, went to Longwood...and because I've been thinking a *lot* about Dos Passos...I undertook as my project a work of contemporary fiction that would somehow encompass the life of the modem metropolis.

"Sometimes I thought of it as a *Vanity Fair* written 150 years later, or, if I was really feeling good about myself, something on the order of *Manhattan Transfer*.... The high life I felt I knew cold...because I lived in Manhattan...but, for the low life, I decided to go to the Bronx. The Bronx to me was sort of like the Arctic Circle: it was north of where I was, and you didn't go there."

The audience titters. "The lowest of the low life of New York is in the Bronx," Wolfe explains. Then he reads a chapter of *Bonfire* that turns upon the unmasking of his protagonist, Sherman McCoy, a Park Avenue liberal who will be exposed as an adulterer when prosecuted for disabling a black youth in a traffic accident in the Bronx. At one point in the novel, in a scene of profound humiliation, Sherman is herded through the Bronx courthouse and penned in a holding cell with the black and Hispanic lowlife that, as a liberal, he has romanticized. Once released, he assures his lawyer, "I'm not going back inside that...place...ever, and I don't care what it takes to keep me out. Even if I have to stick a shotgun barrel in my mouth."

Wolfe leaves his Longwood audience in a park opposite the courthouse, where, "just last week, some poor devil was stabbed to death at 10:00 a.m...for his portable radio, one of the big ones, known upstairs inside the Island as a Bronx attaché case."

There is shocked silence in Farmville, Virginia. Then thunderous applause.

WHEN WOLFE MOVED TO New York in 1962, he dropped a letter to a friend, the legendary practical joker Hugh Troy, that hinted at his ambivalence: "The first thing I knew I was on the 1:20 a.m. bus with fifteen colored brethren, all of us, no doubt, out to make it in New York...Whether I am moving on to bigger and better things, I don't know, but I knew I wouldn't be happy until I gave it a try. This is one big sonofabitch of a town, I have found out, but I guess they are used to boys from the foothills coming in here, and they are probably even tolerant."

Today, Wolfe is still edgy about New York, but for a different reason: it won't let him alone. He is at his Manhattan tailor, Vincent Nicolosi, for a fitting, and his customary politeness becomes strained when he runs into two New Journalists who have been Anglo-dandiacal to the extreme since he published his 1965 piece on "the secret vice" of custom tailoring. Wolfe himself is an extremist, worrying that "my dress is approaching the eccentricity of the wing-collar and spats variety." He owns dozens of suits, seven of which are white, and has his shirts, shoes, hats and even ties made—ordering them from DeCasi, in crepe de chine, a dozen at a clip.

Today his white shoes are scuffed and his cream trousers are dingy from Manhattan air. The flintiness is in his features. He's delighted, however, when his close friend Richard Merkin, the "post-Pop Expressionist" painter, turns up with a silver *The Right Stuff* promo bag. Merkin is dressed in orange slacks, pink tasseled slippers, a striped boating shirt, and a double-breasted jacket.

"Dandyism is a mask," Merkin observes, "but underneath, Tom's not flashy. He does it for effect. Remember Tom Buchanan's outrage at Gatsby's pink suit? I think that's Tom Wolfe in a nutshell: Gatsby in a pink suit. He's a very sensitive creature...and I've never met anyone so responsive to people's feelings. The last thing he would *ever* want to feel is that he's hurt you. Writing is a tremendous escape. What you do there is to assert yourself in a way you can't in real life. It's the invented part of life."

There's a male clubbiness at Nicolosi's this afternoon redolent of Savile Row—or, in Wolfe's case, the house of his father.

Not that Thomas Wolfe, Sr. was a clubby man. He was quiet, self-disciplined and a hard worker, as Wolfe's sister has affirmed. He cultivated a Victorian reserve that had its effect upon his son. "Tom will never tell you his troubles," Merkin says. "You can tell him your troubles all night long, but the last thing you can imagine is Tom being a burden to anyone for an instant." And that reserve is the root of his fierce independence.

"I see certain things of my father in me that I never was aware of," Wolfe says. "He always had his clothes made in Richmond. It was not considered a big deal. I started having mine made in Washington. Unlike him, I became very conscious of it. Then I started wearing large hats... That's something he did, also...And he wore white suits, in the Norfolk style, with a belt in the back and pleats over the shoulder."

Wolfe glances toward the street. "Never underestimate how much of your childhood is sewn into the lining of your garments when you go to New York."

WOLFE CAME TO NEW YORK to become a writer, following an unhappy six-year hiatus in graduate school at Yale— "Tedium of an exquisite sort."

He wanted PhD credentials like his father's to teach, so that he could make a living. But grad school was confining. "There was a monastic model...gothic structures and sitting in dark carrels with slit windows, looking out at the world."

"I shall revolt," wrote Wolfe, as Jocko Thor, at Yale: "I shall burst this placid pink shell / I shall wake up slightly hungover, / Favored, adored, worshiped and / clamored for. / I shall raise Hell and be a real Cut-up."

Wolfe blew off steam by visiting Bill Hoffman, who then was living in New York. Hoffman recalls that Wolfe would check into a welfare hotel on West 103rd Street, and "we'd go down to Greenwich Village to these crummy dives—Tom was very much interested in Bohemia then and he liked engaging these people in talks. But he didn't look like he *belonged* there."

He did not belong at Yale either. It was a rich Yankees' school, liberal and stuffy. "I was a Stevenson man," Wolfe remembers, "but everyone was so liberal and patronizing to Eisenhower that I acted more conservative than I was. I'd kid them by saying, 'You know, Eisenhower's really very bright. He reads seven foreign papers a day. He *has* to. And there's that one from Belgrade.'"

"The professors didn't know what to make of him," Hoffman says. "He was supposed to present scholarly papers, and he would write them in this fireworks style of his and just drive them crazy."

Finally Wolfe buckled down and wrote his American-studies dissertation, "The League of American Writers: Communist Organizational Activity Among American Writers, 1929–1942."

"My theory was that writers, who think of themselves as loners in pursuit of a great goal...actually are lonesome. It's a socializing influence to join these organizations." Increasingly he questioned the enterprise of writing fiction. The regurgitation of an author's deepest fears, hang-ups, and secrets onto the page still went against the grain, and he had begun to find it suspect as art. He wondered if "creativity in prose wasn't embedded in material" and if *reporting* wasn't the key to unlocking it.

After reportorial stints at the Springfield, Massachusetts, *Union* and the *Washington Post,* where he won awards for his writing, Wolfe made it to the *New York Herald Tribune* in 1962. It was the experimental paper in town. Its Sunday magazine, *New York,* was edited by Clay Felker, just over from *Esquire,* and his mandate was liveliness at any cost. Wolfe had been hired as a general-assignment reporter, but soon was writing weekly features.

He preferred the *Tribune* to the *Washington Post,* he told Hugh Troy, noting that "there aren't a lot of spastic bastards running around worried about freedom and immortality." He later would write, "I looked out across the city room of the *Herald Tribune,* 100 moldering yards south of Times Square, with a feeling of amazed bohemian bliss...Either this is the real world, Tom, or there is no real world." He rented an apartment in Greenwich Village and hit the streets.

"The idea," he wrote of his fellow feature writers, in *The New Journalism*, "was to keep body and soul together, pay the rent, get to know 'the world,' accumulate 'experience,' perhaps work some of the fat off your style—then, at some point, quit cold, say goodbye to journalism, move into a shack somewhere...and light up the sky with...The Novel."

Though Wolfe derided this plan publicly, he kept it as an agenda. "He always had an idea of doing a novel about New York, a la *Vanity Fair*," Felker remembers. In the early sixties, as Wolfe pointed out in *The New Journalism*, "the literary upper class were the novelists...the middle class were the 'men of letters'...the lower class were the journalists...As for people who wrote for popular ('slick') magazines and Sunday supplements...they weren't even in the game. They were lumpenproles."

Wolfe toiled as a lumpenprole, writing lively if conventional journalism, until a Hot Rod and Custom Car Show gave him a fundamental insight into the American class system and the 1960s. He talked *Esquire* into sending him to California, where he could further examine the phenomenon; it was his first national-magazine assignment. Back in New York, he had a terrible time lashing the piece together. His editor, Byron Dobell, remembers fearing they would be "stuck with having to write something based on the author's notes, because the author was having a nervous breakdown." In desperation, Wolfe typed up his ideas in the form of a memo to a friend and found a conversational tone that unblocked him and proved exactly right. He wrote all night, listening to manic rock on WABC, and turned in the memo the next morning. Dobell struck out the "Dear Byron," plus "a few 'Chrissake's and things that were too blatantly Holden Caulfield, and we rolled with it."

That was "The Kandy-Kolored Tangerine-Flake Streamline Baby," whose thesis was that the American class system could be beaten, that a reverse snobbery was afoot, in which the old elite was imitating the new. Wolfe characterized the California custom-car designers as artists outside any "ancient, aristocratic aesthetic," free of "the amoeba god of Anglo-European sophistication that gets you in the East." Because of postwar wealth, this new elite had been able to form its own status group.

Wolfe identified other maverick prole groups of the 1960s—rock 'n' rollers, DJs, gangsters, publishers like *Confidential*'s Robert Harrison, stock-car racers, record producers. All were constructing artifacts that polite society considered "vulgar and lower-class-awful beyond comment almost," but that were having a profound effect. He might have been describing his own status as a journalist—and anticipating the furor New Journalism would cause later in the decade.

Wolfe took the techniques of realistic fiction (scene-by-scene construction, dialogue, point of view, and meticulous status detail) and applied them to this new way of reporting. Gay Talese, Tom Morgan, and others had been doing the same thing in *Esquire,* but Wolfe took the form and pushed it to its limits, writing from *inside* his characters like a novelist; his best characters were outsiders—projections of himself. He was hip, the Lenny Bruce of letters. He wrote of the record magnate Phil Spector:

"All these raindrops are *high* or something. They don't roll down the window, they come straight back, toward the tail, wobbling, like all those Mr. Cool snowheads walking on mattresses. The plane is taxiing out toward the runway to take off, and this stupid infarcted water wobbles, sideways, across the window. Phil Spector... America's first teen-age tycoon watches...this watery pathology..."

The pieces were super-eclectic. They incorporated the electronic beeps and chatter of TV, of rock radio; they moved like the spontaneous bop prosody of the Beats; they had a visual quality, on the page; and they were scholarly, with bits of art history and sociology.

Wolfe flung this pastiche at a baby-boom readership raised on television and Top 40 radio, the best-educated generation in the history of the world. "The sixties were a period when fictionists seemed to have abandoned the city as a subject," reflects Wolfe. "Nonfiction writers had a field day."

In New York, styles and manners were changing faster than anyone could record them. *The Social Register* and Four Hundred crowd joined the rabble—in clubs like the Peppermint Lounge and Arthur—and mimicked their dancing, their dress. The new café society, or "Pop Society," as Wolfe preferred to call it, was "made up of people whose status rests not on property and ancestry but on various brilliant ephemera." It accepted Wolfe, the southern émigré, as its chronicler.

Wolfe's first book, *The Kandy-Kolored, Tangerine-Flake Streamline Baby*, a compilation of articles written in that first, manic, fifteen-month period, hit the bestseller lists. He became the Journalist as Superstar, part of an independent statusphere that included Jimmy Breslin (also of the *Trib*), Rex Reed, Pete Hamill, Truman Capote, and Norman Mailer—writers as vilified or adored as rock stars.

"It was a very curious time for me," Wolfe recalls. "I'd spend the day at the *Herald Tribune* getting other people through the publicity mill, and after work I was being interviewed. Suddenly *I* was getting publicity." In 1966 he was photographed by Irving Penn for *Vogue,* and interviewed by a girlfriend, Elaine Dundy, who was Kenneth Tynan's ex-wife and a novelist. Penn caught Wolfe's arrogance of dress and attitude, but Dundy got below the surface flash to what was a driven and isolated young man. She noted his "country air," describing him as "Tom Sawyer drawn by Beardsley." She remembers him today as "pretty wary, and scared of people putting him on...He was very much the Southerner trying to get it right in New York."

Meanwhile, Wolfe had moved to an apartment at Two Beekman Place, one of Manhattan's swankiest addresses—"When I came up north, I didn't come here to fool around"—but kept its interior bohemian and sparsely furnished. A sign over the telephone read, "Hello baby / Just try this little / game one more time."

Wolfe told Dundy that "perfect journalism would deal constantly with one subject: Status," and admitted that what made him angriest was "humiliation. I never forget, I never forgive." He said he'd always wanted to be a writer, but "didn't actually become one until I was thirty-two," the year of *Kandy-Kolored*—"I suppose there was a lot of fear involved." He complained that he had "taken more physical punishment from writing than...from any sport I've ever played." He felt that his greatest talent was for drawing (he'd illustrated the first book, and had had a one-man show in New York), but that he was least talented at "creating stable ties with other people."

Wolfe stayed untied to anything but ambition throughout the mid-sixties (though "a lot of girls were chasing him," remembers Clay Felker), and traveled helter-skelter across America and England in search of new trends or status groups who were "starting their own league," as he had. He "moved constantly," Richard Merkin remembers. "Tom must have lived in fourteen or sixteen different places in New York."

His ambivalence about city life, ignited by Richmond, was heightening. Fame couldn't dampen it. Gay Talese, who has known Wolfe since they were "young men on the street of journalism" together, describes him as "a private man who had a way of separating himself from the city... he [remains] very much the Southerner who feels distance as he moves through the New York scene. It doesn't touch him. He doesn't *want* it to touch him." Wolfe's articles became more critical of New York. "The Big League Complex" and "O Rotten Gotham—Sliding Down into the Behavioral Sink" were openly hostile. It was as if his sensitivity to having grown up the child of rural parents in urban Richmond had been transferred to New York. "Both of us were fascinated with small town guys in large cities—or outsiders," Talese recalls.

Professionally, Wolfe ensured this distance from "the Kentucky colonels of both Journalism and Literature," as he put it, by publishing a two-part *Tribune* article, in April of 1965, characterizing William Shawn, editor of *The New Yorker,* as a "museum custodian, an undertaker, a mortuary scientist" in charge of the magazine's staff—themselves no better than zombies in the liveliness of the copy they produced. E. B. White responded that "Mr. Wolfe's piece on William Shawn...sets some sort of record for journalistic delinquency." Muriel Spark commented that Wolfe's style of attack "is plainly derived from Senator McCarthy," and even J. D. Salinger emerged from his New Hampshire woodshed to sneer that the article was "inaccurate and sub-collegiate and gleeful and unrelievedly poisonous."

"That piece put *New York* magazine on the map," Clay Felker says, "and it put Tom on the map too."

Wolfe responded to his critics with a letter noting that *The New Yorker* "has become a Culture-totem for bourgeois culturati everywhere. Its followers—marvelous!—react just like those of any other totem group when somebody suggests that their holy buffalo knuckle may not be holy after all. They scream like weenies over a wood fire."

Wolfe says today, "There are two ways to make reputations: build up yours, and tear down everyone else's."

AMERICA WEST OF THE Hudson beckoned. Wolfe got out of New York to write a series of articles for the *Trib* about Ken Kesey, a novelist on the lam in Mexico. Kesey had been arrested on drug charges and had jumped bail. He was a good old boy in the mode of stock-car racer Junior Johnson, whom Wolfe had profiled in "The Last American Hero," a protagonist of the sort Wolfe was finding increasingly attractive. Kesey's father, like Wolfe's, had headed a farmers' cooperative, and both writers were committed to experimental realism in prose. They were outsiders who had gathered around them revolutionary constellations.

Kesey's was the Merry Pranksters, post-Beat proto-hippies of a literary bent. One of them was novelist Robert Stone, who had landed an assignment with *Esquire* to write about the group himself. "Wolfe didn't know where Kesey was in Mexico," Stone remembers, "and I did. I immediately got on the phone and told everybody who knew where Kesey was not to tell Wolfe. So Wolfe's sources promptly dried up. When *Esquire* rejected Stone's piece, he bequeathed his notes to Wolfe and agreed to be questioned by him. "He's a dangerous kind of interviewer," Stone observes respectfully, "because he really does put you at your ease."

The *Trib* articles resulted in a contract for *The Electric Kool-Aid Acid Test,* Wolfe's first book-length work. He had begun to work on it in New York, when his father became seriously ill. "I came home to sort of help my mother out," Wolfe recalls, "thinking that I would say good-bye to this book for a while. I was going to the hospital three times a day—and the darndest thing happened. Since I had maybe a couple of hours in the morning, an hour in the afternoon, and maybe an hour at night to work, I was *religious* about it. I never missed those hours. I would sit right down and start writing."

Coming home had unblocked him. Even after Dr. Wolfe recovered, Tom stayed on in Richmond, completing the book in four months.

The Pranksters' experiments with LSD were on the cutting edge of theories about the mind that Wolfe had been exploring for some time. He'd developed a technique "that I thought of as a controlled trance," he says. 'I'd review my notes for a certain chapter, then I would close my eyes and try to imagine myself, as a Method actor would, into the scene...going crazy, for example...how it feels and what it's going to sound like if you translate it into words—which was real writing by radar."

Eventually he decided there was one essential bit of reporting he'd failed to do: take acid. "I had a friend in Buffalo who had access to LSD, so I went up there and took 125 milligrams. At first I thought I was having a gigantic heart attack—I felt like my heart was outside my body with these big veins.... As I began to calm down, I had the feeling that I had entered into the sheen of this nubbly twist carpet-a really *wretched* carpet, made of Acrilan—and somehow this represented the people of America, in their democratic glory. It was cheap and yet it had a certain glossy excitement to it—I even felt sentimental about it. Somehow I was merging with this carpet. At the time, it seemed like a phenomenal insight, a breakthrough."

Though Wolfe dismisses this insight today as not meaning "a goddamn thing," it seemed to free him to write to *Kool-Aid* as a love song to America. The book was American to the core, imitating the workings of the contemporary mind by incorporating stream of consciousness, poetry, and multiple points of view. And it was unreservedly hip. It remains the best book about 1960s America, and it is emotionally free in a way Wolfe's writing has not been since.

Kool-Aid was simultaneously published with *The Pump House Gang* in July of 1968—"Two books!!!!!! Heeeeeeeeeeewack! The same day!!!!!! Too-o-o-o-o-o-o freaking much!" said the *New York Times* review—and became an immediate bestseller. All across the country, students in creative writing programs stared at the photo of Wolfe on its jacket—Tom in a dark shirt, white tie, white step-collared vest, white shoes and suit—and said, "Hey, that ain't Allen Ginsberg." And turned toward the New Journalism.

In the mid-sixties, "fiction moved a long way toward New Journalism," Thomas McGuane says. Today "there's a kind of weird, natural meeting ground. All novelists are trying to fool readers into thinking it's real, and all adventurous journalists are trying to seize the flexibility of fiction."

The New Journalists had seized that flexibility, effecting at the very least a revolution in style. And, as Robert Stone remarks, "a revolution in style can be called a revolution in consciousness...Wolfe reflected it, as I think Kesey reflected it."

Yet *Kool-Aid* had finished on a somber note. Despite a revolution in consciousness, the Pranksters had failed to liberate America with their vision of "now." The hierarchical status groups still reigned. "WE BLEW IT!" the Pranksters chant in Wolfe's final chapter, "WE BLEW IT!" "WE BLEW IT!"

BY 1970, WOLFE thought he had cleared the decks for his big book about New York. In search of material, he crashed a fundraiser for the Black Panthers' legal-defense fund at the Park Avenue apartment of Leonard and Felicia Bernstein. What he found at the Bernsteins' was such gold that it resulted in another postponement of his fiction.

Radical Chic is brilliantly executed and marvelously funny. "As a piece of sheer writing," Wolfe says, "it's my favorite book." In it Wolfe remains the outsider. If he identifies with anyone, it's with the Black Panthers, whom he characterizes as hip, stylish, and aghast at the hypocrisies of Park Avenue liberals.

Radical Chic demolishes New York's rich socialites for their pandering to radical causes (it was authentically damaging, having its effect on both "radical chic" fundraisers and the reputation of Leonard Bernstein) and analyzes the whole shebang, once again in terms of status. As Ellen Willis commented in the *Village Voice,* the piece's "underlying assumption is that political action is inherently ridiculous and irrelevant...The very idea of social conscience pisses him off."

Suddenly the apostle of Pranksterism was being labeled a right-winger. Wolfe blames this on "my having gone against the prevailing orthodoxy" of high liberalism. He had always felt about politics "the way the hippies who were asked to make statements felt about the FBI. *Who cares?* I'm a democrat with a small *d.* I think it would be perfectly okay to have an electrician or a burglar-alarm repairman as president."

Today Robert Stone characterizes Wolfe as "a southern conservative of a very sophisticated kind. I think he sees New York, and political liberalism, as wimpy and posturing and hypocritical."

He was feeling pugnacious in the early seventies. What seemed to anger him most was the Vietnam War and the public's gloom over it. Not only had Vietnam curtailed the "Happiness Explosion" of the 1960s, it had severely divided Wolfe's natural constituency, the college-age baby-boomers. In a 1983 piece about the Vietnam Veterans Memorial, he would note of the war, "The sons of the merchant and managerial classes in America sat this one out, in college, graduate school, Canada and Sweden," and would assert that "the unspeakable and inconfessible goal of the New Left on the campuses had been to transform the shame of the fearful into the guilt of the courageous." Despite Wolfe's conservatism during the early 1970s, he was a huge draw on the campus lecture circuit. "What's Kesey doing now?" became a ritual inquiry that nearly drove him crazy.

Once again during these years, Wolfe was deflected from writing his New York book. "The Truest Sport: Jousting with Sam and Charlie" was an article that presaged *The Right Stuff,* comparing bomber missions over Vietnam to jousting. Later he'd comment, "Sports were...a way of training young men to be warriors in a relatively harmless fashion.... If we want to get into the psychology of it, I think we'll find that men, not so many women, *love war* and they love sports."

The Right Stuff took him six years, during which time he conducted voluminous research and cranked out three other, shorter books to avoid finishing it. "I was stuck with how to handle point of view, I had no main character—no one you could just tell the story through…. I was obsessed with the notion that this book would have no suspense, because everyone knew how it came out."

Changes in his life may have contributed to this block. Wolfe was affected deeply when his father died, and he had become seriously involved with Sheila Berger, a magazine designer whom he'd met in the art department at *Esquire*. And he was unsettled by the desire to write his Manhattan book instead of *The Right Stuff*. He finally created a suitable protagonist by digging within, presenting the Southerner Chuck Yeager as the very embodiment of that good-old-boy, knock-'em-dead spirit that had invigorated his portraits of Kesey and Junior Johnson. The book is a brilliant dissection of the status pyramid in the modern officer corps. At its apex stand the Mercury astronauts: modern knights locked into a Cold War struggle with Soviet cosmonauts for supremacy in the heavens. The right stuff emerged as an amalgam of bravery, style, patriotism, and masculinity. It was the spirit of the rural South, and of his father.

WITH THE PUBLICATION of *The Right Stuff* in 1979, Wolfe became a mature statesman of American letters, a literary oracle reflexively consulted on any number of national events, from the space-shuttle tragedy to the Statue of Liberty's hundredth birthday. The conservatism of *The Right Stuff* did no harm to either Wolfe's sales or his reputation.

"You might say," Clay Felker observes, "that Tom anticipated the whole American conservative movement." *The Right* Stuff certified Wolfe as a historian, and he abandoned his seat as pop-culture critic of the moment. The Victorian collar climbed his neck in *Bauhaus* and *The Painted Word* as his abhorrence of modernism intensified.

"The reaction to *The Painted Word* [in which he outlines the status hierarchies of the art world and argues that modern art would be devoid of meaning without the criticism of the New York culturati] was the most violent of anything I've done," Wolfe remembers, "much more so than *Radical Chic*. The things I was called in print amazed me."

Wolfe's annual retreat from Manhattan is reminiscent of the one his family made from Richmond each summer. The white frame house he rents in Southampton from May through September is late Victorian in style, with gardens out back and an enormous expanse of rolling green yard to Agawan Lake. Though grand in a way, the house offers no competition to the Gatsbyesque mansions that typify Southampton, but is extremely livable, with room for Wolfe's wife, Sheila, and the children (Alexandra, seven, and Thomas, two), and the requisite help, and enough privacy to write.

"I really do a lot of work out there," Wolfe says. "Southampton's an old town, and it's a *real* town...There aren't that many people I know in a literary sense." But, as Richard Merkin quips, "Tom can *dissect* the population of Southampton for you. The Real Stuff is there."

In June of 1986, Wolfe's friend Ed Hayes married the fashion model Susan Gilder in Bellport, and Wolfe attended. "Tom doesn't have that many close friends," Merkin says, "and Eddie's as good a friend as Tom has, maybe his best." The thirty-nine-year-old Hayes, an ex-Bronx D.A. now practicing law in Manhattan, is from an Irish working class family in Queens. He came up the hard way. Wolfe's friendship with him seems an unlikely one. Yet, as Hayes observes, "Tom is fascinated with New York ethnic life, and I'm fascinated with this Wasp warrior class from the South. The real English dandies were aristocrats who were usually soldiers, and aggressive and athletic. Tom sort of represents that. It's that Protestant warrior mentality...similar to what you find in the street life of New York."

Beautifully dressed, Hayes exudes the elegance of a young Cagney. Wolfe has a fatherly affection for him. He is the model for the lawyer Tommy Killian in *Bonfire,* and has served, with Bruce Cutler and others, as Wolfe's guide through the criminal-justice system of the Bronx.

"The hard guys," Hayes says, "without exception love Tom. He's extremely manly in his way of dealing with things.... Actually, he's a police reporter in a nice suit."

When not writing, Wolfe will spend entire afternoons at Hayes's house in Bellport, or Hayes will drive out to Southampton. "I'll kill the day there," he says. "We eat, we talk...I'm the only Irish guy from Sunnyside who got crazed for gardening, and I'll go down to his house and prune his trees for him."

"I think Tom's life in Manhattan is glamorous," Gay Talese says. "And he's found glamour in family life." The years of loneliness when, as Wolfe recalls, he would "haunt the halls of a magazine you're writing for like an odor," are gone. With his children, he gets all the company he needs "at quarter to seven every morning." Wolfe did not marry until he was forty-seven, or become a father until he was nearly fifty. When his son was born in 1985, "it was all I heard about," laughs Hayes. "They climb all over him. They drive him crazy. It's tough to be a father in a white suit."

Despite the extramarital affair so painfully outlined in *Bonfire,* there appears to be no parallel in Wolfe's life. "When I got married," says Hayes, "I had an extensive discussion with him about wearing wedding rings, and about vows. Women really like this guy...but he's one of the few I know who's genuinely faithful. He and Sheila have been together about eighteen years, and the guy comes home nights."

Though Wolfe has friends from most strata of Manhattan life, his closest friends—Hayes and Merkin— are native New Yorkers from different ethnic heritages. Sheila is Jewish. "She's not from a wealthy background," Hayes says, "she's from the Bronx—but 99 percent of the women born to privilege should have her manners, and her looks to boot." He adds that "it's hard to be married to a very famous man, especially in New York. Sheila does that well."

Now forty-one, Sheila was twenty-three when Wolfe met her. "She's very feminine and refined," says Gay Talese. "Tom has a woman who cares greatly for him, and can protect him from a lot of the distractions of New York. She appreciates his need for solitude. Sheila Berger has good judgment. She's no Zelda, in other words."

The East Side townhouse that the Wolfes own is an 1868 brownstone, and with its block shaded by sycamores and its azalea-filled backyard is as close to a southern milieu as one might construct in Manhattan. Wolfe's second-floor study is colorfully functional: high white bookshelves lined with the classics, Chinese-yellow drapes, a desktop computer (his wife's gift, unmastered), and the galleys to *Bonfire* spread about. Wolfe's production quota on revising *Bonfire* for publication in book form has been a fierce two thousand words a day. To overcome inertia, he's kept a clock on his desk "to see if I can do a page and a half an hour." It has taken him a year and a half to revise his novel. "He says he won't buy any clothes until he finishes," Hayes reports. "I said, 'motherfucker, don't go that far.'" Wolfe's anxiety about the book caused him to consult his first *Esquire* editor, Byron Dobell. "I frankly read it with great dread," Dobell reports. "I said, 'Oh shit, the guy always wanted to write a novel and can't'—but I was thrilled, delighted, and somewhat surprised. I told him, 'Absolutely this is a book to be published.'"

Bonfire has been altered substantially since its serialization in *Rolling Stone*. Wolfe has changed the nature of Sherman McCoy's crime, heightened the female characters, and made Sherman a career man on Wall Street rather than a writer. "Maybe the writer was too close to him for comfort," says Jann Wenner, who edited the *Rolling Stone* text. "And maybe if he distances himself from Sherman McCoy, he'll write Sherman McCoy with a little more fervor."

"I can see why he's having trouble with it," Bill

Hoffman says. "Tom's great strength is his intellect. And intellect almost always finds its greatest satisfaction in the satirical. But a lot of times you've got to have real *feelings* for people who are less well equipped than you are."

This afternoon Wolfe seems exhausted by the toll of completing his novel. He is pencil-thin, sniffly, and obviously on edge. We have tea in the elaborate Victorian sitting room off his study; silver-framed photographs of his mother and father look on. Wolfe ushers me to an Art Deco settee he designed as "a memory from my teenage years of what looks swell," and talks about rewriting the ending of *Bonfire*, "making it more complete, and more beautiful." One of his difficulties with the reportorial novel has been that he's repeatedly been scooped by breaking news. "I guess I just have to write faster," he says. Before the Bernhard Goetz incident (during which Goetz shot four young black men trying to mug him), he'd composed a subway scene with nearly identical events, which he had to discard.

"Here was this great piece of city life that I thought I'd introduce. But Bernhard Goetz did it for me—in style. He shot up everyone in sight."

The urge to retreat to pure journalism has been strong: "Often in the midst of writing this novel there were so many resonances with the Goetz case that I really would say, 'Well, why don't I just write about the Goetz case?'" But he's persevered in his drive to join the literary upper class.

"I see the coincidences in the news as an upside-down compliment to my reporting. I'm hitting upon the things that are happening."

Like the Goetz case, *Bonfire* crackles with racial tension. "If the city's going to be in the foreground, you can't duck the factor of ethnic hostility, which is so much a part of life in all our cities." He sniffles, takes a sip of tea. "The point I'm trying to make about status in the novel is that it's so different now from what it might have been fifty years ago, because the ethnic lines in New

York, ironically, are more sharply drawn now than they were before World War II. The black population then was hardly a factor at all politically. Now it's very much a factor."

It's because of this "resort community "paradox, Wolfe explains, that wealthy interlopers (whites) control New York's high life, while the townies (blacks, Latinos, and the new-immigrant New Yorkers) have the real political power.

"Somebody like Sherman McCoy, who you'd think is on top of the status hierarchy in America—he's white, Protestant, old family, best schools, Wall Street—is odd man out once he gets into a political situation. He becomes a victim, a fat turkey to be sliced up."

Ed Hayes has explained it thus: "People with a lot of money and social connections in New York have a power that is very disconnected from ordinary life. You can wake up and become involved in an incident like this in Tom's book, and the people you come in contact with in the criminal-justice system, who are powerful, are so different from you. They're smart, competent people who really give a fuck about what they're doing. And they can hurt you."

Wolfe has given Sherman McCoy a family with roots in Tennessee: "His grandfather was a man of no particular standing, but made some money and came to New York. Sherman's father goes to the right schools and becomes a pillar of Knickerbocker society."

In the first chapter of the book, Wolfe writes of a classmate of Sherman's named Pollard Browning, "who at the age of nine knew how to get across the astonishing news that McCoy was a hick name (and a hick family), as in Hatfields and McCoys, whereas he, Browning, was an Episcopalian Knickerbocker. He used to call Sherman 'Sherman McCoy the Mountain Boy.'" Although there are strong overtones here of Wolfe's early sensitivity to his family's outlander status in Richmond, he seems oblivious to this connection.

"Sherman's from New York, but Pollard's family has been here *longer*," he snorts.

The status of an individual within a group is still his first interest as a writer. "I try to make the characters in this book inseparable from that notion. The psychological development of a person is utterly inseparable from the status that surrounds him. The task of a writer is to show how the social context influences the personal psychology."

Wolfe's passionate feelings about New York's status hierarchy have resulted in a novel that is venomously critical of the city. "New York really is a bonfire of vanity. But there is no villain in my book-unless you consider the human condition villainous. And I don't. Everyone in the book is vain, though. This is the human comedy!" Wolfe says, gesticulating. "We're right in the middle of it. Every ethnic group is mocked equally in *Bonfire*; just about everybody is hypocritical—everybody is 'doing well by doing good.' Everyone is equally shown as a creature of vanity."

This sounds like yet another addendum to Wolfe's diatribe against New York. When I make this assertion, he puts down his teacup and stares.

"I don't see any antipathy at all! It may come out as mockery and so on, but, God, I *love* the cities—I love New York! And often it's hard for me to get across the idea that I don't want it to change. I don't want people like the Bernsteins to stop giving parties like the radical chic. And I really don't want people like the characters in *Bonfire* to act any differently." He's nearly out of his seat. "I don't have an Arcadian bone in my body," he says in outrage. "I'm Addison and Steele, or the early Thackeray! Look at Dickens' *Sketches by Boz*. Are there any sympathetic figures in *Sketches by Boz?* Not really. It's full of mockery, raillery, irony. And yet there is a love of the city. My relish of life in the cities is the very fabric of what I have done! Look at Balzac, who was extremely critical of Paris. Who can say Balzac didn't love the city? He wallowed in the city. He would have *died* anywhere else. And I feel the same way."

Tea, apparently, is over.

Once Wolfe has regained his composure, I ask the key status question: How might he categorize his own reputation among the hierarchical statuspheres of New York?

"I was afraid you'd ask that," he replies morosely. He deliberates a long moment, then says, "I'm either going to make it as a writer...or nothing."

Vanity Fair, 1987

Seasons through the Park

It's a perfect October day: sixty degrees, the spires above Central Park West bathed in aquamarine, hundreds of people gathered near Bethesda Fountain or passing through its esplanade. A man in tailcoat and spats is telling stories by the Lake. Children sit on the grass as he paces, gesturing broadly. What he says is unintelligible from this distance, but a sign, GHOST TALES, gives him away. The children don't look apprehensive. Their glances drift to the lake with its rowboats, dawdling lovers, lush willows, and the art nouveau curve of Bow Bridge—but soon return. For they are city kids, trained to esteem theatricality.

Which is omnipresent. A classical guitarist plucks New Age riffs as an accomplice hawks cassettes. A fusion band, New Hype Jazz, plays as their leader, a Latino trumpeter in beret and motorcycle jacket (a hockey mask capping its right shoulder) passes a bowl for contributions. The music is infectious; an aging hipster in zoot suit and stingy brim starts to rhumba. Above the terrace, a puppet troupe called the Crowtations—its birds costumed like Motowners—lip synchs to rhythm and blues. Its choreography is hilarious, and the crowd tips big. Beside a lakeside willow, white-coated technicians, expert in reflexology, acupuncture, and related therapies, knead backs of clients (ten minutes for ten dollars) who splay face-down on orthopedic chairs. One masseur's placard reads, "Bodywork from China, Japan, Egypt, Israel, Tibet, the Bronx, and Heaven."

A few yards distant, by an overhanging branch, a largemouth bass swirls at the pond's surface. I spot it and cast a black surface popper, jigging it lightly across the water. I've been fishing half an hour, and except for two small bluegills, have caught nothing. The Lake is rich in marine life, and it is not unheard-of to take six-to-eight-pound bass here. I jerk the popper and the fish strikes, tugging twice then pulling hard for deep water. As my rod bows, I hear a father say, "Look Josh, the man's fishing." Guitar music pauses. I fight the bass to shoreline, where a small crowd of children is gathering. I palm the fish—twelve inches—before releasing it, and turn to see some twenty people watching. The reflexologists seem annoyed as does the storyteller; I've diverted their crowd. I strip out line and cast deliberately so the children might watch, as curses from musicians and acupuncturists fill the air.

WHO DECIDES CENTRAL PARK'S use, and to whom it belongs, are questions that have been argued since Frederick Law Olmsted's and Calvert Vaux's Greensward Plan was effected in 1858. Central Park was America's first landscaped public park—and its first democratic one, an archetype for all that followed. It was conceived at a moment when the perils of city life first became evident to Americans. In 1856, New York was growing exponentially with its wealth, industry, and immigrant population. Andrew Jackson Downing, the preeminent landscape architect of his day, had lobbied as early as 1849 for "the necessity of a great park" as palliative for Manhattan's tensions. He'd long felt that the romantic tradition and its "rural embellishments" were needed "to soften and humanize the rude...and give continual education to the educated." This was at the heart of the romantic thesis of *rus in urbe*, or country in city, as made practical in Olmsted and Vaux's Greensward design. Despite Americans' love of theatrical excess, Vaux, a disciple of Downing's, had praised their "innate homage to the natural in contradistinction to the artificial," and Olmsted believed a naturalistic park would have "a distinctly harmonizing and refining influence upon the most unfortunate and most lawless classes of the city." It would calm then activate their imaginations by creating a romantic world of improved nature, where the rough edges of city life were smoothed and the exigencies of industrialism temporarily suspended.

Today, Central Park is synonymous with what's best and worst about urban life. It's where Woody Allen cavorted with Mariel Hemingway in *Manhattan*, but where the celebrated Jogger was raped and nearly murdered in 1989. It's where Paul Simon played to 750,000 fans in 1991, but where Jennifer Levin was strangled in 1986's Preppy Murder. It's where the New York City marathon ends, but where many a drug habit starts. It's where thousands line the sidewalk to enjoy Macy's Thanksgiving Day parade—a few yards from where John Lennon was slain in 1980.

Through popular art, Central Park has been laminated onto our psyches. It's where Stuart Little raced his boat on Conservatory Water, where Holden Caulfield fretted about ducks wintering on the Pond, and where *The Fisher King*'s Robin Williams urged Jeff Bridges to disrobe and "give the little guy some air." Central Park *is* Manhattan. And since Manhattan is centerpiece to America's greatest city, what happens there is of interest to the world.

THEATRICALITY IN CENTRAL PARK (of the type Lillian Russell displayed there, by riding a gold-plated bicycle with jewel-encrusted spokes) has always been prevalent and in some ways conflictual with the park's natural subtleties—which are less apparent. In summer they're cloaked by the greenery of 26,000 trees. On the Atlantic and Hudson flyways, the park's foliage is prime birding territory. Some 259 species have been identified resting and recuperating there. Twenty species nest in the park, including downy woodpeckers, eastern kingbirds, tufted titmice, gray catbirds, and brown thrashers. More exotic species, such as white egrets, blue herons, snowy owls, cormorants, short-eared owls, and fish crows are spotted. Last spring two red-tailed hawks nested on the cornice of Mary Tyler Moore's building, overlooking the park at Seventy-Fourth Street and Fifth Avenue. As hawkers sat with binoculars off Conservatory Water, they watched the pair mate on Woody Allen's TV antenna, as Allen and Soon-Yi Previn strolled hand in hand.

Sarah Elliott, a Chicagoan who birded with her mother in Olmsted's Wooded Island as a child, has led the National Audubon's Christmas Count in Central Park since 1988. "We only found fifty birds this year," she regrets, "but the weather was terrible." Counters met on December 19 at the Reservoir for what is among the nation's oldest Christmas counts. Elliott, in her mid-sixties, has birdwatched in Central Park for thirty-four years. In good weather, she's birding every day or working as a park volunteer. "In 1973," she says nonchalantly, "I was packing mud around trees in the Ramble and a kid tried to rape me. I talked him out of it—gave him a wheelbarrow instead."

Most birding territories are in the park's secluded regions: the North Woods, the four-acre Hallett Nature Sanctuary near Fifty-Ninth Street, or the thirty-six-acre Ramble at park center. Their winding paths and verdancy cloak what Central Park Precinct Captain, Bill Bayer, calls "predators": not cougars or grizzlies, but the five to thirty-five muggers, the dozen rapists, and two murderers who each year ply their craft. Though administrators praise Central Park as the safest 848 acres in New York

City, its predators' brutality is notable when it strikes. And usually well publicized. Commissioner Stern smirks, "If you have the misfortune of being raped or murdered in Central Park, you become a celebrity."

My uncle, William Nichols—a writer and producer of network television shows, and a devotee of theatricality—was already celebrated when, in 1963, he was attacked by several youths while birding in the Ramble. He was robbed, pummeled, and left for dead. His friend, James Schuyler, described the incident in a poem, "Dining Out with Doug and Frank." *My abstention from the Park / is for Billy Nichols who went / bird-watching there and... got his / head beat in....*"

My dalliances in Central Park are invariably colored by my uncle's experience. Part of me is wary, another incautious to the point of danger—exploring late at night, for example. It's a call of the wild, where one isn't top of the food chain. So on an evening in July, right after moving near the park, I'm both startled and pleased to encounter a young African American spin casting in the algae-covered Lake off the Ramble. I've fished for striped bass in the East and Hudson Rivers (where pier fisherman brandish axe handles to discourage muggers), and know of street kids that angle for the many species thriving there. But I don't realize fishermen work the Lake. "There's big ones," the young man claims. Then reluctantly divulges favorite angling spots within the park: beneath the Pool's willows, at the northeast tip of the Reservoir, and deep in the Turtle Pond. As bats dip below tree line, he hooks something solid as a tire. He fights it to the shallows, then loses it in a swirl of gray. "Definitely a bass," he sputters. "Though when they drained the Meer," he adds, "they found a twenty-pound carp and put it here."

The Meer was renovated in 1992—as part of Central Park's current restoration, inaugurated in 1982—then refilled and stocked with 50,000 bass, bluegill, sand catfish fingerlings. In September I bicycle north to find dozens of black and Hispanic anglers working its banks. Some own tackle, even fly rods, but most use bamboo poles with bobbers and barbless hooks that park volunteers provide, free, for catch-and-release fishing. As a jazz group plays before Dana Center, I watch a grandmother teach her grandson to fish in a body of water previously thought dead.

In 1856 the 848 acres that Central Park would encompass had been settled largely by minorities: "poor Irish, German and black families," according to Ron Rosenzweig and Elizabeth Blackmar's superb *The Park and The People*, "who raised vegetables and tended hogs." They were characterized as squatters, their territory portrayed as a "scene of plunder and depredations," the *Evening Post* wrote, "the headquarters of vagabonds and scoundrels of every description." Adjoining landowners desired a park to improve their neighborhood and to increase property values. Despite Olmsted's democratic intentions, the squatters would have to move.

But as records show, some park residents, including African Americans, owned land—a rare circumstance pre-Emancipation. Seneca Village, "one of the city's best-established black communities, with three churches and a school," Rosenzweig and Blackmar report, was razed for Central Park, as were other minority settlements.

Central Park Administrator, Betsy Barlow Rogers, calls restoration of the park's northeast corner—long a wasteland to its black and Latin neighbors—her "most thrilling" success. She remembers, "When we opened Dana and the Meer this fall, I was feeling all that delight. 'You gave us back the park,' [residents] said. They remembered when it was nice, then how it got bad. Now it's nice again."

BETSY ROGERS IS THE PARK'S chief renovator and foremost spokesperson. "I was *born* in Central Park," she jokes. In fact, she was appointed Administrator in 1979, after serving as Executive Director of the Central Park Task Force, and working with the Parks Council.

Rosenzweig and Blackmar rate her as "one of the five most influential figures in the park's history." Two-term Parks Commissioner, Henry J. Stern—a man of storied impishness—says that "Betsy is the key figure in this twentieth century renaissance of Central Park. Every century someone comes along with a vision. [Under her direction] it's become *the* most widely supported public park in the country."

A fifty-seven-year-old of aristocratic mien, wispy brown hair, and a wide smile, she's the perfect go-between for New York City's Parks Department and the Central Park Conservancy—a private fund raising group, coordinating gifts from the vastly rich denizens of Fifth Avenue, Central Park West, Central Park South, and neighboring locations, that's raised nearly 100 million dollars to date. The Conservancy matches, and at times betters, the city's budget for park restoration.

Rogers is conservative, an Olmstedian—though she has no desire to return Central Park to the nineteenth century. "To be Olmstedian is to honor a certain tradition of design," she maintains, "which is the pastoral tradition that comes out of the estate gardening of England." The work she has overseen, and largely paid for as founder of the Conservancy, is in that mode.

She has written three books, including *The Forest and Wetlands of New York City*, that was nominated for a National Book Award in 1971. She has taken the park from what was a graffiti-ridden lair of dope peddlers and vandals, through a magnificent restoration, 60 percent finished, that includes the hiring of a woodlands manager to oversee a naturalistic revival of the ninety-acre North Woods. She's done this largely through public/private partnering.

That fundraising model has become an international panacea to preservationist distress. "If the [parks are] going to be truly great," Stern says, "there has to be some kind of partnership, with the city providing basic maintenance and the frills and the special things that make [them] great being paid for privately. You can't have a series of royal gardens, paid for by tax funds." Rogers has traveled to Japan, Ireland, Italy, and France to detail plans for restoring urban parks.

"They're all in trouble now," she laments. "We had such vision, in the nineteenth century, when we built these great park systems. Now it's both a psychic and financial disinvestment in public space that's going on. There are some of us who are optimists, and we believe that there is an essential good [in public spaces]. We think that you can overwhelm unsavory uses by bringing in positive uses. If you make the park look like it isn't a lawless and abandoned environment, if, to use a really old-fashioned word, you invest in beauty...I have found in my work that there has been a corresponding appreciation. People have come back enthusiastically. It's a great and successful experiment in democracy."

THOSE ENGLISH PARKS that were Olmsted's models have their roots in the medieval enclosure movement— where vast tracts of commonly held land, or commons, were granted to lords for private hunting and angling. Gary Snyder writes in *The Practice of the Wild* that "The commons is the contract a people make with their local natural system." In September, when I mention to him that I've seen immigrant or previously-absent populations in Central Park fishing, he observes, "These people are getting involved in the subsistence relation to [New York], which a lot of the people who are already there don't have." I note that races seem to mix better in the park. He says, "Maybe the only identity that we can all agree on, in this culturally diverse and racially diverse world we're moving into, is a respect for place. And that by literally *sharing the ground,* we have something that we share together."

Much of Central Park's attractiveness is anchored to the backbone accessibility of it as *place.* Excepting the rivers, it's the only sizeable expanse where Manhattanites

may embrace the natural world. New immigrants—
Latins and Asians especially—are drawn to Central Park,
some fishing, some hunting crayfish in the Meer, some
picking ginkgo nuts or mulberries, some scouring the
understory for pigweed or field garlic, others cleaving to
rock outcroppings as if they were the spine of the island—
which they are. One such is a Japanese boulderer named
Yuki Ikumori. I meet him in October at Umpire Rock,
a 400-million-year-old chunk of mica schist, containing
grooves made by the glaciers 40,000 years ago, which
mark its northwest face like finger swipes in chocolate
icing. Many such rocks—stumps of a decapitated
mountain range—protrude from the park's landscape,
and elsewhere support Manhattan's skyscrapers. But no
outcropping is so dramatically grooved as Umpire.

On its northeast side I spot Ikumori, plastered to the
rockface in khaki pants and pink drover's shirt, his only
concession to gear a pair of chartreuse-laced climbing
shoes. In his forties, he's lean with powerful arms and
back, has a warrior's face, shoulder-length hair and
samurai mustache. He's coaching a young climber,
leaving chalk prints on the schist as he fingers the way,
while a Spanish television crew films him. He climbs
with primitive grace—as a slow loris or a sloth might,
negotiating a tree. He studies the rock, noting hand and
toe holds, then moves with the fluidity of aikido.

New York climbers have written a book, *Climbing in
the Manhattan Area*, that Ikumori contributed to. "Yuki's
unbelievably good," a climbing bum says, adding that he's
considered the park's master boulderer.

Isumori introduces himself, explaining that he's a native
Japanese who's lived in New York for ten years, and is a
visual artist who sleeps and works in the storeroom of a
Greenwich Village restaurant, in return for odd jobs and
gardening. He spends much time painting, but otherwise
lives to creep up the face of Manhattan bedrock. His
paintings are geometrical pastels, intricately linked,
"like cells." He notes, "The climbing has made me more

flexible in my art. In clear weather I'm here every day."
He's been climbing six years, does no other sport and
appreciates that "there are no champions in bouldering—
you compete with the rock." The concentration it takes
to best a boulder is similar to that necessary to create art.
"And like art," he observes, "you have to find the route...I
do ten new paintings a year, and find ten new routes up
the rock." As I watch him climb toward lovers seated at
the boulder's summit, music drifts from the Carousel and
Essex House's tower seems to dare him from Central Park
South.

MANHATTANITES' HUNGER FOR the land is so great that
"Wildman" Steve Brill, since his arrest for picking and
eating a dandelion in 1986, has led over 18,000 people on
Edible Tours of Central Park. Wildman's book, *Identifying
and Harvesting Edible and Medicinal Plants In Wild
(And Not So Wild) Places*, is to be published this spring.
Meanwhile, artist Walter De Maria's installation, *The
Earth Room*, has been on display in a SoHo loft since 1980.
It is 36,000 square feet of black dirt, microorganisms, and
worms, with which visitors silently commune. Its keeper,
Bill Dillworth, tells the *New York Times* in November:
"When people become disoriented and troubled, they will
isolate themselves with the earth—and renew themselves."
The same week, local TV reports that New Yorkers' innate
sense of fecundity has transformed some forty-one vacant
lots on the lower east side to vegetable or flower gardens.
That is underlined, three weeks later, by a second *Times*
piece, on the biophilia hypothesis, positing that humans
have "a deep, genetically based emotional need to affiliate
with the rest of the living world," that people prefer "park
like settings rather than enclosed ones," and that there is
scientific evidence that "If we complete the destruction
of nature, we will have succeeded in cutting ourselves off
from the source of sanity itself."

As if in response, visitors hurry to Central Park's
woods, I among them. On a brisk December day, the park's

woodlands manager, Dennis Burton, accompanies me on a tour of the restored, ninety-acre North Woods. Burton is a fortyish fellow with frizzy brown hair that, this afternoon, is flecked with sawdust from cutting a fallen black willow. "Huge," he assures me, "and planted about sixty years ago." Burton wears neither uniform nor suit coat, but a backpacker's parka and mountain boots—unusual for a park employee. He speaks, through a slight New York accent, of how he came to be an environmentalist: "I have a degree in English from Stonybrook. When I got my degree there was no job, so somebody offered me one doing tree work. Just the names of the trees, *viburnum dentatum*, it all sounded so poetic…it kind of blossomed, so to speak, into this."

We stand a quarter mile from Harlem, but this section of park could not feel more remote. In Olmsted's plan, its modest forest was left unimproved, suggesting the Adirondacks. It had been trampled by British and Hessian troops during the Revolutionary War, and largely denuded by American forces during the War of 1812. Villages were cropping up when Olmsted acquired the land in 1863. The park's oldest building—its military Blockhouse #1— sits ruined on an adjacent hilltop.

I follow Burton south through Huddlestone Arch, a gravity bridge and tunnel made from elephantine rocks of black schist. "The idea was that you would walk from that open vista into this," Burton says, indicating the forest. "It's kind of like the magic gate." Water drips from its stones, and I think of *Beauty and the Beast*, the TV series in which Vincent, a leonine tunnel dweller, rescues and comes to love Catherine, an attorney beaten unconscious in the park. We emerge at the Ravine, walking past a restored waterfall—the Cascade—to Manhattan's last surviving stream bed, from which Olmsted later created the Loch—his "long lake."

Burton pauses above a marsh, crowded with aster and fallen willows. "We're starting to lose them," he says evenly, "but you can see the canopy has opened up. That's become one of our best bird habitats. On any given weekend, we'll find a line of birders on this path, with their binoculars looking in and spotting all kinds of stuff." He swivels. "In these open areas I'm putting plant material that's more of a sun lover, also plant material that provides berries, like elderberries and hardhack, that provides food for wildlife."

Burton gestures toward the tree line. "What we're doing here is making kind of a model of the northeast deciduous forest...an oak, hickory, chestnut, tulip forest, which is what we still have. That's what was here when the Europeans first discovered it." He walks on, pausing to toe a hillock. "We started replanting and restabilizing these slopes," he says. "We've used only native vegetation so far, mountain laurel and witch hazel, pin oaks, ironwood, and the ground vegetation, plus different kinds of wildflowers that we would normally expect in here. The theory being that if you return a habitat, an environment or an ecosystem to its original [state], then you'll get wildlife to come back."

But Burton hasn't waited: "Because we're on an island, the best we can really hope to return naturally would be winged animals. Birds, butterflies, bees, wasps, flies, that sort of thing. But we started a program where we're introducing some herpetiles—frogs, snakes, turtles. Now the problem is that this is an urban setting, and a lot of kids use the area. So turtles would be difficult to bring in here, because they would be captured. Snakes pretty much the same. So we have, since last spring, introduced great tree frogs, green frogs and the spring peeper. We've actually dug holes for them to lay their eggs." Raccoons, groundhogs, and rabbits are already well-established. "We have a number of feral cats," Burton adds. "We had a couple of dogs that had puppies over at Huddlestone. But they disappeared."

I ask whose idea it was to restore plant and animal life to its pre-Columbian state. "The designers, the planners," Burton says. "But there were so many constituencies that were concerned about what we were going to put in here, what we were going to cut, and what kinds of projects we were going to do, that we didn't do anything." Birdwatchers, for example, didn't want the underbrush cut back, and the Historical Society and Arts Council wrangled over every architectural maneuver. "So we hired a consultant from Philadelphia—Leslie Sauer of Andropogon Associates—who's very cutting edge on this restoration of urban woodland ecosystems. Leslie wrote us a fifty-six-page report. We took all of that information and created a Woodlands Advisory Board"— with representatives from the Audubon Society, Sierra Club, Parks Department, Conservancy, and others— "which hashed over the information, and slowly started approaching the restoration."

Sauer's report cites four major contributors to North Woods' deterioration: off-trail use of bicycles and vehicles, hiker trampling, improper storm drainage, and the spread of exotic invasive vegetation. She recommends banning exotic species and replanting mostly native vegetation.

She later tells me, "Most [urban parks] are going through a similar evaluation of the issues of landscape management—how they're going to protect natural areas. We're reviewing the final draft of a master plan for [Brooklyn's] Prospect Park. We also did a master plan for [Manhattan's] Inwood Park, and we just completed one for the whole Olmsted park system in Louisville, Kentucky." Andropogon—named for a grass that reinhabits burned areas—also works with the National Park Service to restore earthen fortifications at Civil War battle sites, and with Philadelphia to reclaim "derelict industrial land." She praises the work of both the St. Louis Botanical Garden, and the Nature Conservancy, which helps restore Midwestern prairies.

"But," she insists, "the difference is that Central Park is the most intense, and probably the most rich [program] from that perspective. There's a level of expert staffing that's really exceptional. So in that sense I think it's kind of the leader."

After examining Glenspan Arch, a restored portal at the Ravine's western entrance, and its fourteen-foot Cascade, Burton and I backtrack to a small meadow below the 102nd Street transverse. "We're slowly trying to establish this as a native grass and wildflower meadow," he says, "but it's slow because right now it's mostly inhabited by lawn grasses and that sort of thing." He grins. "So I got myself a kerosene torch, and what I'm going to start doing is burning off little sections and uprooting those grasses. Then burning it to stimulate the soil and put seeding or plugs in of the natural grasses and wildflowers." He steps back. "It's a gorgeous meadow, with goldenrod and different kinds of asters, heath asters, and a lot of different kinds of grasses in it. [In late summer] when you walk through, it's hip height."

Sitting on a rail built to deter mountain bikers, I ask about Burton's philosophy. "It's to develop a woodlands in the middle of Manhattan that is as much as possible self-sufficient," he says. "We want everything to survive out here on its own." An older couple passes, arm in arm. Burton glows. "Within a year and a half," he murmurs, "people started coming who say they haven't been down here in five or ten years. The perception was [that it wasn't] safe. But we're starting to change that perception. On weekends, I've seen more and more families coming through here. It seems to bring people together democratically, which was the original intent of this park."

ON NEW YEAR'S EVE, I join 5,000 New Yorkers for a midnight costume competition and race, beginning at Tavern on the Green's light-bespangled trees, extending two-and-one-half miles to West Ninety-Fifth Street and back. It is twenty-four degrees Fahrenheit. Some runners wear tuxedos or gowns, others are costumed as 101 Dalmatians, the A train, Energizer Bunny, two Running

Noses, various Big Apples, and a Wolverine. One runner is naked but for a Santa Claus hat, his number, and sneakers. Representatives of every color, class, age, sex, and sexual proclivity are represented. At midnight fireworks explode, the race begins, and as spectators cheer beneath arcs of blue and red, it's obvious that *here* are true Manhattanites, not in Times Square.

Running in Central Park after dark is so attractive to New Yorkers that, at 9:00 p.m. on a warm spring evening in 1989, the activity's silkiness drew a woman jogger eight blocks south of Harlem, where she was attacked, it was said, by a "teen wolfpack" of perhaps fifteen youths, was raped and beaten so terribly that, when found in a coma, her skull was crushed, her left eyeball was pushed back through its socket, dirt and twigs fouled her vagina, and she'd lost 75 percent of her blood. (Later a lone rapist confessed to the crime.) Despite the Jogger's eventual celebrity—which drew more, not less donations to Central Park Conservancy—unescorted women still run at night past the spot where she fell.

Part of the park's attractiveness, day or night, is that it reminds New Yorkers of someplace else: the Poconos, Lake Placid, the Shenandoah Valley or a New England commons. This illusory quality was Olmsted's intent—to suspend disbelief in a manner crucial to romantic flights of fancy. When I run the park each afternoon, I meditate upon that last sliver of nature, still percolating beneath Manhattan sidewalks, that compelled settlers to make New York *the* city of the second half of the twentieth century. What Scott Fitzgerald called "the old island here that flowered once for Dutch sailors' eyes—a fresh, green breast of the new world."

But there's part of me that's home jogging the C&O Canal's towpath near Washington, DC, or circling the Tidal Basin when cherry trees are in blossom, or playing in the tiny park below my grandparents' building on Manhattan's East Fifty-First Street. Ultimately, in Central Park, one returns to childhood. Which may be why, as

Commissioner Stern notes, "a lot of people, if they could, would like to be *buried* in Central Park. It's the end of a cycle: when you're a baby you're taken there in a baby carriage by your parents, then as a kid you're taken sledding, then you go out with your girlfriend there, then you play tennis, then you take *your* baby out to Central Park. And when you're old you get wheeled around Central Park in a wheelchair."

QUITE A LEAP FROM the nineteenth century's contemplation of pastoral delights, when sheep grazed the Meadow and barouche carriage rides were the entertainment of choice. But professional outrageousness and native theatricality have always chipped at the park's gentility. From the first, working people preferred less fettered, commercial parks such as Jones Wood or Hoboken's Elysian Fields, where beer drinking, ball playing, militia drills, gambling, picnicking on the grass, and Coney Island-type diversions were prevalent. Central Park had too many rules; its prohibition against commerce extended to butchers or bakers who might drive their wagons on Sundays among the genteel traffic. And its acreage was removed from where poor New Yorkers lived. Populist voices such as that of the *Irish News* cried, "New York wants a place to play leap-frog in."

Olmsted included several small playgrounds and a parade field in his Greensward Plan. But as the city grew northward, Boss Tweed paid off political debts with pork barrel construction projects, and in the 1930s Commissioner Robert Moses reshaped the park with countless new paths, buildings, recreational, and commercial facilities. Today's fifteen-million annual visitors are served by two skating rinks, a gigantic swimming pool, numerous tennis courts and ball fields with backstops, formal gardens, a model boat basin, two major restaurants, rowboats for rent, a zoo, a chess and checkers house, the Delacorte Theater, a cricket green, a concert stage, a police precinct, and two museums—the

Natural History and the Metropolitan.

Which never seem enough. Conflict between recreational and romantic factions will again erupt when fate of the recently decommissioned Central Park Reservoir will be decided in 1999. One hundred and ten acres wide, it has, for a century and a half, quenched New Yorkers' thirsts while providing a staggering aquatic vista that's home to waterfowl species, huge trout, bass, bluegills, catfish and turtles. Yet some would prefer it drained for tennis courts, softball fields and horseshoe pits. Rogers notes that "We have to feed the streams in the park" with the reservoir, promising that, "It's going to be a water body for a long, long time."

Olmstedians, such as former park Curator, Henry Hope Reed, see Central Park as New York's premier work of architecture, and welcome a return to Olmsted's intentions, if not his plan. Reed advised Commissioner Thomas Hoving in 1966 that "what makes the park is the landscape, the green lawns, leafy vistas, and mirrors of water," not theatrical happenings that would "desecrate one of the finest American examples of public art." Reed's constituency, Friends of Central Park, advises Rogers in a thorn-in-the-side manner. It has criticized the Conservancy's allocation of plaques to playgrounds, statues, gardens or park benches as door prizes to those "determined philanthropists anxious to have their names embedded everlastingly in concrete." And its current director, Robert Makla, thinks asphalt paths in the Ravine "a disaster," and the Dana Discovery Center and its planned restaurant "*outrageous*," ruining the country lake atmosphere of that end of the park. "This is where Olmsted intended poor people who can't leave New York," Makla says, "to spend their two weeks' vacation in a landscape resembling the Catskills or Adirondacks."

Equally outrageous, critics claim, are events such as last October's "Woofstock," (which I attended) its canine celebrants wearing tie-dye, love beads, and bandannas, present for a march to benefit homeless animals. The movie star, Beethoven, served as Honorary Chairdog. Seventeen-hundred pet addicts congregated to greet him and fellow celebrities Matthew Broderick, Sarah Jessica Parker, and Tama Janowitz, all dog lovers. On Rumsey Playfield were paper-fetching contests, obedience trials, dog vaudeville acts, and more subcaudal sniffing than in any porn palace along Forty-Second Street. One woman brandished a sign reading, THERE IS NO SAFE SEX FOR PETS—SPAY OR NEUTER, as I heard another screech, "I wanna *wawk*, I gotta brunch date!"

The Woofstockers motivated past joggers, roller bladers, bicyclists, a race walker reading from a script, and—an Asian couple being photographed for a wedding. The bride and groom, each immaculate in white silk, stood on steps leading below ground to the Bethesda Arcade. Beneath its arches, Francis Ford Coppola shot party scenes for *New York Stories*. And here some dozen homeless live. As the wedding couple smiled, ragged men and women crouched a few feet distant on filthy sleeping pallets as a troubled fellow shrieked, "Got your foreign policy, your *deficit*," then whispered to a muraled wall, "This country, goddamn, goddamn."

Betsy Rogers admits that homelessness is "a terrible social problem that we have" within the park. "One tries to deal with it compassionately. We've spent millions of dollars restoring the Arcade. They aren't harming anything, but it's not nice to smell urine down there, and it's not a scene that makes other park users happy. On the other hand, how far do you go, and to where do you displace these people?"

That dilemma has been at the heart of the current restoration. Some 200 homeless sleep in the park during temperate months, are rousted mornings and ordered to move along. Though Rogers works with outreach groups to assist them, and employs some as laborers for a project called Cash for Trash, they won't disappear. "What you *don't* want is something like Tompkins Square Park," she exclaims, "where the whole place becomes colonized.

Because that interferes with our basic mission, which is a recreational one."

The newest recreational addition mid-park is Summer Stage, an iron-railed platform near Seventy-Second Street that Rogers admits is "my Frankenstein." She started its program as a multi-ethnic venue for local artists, but expanded to include free concerts which, last summer, included ones by Joan Baez, Jimmy Dale Gilmore, Buddy Guy, Dance Brazil, and others, plus ticketed performances by 10,000 Maniacs, the Neville Brothers, Al Jarreau and David Sanborn. Crowds frequenting these events often dismay park regulars and discombobulate the neighborhood.

"When the concerts have driven the people crazy on Fifth Avenue," Rogers admits, "I've been very sympathetic to their complaint. The stage is a nightmare, too." Critics of the program agree. "It's like the old Dr. Pepper concerts at Wollman Skating Rink," says Richard Karp, a writer living nearby. "The park wasn't meant to be commercial and it wasn't meant to be 'entertaining.' You were supposed to entertain yourself." To escape the chaos of two children in a small apartment, Karp has for the past six months been reading Gibbons' *The History of the Decline and Fall of the Roman Empire* on a bench near Inventors Gate. Living by Central Park since 1974, he's enjoyed its rusticity for thirty-odd years. "Beginning in 1979," he recalls, "my brother Walter and I, as duffers, began a scientific identification of all the park's trees. We'd hike everyplace, then visit the American Wing of the Metropolitan Museum, where Walter would say, 'The greatest work of American art isn't on these walls, its out that window—Central Park."

Karp's deepest anger is over Betsy Rogers's renovation of the Boathouse Restaurant. "It used to be you could sit there all sweaty from tennis, drink a beer and enjoy the best view in New York. Every class and race. Now it's more expensive to sit by the water, cheaper out back. The only people who can afford to sit in front are art dealers and German tourists. That doesn't go with Olmsted's egalitarian intention."

AT THREE O'CLOCK one February morning, I awake and am denied further sleep. I can hear wind rattling lamp posts outside; there's little traffic. This has been Manhattan's coldest winter in memory: two degrees below zero on January 19. A foot of ice-capped snow blankets Central Park, skiers and skaters zipping daily across it surface. I've had a rucksack packed, awaiting a thaw. Which appears distant. If I'm to explore the North Woods by night, it's now or never.

My intention has been to camp, but Dennis Burton has convinced me the restored landscape is too fragile for that. Camping is, in fact, illegal in Central Park. Nevertheless I've packed a mummy sack and air mattress; I'll meditate.

It's twelve above zero when I hit Fifth Avenue, and doormen yawn spotting a rucksacked pilgrim, they're used to us. I enter the park at Seventy-Second Street, boots skidding down the walk to Conservatory Water, then digging into snow dusting its frozen surface. Crayfish sleep in this boat basin, a chilly nest. No human is abroad. The apartments above Fifth are Delphic on the horizon. I hump to Bethesda Terrace, where revelers congregated last fall, and its esplanade is empty. But under the Arcade is a sizeable encampment: several dozen homeless in cardboard shelters or tents, huddled against the cold. I cross the Lake's surface toward Bow Bridge, pausing to admire Central Park West's darkened spires against a moonlit sky. Ducking under the bridge, pigeons flutter as I disturb their perches.

I cut to land, tracking the Ramble's walks past Olmsted's rustic shelters, where more homeless camp, through dark woods where no creature stirs. Here my uncle was attacked, but my only thought is of the landscape's beauty, its boulders capped with snow, its gently waving trees. At Belvedere Castle—a turreted structure on a cliff overlooking Turtle Pond—I disturb one camper, who grunts and turns in his blanket. I cross the Pond to a windswept Great Lawn, where I hunch my pack against the gale.

Passing the 1870 stables—now police headquarters for the park—I cross Eighty-Sixth Street to the Reservoir's cinder track, Manhattan's finest running path. Ducks huddle in the Pump House lee, and standing before this vast space, framed by Art Deco towers to the east and the garishly lit skyscrapers of midtown, is like viewing the Rockies at sunset. I cross North Meadow and the 102nd Street transverse, where the Jogger was raped, and duck toward North Woods.

I half climb, half skid to the Ravine, where all is quiet. The Loch is frozen to invisibility, but remnants of footprints show me a path. I hike southwest to Glenspan Arch, backtrack to Huddlestone, then move north through the forest to Block House #1. There is wind and the rattling of tree limbs, but no other sound. Santeria is practiced here, and the carcasses of sacrificial animals are periodically discovered. In the early sixties, a human torso was found in the park—with no arms, legs or head. I remember Ed Abbey's comment that, "Wilderness is and should be a place where, as in Central Park, New York City, you have a fair chance of being mugged and buggered by a shaggy fellow in a fur coat—" The Block House's great stones, atop the park's highest point, protrude from the ice like a glacially born hillock. From here, Harlem and the Bronx stretch toward Long Island Sound. Headlights dart along Malcolm X Boulevard, but they're all that move.

Backtracking, I spook an owl who rattles a branch then glides off eerily. Raccoons inhabit this forest, and though I detect scampering, no doubt they are nesting. Escaped parrots live here, and I recall a story my uncle wrote for me, about a canary named Henry who flees his cage to become lost in Central Park. I cross the Loch's marsh and unsling my pack at Dennis Burton's meadow. Whose snow is pearly in the moonlight.

I lay my gear on ice where no foliage will be harmed, then ease into my bag. A light snow is falling. I think of All Angel's Church—its earliest structure razed to build the park—which has an outreach program teaching homeless to make their own sleepsacks. I ball my parka to a pillow, then lie back to contemplate the sky.

I'm awakened by sunlight. It's 7:30. The meadow is powdered with fresh snow. A squirrel scolds me from an overhanging branch, and rabbit tracks encircle my bag. Sparrows chatter, and as I sit up I catch a scarlet flash in the bushes—a cardinal. I scrunch back against a tree and study the brush. A blue jay dips, trailed by the russet whir of a female cardinal. One week later, the first warm day will drench the park in sunlight. Musicians will pack Bethesda Terrace, and crowds will be so thick on East and West Drives it will be difficult to walk. I'll be challenged twice by street kids, and jogging past the Meer, will watch two youths goad leashed pit bulls to fight.

But now I sit alone with the forest. A magnificent respite. Forty-five minutes later I pack my gear, then grudgingly rejoin the city.

Outside, 1994

Loyalties:
Carl Bernstein

The blue vinyl gloves Prince affects at Nell's to offset his red, purple, and yellow jester's suit are tough to accept, and Carl Bernstein keeps stealing looks into the next booth to make certain he's seen them. Prince's tiny hands, swathed in blue, flutter above his plate as Nell Campbell chats intently and the club's bodyguards fend off well-wishers. Bernstein is no starer. But despite his own banquette here, he's compelled to peek. It's his reportorial eye that won't let him rest—not when celebrity minutiae like blue vinyl gloves are there for the cataloguing.

Bernstein himself has discouraged well-wishers tonight, but momentarily is accepting compliments from a young staffer of the Republican National Committee, who converses adamantly with him about 1988's politics. It is nearly election eve. Close by, Manhattan literati such as Bret Easton Ellis, Morgan Entrekin, and Tama Janowitz socialize amid the lush Victoriana and tepid jazz that is Nell's.

"Ronald Reagan is a *leader*," Bernstein intones. "However awful his policies are, you get a sense of somebody who's willing to fight for what he believes in...."

The young staffer nods, smiling. Politics is an eccentric topic for Nell's, and Bernstein is an oddly-turned out pundit. In black T-shirt, black suit, and gray cowboy boots—his silver hair styled like an aging rocker's—he looks more like Don Everly than David Broder. At forty-five, Bernstein owns a feline grace that belies a pug-dog countenance. His wide shoulders roll with each declamation, his deep chest heaves as one arm snakes across the banquette's top, fingers tapping, and an expensively-shod foot scoots across its seat.

Prince's blue-vinyl gloves are a flurry. Glancing over, Bernstein declaims, "what interests me about Dukakis is his unwillingness to say what he *believes* in. Instead of getting up, when Bush accuses him of belonging to the ACLU, and saying, 'yeah, I belong to the ACLU, I'm *proud* to belong to it,' he lies down. When a presidential candidate can't say what he believes in, that's bothersome."

Not saying what one believes in, nor enjoying the right, is a principal theme of *Loyalties*—the book he's wrestled with for a decade, has just completed, and will deliver to Simon & Schuster tomorrow. It concerns the Truman Loyalty Order, and his parents having taken the Fifth before Congress during the McCarthyite frenzy of the late forties and early fifties. It's a book very much about Washington, where Carl was born, and about who he is: The "real" Carl, not the philanderer of *Heartburn*, the café socialite, or lover of glamorous women. As autobiography, it sheds light on these personae; but its intentions are writerly, and by its pages Bernstein emerges from the fog of celebrity that's obscured him since Watergate as a serious and thoughtful writer.

"The press is the most powerful institution in this society," Bernstein declares above the music. "And the wonderful thing about being able to write," he adds, "is that you get to *say* what it is you think."

HAVING ONE'S SAY is not always pleasant. Six months earlier, on Easter morning, Bernstein is double-checking locales for *Loyalties*, by scouting childhood haunts in Washington. He motors north on Wisconsin Avenue, to that end. Last night he's camped at Bob Woodward's in Georgetown; at this moment his younger son, Max, aged ten, is hunting Easter eggs with Sally Quinn's and Ben Bradlee's son at the Bradlee mansion on N Street. Bernstein is in Washington to "negotiate paragraphs" of *Loyalties* with his parents (he's changed its title from *Disloyal*, at their request), and soon will show them a draft. It's an unsettling time. They are less than happy about the book's publication. "It's a question of acceptance," Bernstein explains. "Certainly there are going to be a lot of people who'll be accusatory about their lives."

Though *Loyalties* is, on balance, a loving portrait of Al and Sylvia Bernstein—radical parents of the 1950s standing up for their beliefs—its pages are laden with Carl's angry reminiscence: of "the chaos that ruled our house," and "the inability of my mother to get a grip on running the household and what seemed like the accompanying abdication of parenthood by my father."

Bernstein adds, "There was some chaos around that place. My father couldn't earn a living at what he wanted to do, and my mother was all over the newspapers for taking the Fifth Amendment."

Al Bernstein was a Columbia Law School graduate and New Yorker who'd migrated to Washington during the New Deal. He'd been a Senate investigator, had worked briefly for OPA, then allied with the United Public Workers union, to organize federal employees. When Harry Truman's Loyalty Order was issued in 1947, requiring all government workers to sign loyalty oaths, he defended more than 700 politically-suspect employees. He won 90 percent of his cases. When James Eastland's Internal Security Committee convened in 1951 to investigate Communist-affiliated unions, they targeted UPW and its lawyer, Al Bernstein. During World War II,

Bernstein had joined the Communist Party. He appeared before Eastland's committee and rather than testify, pleaded the Fifth. The CIO already had dismissed UPW from its ranks as too far left, and Al Bernstein was minus a job. Publicity rendered him unemployable, and until the mid-fifties he supported his family by running a laundry in a black neighborhood near Howard University. Sylvia Bernstein was no less radical. Or "progressive," as the Bernsteins preferred. "It is my mother who...always seemed to me the more militant, the more active," the book states. She'd joined the Communist Party, was a linchpin of the desegregation movement in Washington (Carl, age seven, sat in regularly with black children at segregated lunch counters), a consumer-rights advocate, and co-organizer of the Washington Committee to Secure Justice for Julius and Ethel Rosenberg. The similarity of the Rosenbergs' predicament to his parents' was not lost on Carl: "The Rosenbergs, too, were progressive people— and they were going to die for it; they were going to fry." He spent the afternoon of their execution demonstrating before the White House with his mother, and at news of the Rosenbergs' deaths, became hysterical: "I shook and cried uncontrollably that night, can still summon the terror—and the fury at my mother for risking her life...I thought she was going to die."

The house where the Bernsteins lived stands at 4230 Chesapeake Street, in a Northwest neighborhood called Tenleytown. It is the same semi-detached, white stucco shoebox Carl remembers from his childhood. "Look, there's our base path," he says, pointing to the lawn. "I can't believe it's still there." Tenleytown had been a working class quarter, "Catholic and nearly hillbilly." A friend's dad taught Carl bluegrass guitar, another's uncle, head of the Washington numbers racket, piqued his curiosity about gambling. Carl's parents held regular poker games, and Al Bernstein was a winner. Carl's moniker became Chips, for the markers he loved to fondle. "I felt very secure here," Carl says, beaming.

But security vanished, the morning after Sylvia Bernstein's testimony before HUAC, with her photograph as front page news in all three Washington papers, including the *Post*. RED PARTY "HARD CORE" IN CAPITAL, VELDE SAYS, was the latter's headline. "*The suggestion of espionage hung over the story like the asphyxiating cloud of the epoch itself.*" Ben Gilbert, *Post* city-editor, was a neighbor of the Bernsteins. His children were Carl's friends. They and other kids, according to Carl, shunned him and his sister Mary after the publicity (though Gilbert denies this). His mother's friends and cousins turned their backs. It was a shattering moment. For Carl, age ten, the Gilberts' abdication was most painful: "Because my best friends really were the Gilbert children. And I knew that the Gilbert kids were out of my life. Forever."

Tenleytown's blue-collar folk stayed loyal, a steadfastness Carl would remember: "I loved that neighborhood and the kids in it and our city, which was defined not by the symbols of the national capital but by the places our bikes took us." This dichotomy—of real city versus federal, of us versus them—became for him a nagging thorn.

Carl's maternal grandparents, the Thomas Walkers (formerly Walkowitz), ran a dry cleaning and tailor's shop in the basement of a middleclass apartment building in Adams Morgan. The shop was the Argonne Valet. Walking toward it now, in James Dean windbreaker, jeans, and ocher cat shoes—a phantom from the fifties— Bernstein speaks of his grandparents' family as "poor and political—radicals." They were Russian Jews in a southern city, inhospitable to immigrants: "But my Washington isn't about Capitol Hill or the federal buildings," he says, "it's about neighborhoods like this...a kind of servants' quarters for people who come in every four years. My grandfather did their pants. My grandmother sewed their buttons on."

Carl was closest to his grandfather: "He loved books and music and whiskey, he was "carefree, charming, warm, impetuous." He kept a cache of French postcards in his drawer, and took Carl on cleaning errands. One day, when he was three, they strode past the iron grillwork and marble columns of the Ontario Apartments' lobby, and rode to the sixth floor. The Ontario was Adams Morgan's grandest residence. They made delivery at Judge Henry W. Edgerton's—number 605. Carl forgot neither the experience nor the apartment. In 1973, his pockets swollen with Watergate cash, he bought it. He lived there, alone or with Nora Ephron, for a decade.

The Argonne, now Park Plaza apartments, stands at 1629 Columbia Road; approaching it Bernstein looks apprehensive. "I describe the shop as maybe fifteen-by-fifteen feet, with overhead pipes, but I want to make sure."

The basement valet is an Asian grocery, loud with rock music and bartering. Bernstein is all swagger. "Over there was the steam press, which my grandfather worked. And in that corner was my grandmother's sewing machine." To the proprietor, he barks, "How long have you had it? Was it a cleaner's then?" Every gaze is on this blustery presence.

Outside, he starts to speak, then chokes. Tears dampen his cheeks. "In all the years I lived in Adams Morgan," he whispers, "I never walked back in there." He rubs his eyes. "I really loved my grandfather."

BERNSTEIN LOVES CELEBRITY, of that there's no doubt. Since Watergate, he notes, "I haven't had a dozen people say anything nasty to me. It makes you feel good when somebody comes up and says, 'That's a terrific thing you did.'" Tonight, at SoHo's chic Canal Bar, any number of folks have paused to greet him: Barry Goldwater's granddaughter Ceci, *Fame's* publisher Steven Greenberg, the Hotel Royalton's Steve Rubell and Ian Schrager, Indochine's and Canal Bar's Brian McNally—saluting him with a smacker of a kiss—and various stunning women. Bernstein's rep as a journalistic Warren Beatty precedes him. Having escorted, in his day, Bianca Jagger,

Betty Thomas, Frances Fitzgerald, Kathleen Tynan, Elizabeth Taylor, and—not to forget—Nora Ephron, he's comfortable stag in a Canal front booth, merely studying the crush about him.

Saloon society is a milieu Bernstein discovered young— at the Washington *Star*. It can be said his adulthood began when, as a sixteen-year-old copy boy, he strode into that paper's city room. *New York Times'* assistant managing-editor, Warren Hoge, who apprenticed with Bernstein at the *Star*, recalls, "It was a place where, as Evelyn Waugh wrote in *Scoop*, 'neurotic men in shirtsleeves and eyeshades rush from telephone to tape machine, insulting and betraying one other in surroundings of unredeemed squalor.'" After work at Harrigan's, the *Star's* saloon, Bernstein learned to hail bartenders by name and quaff martinis with older reporters. He was precociously adept at café socializing.

"When I see Carl work Elaine's," says Hoge, still a close friend, "it's like Carl working Harrigan's twenty-five years ago."

Bernstein adds, "I've always been attracted to action. I like to see what's really happening. That's why you become a journalist. It's a kind of vicarious participation."

During grade school, he'd kibitzed with announcers at WMAL radio each morning, and afternoons played guitar on television's *Pick Temple Show*. At Montgomery Blair high school, he danced two days a week for Washington's spinoff of *American Bandstand*. He had so much action, from shooting pool to politics, that he was suspended, in debt for gambling, and arrested twice—for drag racing, and for smashing the windows of a local anti-Semite. His only constructive activities at Montgomery Blair were as Aleph Zadik Aleph chapter-president, and editor of its chapter newspaper. He barely graduated.

Al Bernstein knew a columnist at the *Star*, so in the spring of 1960, he wrangled Carl a job: "It was unthinkable that I would go to the *Post*: Ben Gilbert was still the city editor, and Jerry Klutz, who wrote the

Federal Diary column, had treated the union—and my father—with disdain." Carl recalled his father saying, of journalism and Truman's Loyalty Order, that "someday he'd try a book on the subject" and suggested "we do it together...."

The Bernsteins had emigrated from Chesapeake Street to Silver Spring, where they were political and economic outsiders. Their new block was Jewish, but financially it was middle to upper-middle class. And decidedly conservative. "Since moving," Bernstein would write, "I had clutched at almost anything to win acceptance, to regain the security of Chesapeake Street." That security would return in the Runyonesque world of journalism.

From the first, Carl loved the *Star*. He remembers confronting its massive city room—with ticker tapes and typewriters clattering, police radios barking, reporters shouting "copy" and bustling to produce five editions a day—as "one of the indelible moments of my life." The *Star* had "a sense of energy, of people doing important things. It was about something *real*. I didn't think school was about anything real. And there was a camaraderie... not to speak of the delight we took in beating the *Washington Post*. That's what we *really* loved to do, kick the shit out of the *Post*."

The buffer between Washington's servant class and its government was the Fourth Estate. But, Al Bernstein reminded him, the real damage to Carl's mother had been through "the role of the press—her picture in the paper." So Carl took his ambivalence at joining the press's ranks and fueled his anger at the *Post*—by reveling in the *Star*.

It was the prestige paper in Washington, had been for eighty years. But it was losing ground to the *Post*, the city's liberal upstart. The *Star* was Washington's establishment paper, conservative and Republican. Bernstein kept his radical pedigree quiet. "The *Star* was the mouthpiece for the FBI. They would always be over there peddling shit, really nasty stuff." As his family was under surveillance, and would remain so for thirty-five years (the FBI attended Carl's Bar Mitzvah) this presented a conflict. "I had trouble with it." Despite its conservatism, the *Star* drew bright young staffers like David Broder, Mary McGrory, Haynes Johnson, Lance Morrow, Ben Forgey, Warren Hoge, and had the city's best Supreme Court and Capitol Hill reporters.

Carl found a second family at the *Star*. "Clearly there are a lot of feelings I had as a child that made me feel separate, or different, or apart from other kids. The minute I went to work at the *Star*, I had great friends. We were really close. It was probably the happiest period of my life. And the most wonderful way to grow up."

Bernstein, in 1960, was a five-foot-four inch copy boy with a flattop haircut and Howdy Doody smile, with which he charmed senior editors. By 1964, when Hoge met him, "he was already a persona in that newsroom. He was incredibly savvy for a young guy...rambunctious and something of a prankster. He *loved* the newsroom. He fit into it wonderfully, and he conquered it at a very tender age. That seemed to be a destiny he found earlier than most people find their destiny."

Bernstein's free time was spent strumming guitar at parties, or chasing the tide of young women that flooded Washington during Camelot and the Great Society. "I screwed around a *lot* in my twenties." He and Hoge, dressed in secondhand tuxes, crashed many an embassy party "living off pigs in blankets," Bernstein remembers. "We were only making $44 a week."

But the corridors of power were seductive. "Unfortunately," Hoge says, "journalists learn a taste that they can't afford. In Washington we were surrounded by power and money, but we had neither."

Hoge believes there may have been "a part of Carl that was upwardly mobile—to the extent that he navigated the newsroom of the Washington *Star* extraordinarily well for an extremely young guy. He could work a room wonderfully well. The talent was there. But the opportunity was to come later on."

Bernstein tonight is upbeat about his fame. And protective. "I think people who sit around pissing and moaning about celebrity—if it comes from something you've achieved in your work—and go around punching photographers and getting nasty and sassy, are appalling."

He pauses in his superstar booth to eye a clutch of leggy women. "It's a good place to look at the customers." He chuckles. "I'm sitting here giving speeches and the world's going by."

ONE EVENING IN 1985, *Time* senior writer John Leo—an organizer of Sag Harbor's writers' and artists' softball game—was addressing the team's annual roast, when he segued into an elaborate routine about members' contributions to the state of New Jersey. Holding up its Great Seal, and alluding to Bernstein's dalliance with Liz Taylor, he announced the New Jersey Award for 1985 would go to Carl, "for spending the most amount of time in Elizabeth."

Leo says his quip "was an accidental double entendre. It turned out Carl actually had spent a year working for the *Daily Journal* in Elizabeth."

Bernstein had followed a favorite editor there in 1965, when bosses at the *Star* refused to hire him full time. *Star* policy required staff reporters to have college degrees. He'd been attending classes at Maryland, but the academic life was not for him. "When I saw Elizabeth, New Jersey," he says, taxiing through late-night New York, "I knew I couldn't stand to work *and* live there. So I found a place in the Village." It was an apartment shared with two stewardesses—demographics insuring some memorable evenings. That year offered Bernstein his first bite of the Apple, and he relished it. He performed well at the *Journal*, winning three AP awards for best feature writing, best investigative reporting, and best news story on deadline. But his cockiness earned him a nickname: "The Rotten Kid."

He was cocky enough to again try Washington. The *Post*

had hired Ben Bradlee as managing editor. "Bradlee had an idea for a metropolitan newspaper that took reporting and newspapering into the next generation," Bernstein says. Bradlee despised ideology in newspapering, as he did "spin," or subjective reporting. That was fine with Bernstein; ideology had ruined his parents, and "spin" had cost him his friends.

The *Post* had a job open, but it also had Ben Gilbert, then deputy managing editor. Gilbert wanted an interview. He inquired after Bernstein's parents—they were fine, his father worked now as a fundraiser for the National Conference of Christians and Jews, his mother as a salesclerk at Garfinckle's. Then Gilbert asked, "Are you political?" Carl answered, "Ben—the only two organizations I've ever belonged to are B'nai B'rith youth and the Newspaper Guild." He stalked out, feeling "rage and disgust," but joined the *Post* in October of 1966.

He knew the city, and was perfect for the Metro desk. Young Ivy Leaguers were trickling to newspapers, hoping to make a difference, but few were trained as Bernstein had been. He'd done everything at the *Star* from attending Jack Kennedy's press conferences as a copy boy, to working the rewrite desk as night editor and dictationist. He'd done police and court reporting, and he'd written features. His first reportorial byline had been at eighteen, on "an obit about an old lady who fed pigeons at Eleventh and Pennsylvania. She had a newsstand. I went down and got a lot of quotes from people. Haynes Johnson put it on page one."

The *Post* wasn't as Runyonesque as the *Star*, and Bernstein did not fit in. He was arrogant and cantankerous, suffered debilitating migraines, was the office deadbeat, failed to respect his editors, and was otherwise difficult. "I *am* difficult, I thought I was better than other people." Covering the District Building, he was caught sleeping in its press shack; covering Virginia, he rented a car and forgot it in a parking garage for two months—until Hertz reminded. He was terrible about money, his and the

Post's. Managing Editor Howard Simons complained that "Bernstein just spent more money covering Virginia than Murrey Marder did covering the Paris peace talks." He wore his hair long, dressing in fatigue jackets and combat boots. He raged against *Post* hierarchy in guild meetings. Bradlee wanted to fire him. As David Halberstam wrote, in *The Powers That Be*, "Bradlee could never make up his mind whether Bernstein was a winner or a loser. A winner determined to be a loser, most probably."

His favorite assignments were discursive pieces about the city that only a reporter who'd been raised in Washington might imagine. More often than not they held a personal resonance. He did not wish to write yet of his childhood, but "I always wanted to cover things associated—civil rights, the antiwar movement, and Vietnam." The local pieces were closest to home. He did a split-page feature on Eighteenth Street, where his mother was born. And one on Southern Maryland's "Wesorts": triracial isolates—part American Indian, part white, and part black—named "from the expression, 'We sorts of people are different from you sorts.'" Bernstein's sort, a clan of far-left radicals, was different from most *Post* reporters', and it ate at him.

The first line of *Loyalties* quotes Nora Ephron saying, "At some point you're going to confront your feelings." Bernstein then reflects, "I'm not sure that she comprehends the depth of pain and anger and rage." At the *Post* he raged indirectly at his childhood, but did not acknowledge other feelings. "Part of my security for many years has been not to look at myself," he says. "I'm sure one of the reasons I've always found journalism so appealing is that it doesn't require commitment, and it doesn't require introspection." He wrote about other people's lives, creatively and well, in a genre that did not require sustained attention. As *Post* national editor, Bob Kaiser (a person Bernstein says "knows me the best") remarks: "the thing about journalism that was so appealing to Carl was the instant gratification...you could honestly say to yourself, and have people say to you, 'this sort of passes for something literary...this is really creative.' And yet you woke up yesterday morning and you didn't know it was going to happen, and by seven o'clock at night it was done."

Other pastimes that deflected negative feelings were the pursuit of women and drinking. The former he had an insatiable capacity for, the latter none at all. "*Some loose gene there that brings out the worst tendencies of us Walker-Bernsteins.*" He'd tried marriage—to *Post* reporter Carol Honsa—but that lasted about a year. "They didn't seem to be on the same wavelength," columnist Richard Cohen remembers. "If Carl got five dollars he'd spend six, if Carol got five dollars she'd save six." He was seeking stability, and as his best-man, Bob Kaiser, observes: "Carol was very important in helping him to grow up some. Teaching him that he really did have to keep a checkbook, and meet certain other very minimal, basic adult requirements." But on his wedding day, Bernstein had turned in panic to Warren Hoge and begged, "Get me out of here." Kaiser led him to the Old Stein Grill and convinced him not to bolt.

His tension was interior, but it was directed outward, at the *Post*. He wanted Vietnam; they wouldn't send him. He wanted the national desk; they wouldn't transfer him. He wanted to be rock critic; they assigned another writer, William C. Woods. He wanted Hunter Thompson's job as political reporter for *Rolling Stone*; Jann Wenner wouldn't hire him. "'What a creep, what an arrogant asshole,'" Wenner recalls his interviewer reporting. He was burning bridges, and the *Post* was fed up.

"Before I went to Moscow in 1971," Kaiser remembers, "I had a conversation with [Metro editor] Harry Rosenfeld telling him not to fire Carl. His essential irresponsibility—and irresponsibility is an important part of his character, his unwillingness to accept responsibility, to be burdened by conventional responsibility—did always get him into trouble here." But Kaiser felt Carl worth salvaging.

THEN WATERGATE. It has been said authors compose but one book during their careers, the book of their own lives. For Bernstein, and perhaps Bob Woodward, the stories they wrote (two-hundred-and-twenty-five from June 17, 1972, the break-in, to August 9, 1974, Nixon's resignation) and *All the President's Men* comprised a first chapter in that saga. They were the courtship to a marriage that's lasted. Their friendship "*is* like a good marriage," Bernstein says. "It's about as wonderful a relationship as you get to have in this life. We're always there for each other."

They were opposites who attracted. Bernstein, as Woodward wrote, "looked like one of those counterculture journalists that [he] despised." And Woodward, as Bernstein sniped, was "a prima donna who played heavily at office politics. Yale...Lawns, greensward, staterooms and grass tennis courts." They were, J. Anthony Lukas observed later, "a kind of journalistic centaur with an aristocratic Republican head and runty Jewish hindquarters."

For Bernstein, the Watergate break-in was from the first, riveting. It was a black-bag job, involving anti-Communists and an ex-CIA agent, a violation of civil rights like those his parents had long decried. The initial break-in was shocking, but that of Daniel Ellsberg's psychiatrist's office was "*the* most stunning moment for me in Watergate." He'd been reading news wires, when one reported that the case against Daniel Ellsberg had been dismissed, because Watergate plumbers had burglarized his doctor's office and bugged an NSC staffer's phone upon which Ellsberg spoke. "I was disbelieving," Bernstein says. "I came running up to the front of the newsroom saying, 'can you *believe* this? Look at this!' I was astounded. And yet this was indeed what people around my parents had been saying for years about what the FBI was doing...."

They worked it as a police story, following leads and grilling sources as Bernstein had at the *Star*. Woodward had not yet earned Ben Bradlee's accolade as "the best reporter I've ever seen, period." He was quite green. "Carl, in a sense, taught me journalism," he says. "I had less than two years' experience when we started working together on Watergate, and how much did he have? I think he started typing in the crib."

Bernstein got to Woodward personally. He circumvented the fabled "block of ice" in Woodward's gut, and helped to melt it. "The extent to which I've learned to try to be a better friend to people, I've largely learned from Carl," he says. "I remember there'd been some copy aid I'd brushed off, or been rude to, and Carl really kind of grabbed me by the ear and said, 'You can't treat people like that, no matter who they are.' It was direct and unequivocal… obviously he'd been there, he'd *been* a copy aid."

The two immediately gauged their working strengths: Woodward's was persistence and order, Bernstein's creative analysis. Yet they switched roles, shouting, arguing, driving each other harder. Bernstein proved more orderly than his reputation suggested. Woodward remembers "leaving on a Friday night and Carl said 'I'm going to stay here a while.' I came in on Saturday morning and he had stayed up the whole night rewriting the story on that six-ply with red borders we used to have, and he had each page of it laid out on a couple of desks. He had this obsession about having the first couple of paragraphs typed perfectly—not only did they have to read perfectly, they had to be typed perfectly—without a mark on them, or a correction, or an overstroke."

They reported Watergate as a hometown-Washington story, minus the "spin" that pack journalists employed to shield sources with whom they were chummy. As early as September, 1972, it was clear to both reporters where the trail led. Bernstein whispered, "You know, Nixon is going to get impeached." Woodward said, "I think you're right, but neither you nor I can tell anybody we have any inkling of what we're looking for."

To Bernstein, this was more than a political story, it

was Washington City (himself and his family as servant class) versus the government. Nixon was never targeted for revenge—"it's not the kind of person I am...I don't believe in that shit"—but the irony of his fall as both president and mythic Communist-baiter was not lost on him. Nor on his family.

Years later Bob Kaiser and Dick Cohen attended Bernstein's Grandmother-Walker's funeral, where he spoke. Kaiser recalls that "Carl moved everyone," because "he was such an important symbol. Here was this nutty family, full of Communists and other left-wing crusaders of various hopeless kinds, on the outs in American life for years...but here was their progeny who had slain one of the great devil-figures of the twentieth century. Nothing had turned out quite right for them, except this."

Watergate turned out far better than Bernstein had ever imagined. A Pulitzer was awarded for his and Woodward's reporting (not to them, but to the *Post*—another source of resentment), they signed a hardcover contract for *All the President's Men* for $60,000, auctioning the paperback rights for an unprecedented $1,050,000. *President's* would sell 600,000 copies in hardcover, over a million in paper. *The Final Days*, published in 1976, would sell 900,000 in hardcover, over a million in paper, becoming the fastest-selling nonfiction book in history. Dustin Hoffman would play Bernstein, opposite Redford's Woodward, in the film of *President's*—catapulting both reporters to superstardom. Bernstein metamorphosed from a fatigue-jacketed denizen of the *Post's* newsroom, to a swashbuckling celebrity commanding suites at the Carlyle and St. Regis. His success flabbergasted him. "I never thought you could make any money in this business," he says. The $60,000 advance for *President's* was "an unbelievable sum...It was two-and-a-half times as much as we were making at the *Post*—combined."

Success was culture shock. Overnight he went from "a real nobody in every sense of the word," Kaiser remembers, "whose only way to make the impression on people that he loves to make was by words—spoken or written," to a national hero: The paradigm of a counterculture journalist, alerting America to what its Left had long known...that government was corrupt, and could be more foe than friend.

It was a staggering revelation—one Americans had avoided for decades—which prompted numerous investigations into government misconduct, and served as much as any one factor to color the seventies in desolate shades. But it was a bright moment for Carl Bernstein. As he said to colleague William C. Woods, "It's been a hard year for the country, but I've had a hell of a good time." He and Woodward were the white knights of investigative reporting, private eyes of the new nonfiction. Journalism schools swelled with aspiring investigators. Bernstein hit the lecture trail (commanding $5,000 a speech), proselytizing mightily for his tribe of journalistic Wesorts.

Suddenly women were chasing *him*. And they weren't interested in his reporting. One admirer, post-coitally, telephoned a friend and said, "Guess what—I just fucked my second Pulitzer Prize winner."

Enter Nora Ephron. They met in 1973 at a party thrown by Marie Brenner, herself an ex-Bernstein lover, and were married in 1976. Theirs was a meeting "ripe with promise," Brenner recalls. Ephron had recently divorced Dan Greenburg, was edgy and insecure about having children, and here was Bernstein—a bachelor hero of Watergate. He was a writer, he was Jewish, they shared current-celebrity, and a childhood oddly-shaped by the media.

She'd grown up wealthy in Beverly Hills; her parents were playwrights and scenarists. They'd written two plays about her, *Three's A Family*, at her birth, and *Take Her She's Mine*, during her years at Wellesley...quoting directly from her letters. Bernstein claims "she never got over that," but assessing her penchant for celebrity, thinks it might have been because the plays didn't make her celebrated enough. Ephron, as a writer, mined her life as an unabashed mother lode. Her column for *Esquire* and a book, *Crazy Salad*, advertised that fact. She'd warned Bernstein, "Everything in your life is material." It's surprising she waited ten years to cash in.

Their time together would prove tumultuous. After *The Final Days* (a curiously-empathetic view of Nixon, presaging Bernstein's portrait of his father in *Loyalties*) he tired of government reporting and resigned from the *Post*. Woodward wanted to write about the Supreme Court, Bernstein a major corporation, and they weren't getting along. "He was leaving the paper," Woodward says, "he was drawn to New York and Nora Ephron, and I did not agree with that. I didn't think that was good for him." Woodward felt "Nora's pretenses for him on all kinds of levels, literary, social, and so forth, didn't fit the person. I saw somebody who was one of the best reporters and writers I'd ever encountered, and he was essentially uprooting himself from that."

Bernstein and Ephron, as the Nick and Nora Charles of literary journalism, were splattered across America's gossip columns. They shuttled between parties in Manhattan and Washington (he enlarged Judge Edgerton's apartment for her), until "we both came to believe a little too much of what we were reading in the papers about the marriage," Bernstein remarks. "We had come to expect that it had to be storybook perfect...."

Kaiser says that he and Woodward "both resisted becoming totally charmed by Nora. And she by us. Nora's affection for Carl, I felt, was based on a total misperception on who and what he was. She had an idealized image of the guy she wanted to marry, and forced Carl into it. And it had nothing to do with my Carl."

But as Ephron later wrote: "I married him against all the evidence...and in so doing became the kind of romantic only a cynic is truly capable of being."

Bernstein's attraction to her was upwardly motivated, Kaiser theorizes, and had "a lot to do with the glamour of her life and his new celebrity status. That whole thing was incredibly important—to become a celebrity was just an enormous accomplishment for Carl, and still is." Woodward characterizes Bernstein's infatuation with Ephron more succinctly: "She knew the right lettuce and she knew the right shoes."

Woodward had lost Bernstein. It was like McCartney losing Lennon. Watergate had married them in history, their relationship was so complex...as Bernstein explains, "Any two, strong-willed people who are going through a lot together, and the closer the relationship is, the more subject it is to anger or to hurt—because there is that element of love."

The facts of his childhood as a red-diaper baby nagged. He'd begun confiding in people—first to Hoge, Cohen and Kaiser, then to Woodward, then Bradlee—until by 1972, when Marie Brenner met him, "within two days, he told me that whole story—this was the essential fact of his life."

His work circled about that subject, without hitting it directly. "I was sort of desperately looking for something to do," he remembers. He wrote a 12,000 word article for *Rolling Stone*, about the CIA's recruitment of journalists during the cold war, that moved him a little closer to home. (Wenner paid him $30,000 dollars for it.) But his subconscious energy was already focused on *Loyalties*.

Then, "Nora said, 'What about what happened with your parents, you're always talking about it?' It seemed like a really good idea, for about six weeks. I hated it almost from the beginning." He spent the next year and a half interviewing his parents, their friends, people in the Party, other red-diaper babies, and political advisers from the Truman era. "Reliving it was just not a lot of fun. Most people spend their lives avoiding subjects which are painful or have been traumatic. Here I'd left what I'd done all my life, and then for a year and a half I was doing nothing but looking at my past in the face. It was very unsettling."

He started to write after a year of reporting, and did "what's about the first thirty or forty pages of the book, and then the Rosenberg section. I hated doing it. I hated working on it. I hated the feelings that it brought up." He laid the manuscript aside, went into psychotherapy. "Some of it was maybe too painful...this is very much a book about fathers and sons...and I wasn't a father yet."

He and Ephron had bought "Trees," a $250,000 nineteenth-century, country house in Bridgehampton, with a cottage out back they'd refurbished for Carl to use as an office. There he sat, blocked. "It didn't make any sense to me that I was blocked." But, "my marriage was falling apart. Really what I wanted was to be back at work in journalism. I missed it. I'd spent every day of my life from when I was sixteen going to work at a newspaper. Now here I was off in Bridgehampton, walking around like some kind of literary landed-gentry, and I *hated* it."

The magnitude of *Loyalties* had sunk in. His parents were not happy with the book under any circumstances, and adamant that he skirt the Communist Party issue. "There was no way I was willing to do that," he says. "To tell this story honestly I have to say what I've said." But he bore tremendous guilt, coming to wonder if he weren't a "son loose in the land as witch hunter in lamb's disguise," and in darker moments, whether "this book isn't the equivalent of [my father's] politics, if the whole subject isn't some terrible poison, some family toxin that eats away your piece of mind—and sends your life off the tracks."

It would assist in derailing his life. In Washington, he inaugurated a highly-public affair with Margaret Jay, daughter of the British Prime Minister, James Callaghan, and wife of the British ambassador, Peter Jay—the one act certain to shatter concentration on his book, giving Ephron the opportunity to expose him as he'd wished to expose his parents. From the publicity, he would become, like Al Bernstein—"a man who wanted more than anything to participate in the events of his day," and who "by the age of forty, found himself excluded"—blackballed and trivialized.

Heartburn, published in 1983, was the comic roman à clef that Bernstein describes as "absolutely the perfect book for the eighties. It is prurient, it obliterates everybody's dignity, even the dignity that children ought to have by having a private childhood." (Bernstein and Ephron will not speak on the record about their marriage; he stands by his 1986 *Playboy* interview—a curious platform for a man Ephron characterized as "a piece of work in the sack...capable of having sex with a Venetian blind.") *Heartburn* starred a faithless husband (Carl) who betrayed his wife (Nora), seven months pregnant with their second child (Max), for a Washington woman (Margaret Jay). It became, as Bernstein dubbed it "our national soap opera."

Bernstein readily admits that "the breakup of my marriage is a consequence of my actions," but vilifies *Heartburn* as an inexcusable violation of privacy, most damaging to the couple's children. Theirs had been matrimony lived in public. "First the marriage was announced in a gossip column," Bernstein told *Playboy*. "Then Nora's way of ending the marriage...was to go to a gossip columnist, Liz Smith in this case, and say, 'The marriage is over; here's why.' And then the purported story of the marriage and its disintegration becomes a book...." Details of their divorce agreement were published in *Harper's*. The public eagerly awaited a movie version of the soap opera that had been Ephron's bestseller.

Heartburn was, in some ways, the least-vitriolic criticism Bernstein would receive during the eighties. The bloom was off the rose for investigative journalism—in fact, the press. He became the court fool of gossip columnists and moralists alike, his social life vilified, and the downtime necessary to produce *Loyalties* endlessly contrasted with Woodward's prodigious output. Woodward himself would take knocks for *Wired: The Short Life & Fast Times of John Belushi*, for *Post* reporter Janet Cooke's returned Pulitzer, lost on his shift as Metro editor, and for *Veil: The Secret Wars of the CIA, 1981-1987*. The press had turned against its bearers of bad news, as had the public.

The question arose as to whether Woodward's depiction of Belushi's downward spiral, in *Wired*, was not a subconscious portrait of Bernstein. "No," Woodward says, but "the issue of instant success and how you deal with it is something I related to both of us—there are some parallels."

In the midst of this, Bernstein retreated to daily journalism. "I wanted to get back to what was familiar and comfortable," he says, "back to that experience of the *Star*." He'd been set to return to the *Post* as an editor, but part of him didn't want to get back into competition with Woodward (both ultimately wanted Bradlee's job), as they were patching up their relationship. At a party in Sagaponik, he asked Roone Arledge if he might try some television pieces for ABC, and was offered a job as Washington bureau chief. "I was greatly relieved at this, because I really didn't want to go back to the *Washington Post*. I thought, you know, be an editor in television... learn something new, take a chance." He'd put the book aside, "but I always knew I'd go back to it." He lasted fourteen months as bureau chief, and was a disaster. "I did a lousy job at it...I came in with not nearly enough humility about not knowing television, and I'm dealing with guys with bigger egos than I *ever* had. That's saying something."

"He was widely laughed at," one ABC ego recalls. "He was never taken seriously," and Arledge's experiment "was a failure the day it began."

Bernstein's personal life was in disarray, with too many late nights at Elaine's and not enough mornings on the job. "I kept reading that I was going to be removed, and there came a point where it became a self-fulfilling prophecy. I went to Roone and said, 'I don't want to be in this job, either.'" Arledge reassigned him to a *World*

News Tonight, 20/20 and *Nightline* correspondent, and Bernstein loved it. He was back reporting. "I was not a traditional TV reporter, I did not change my accent [one of Washington's last working-class drawls]. I was competent at the on-air part, and I was just as good a reporter as I've ever been." On assignment in London, he met Elizabeth Taylor—Lillian Hellman introduced them, backstage at *The Little Foxes*—and began what for a time was a private affair. The day before its announcement in the press, he mentioned it to Ephron. "Carl," she said, "would you please leave now so I can call my friends?"

Bernstein produced solid reports on the Falklands and Beirut wars for *Nightline*, and though his on-air persona often was "wild," one staffer recalls, he worked comfortably with Ted Koppel, his best friend at the network. "He did very, very well," Koppel remembers. "Carl is an incredibly hard-nosed, hard-working reporter. Put him together with a producer, and he'll get the story for you."

Then *Heartburn.* Shortly after its publication, Bernstein was arrested for driving drunk, on duty for ABC in Washington, after wrecking his car at three in the afternoon. Earlier that morning, he'd been stopped on suspicion of driving drunk, with his breathalyzer a hair above legal. Things were out of control. Bernstein knew he was in trouble, and asked Woodward to drive him to Sibley Hospital, where he admitted himself for depression, exhaustion, and severe migraines. He ordered a CAT scan and stayed four days. "I was feeling some real depression about *Heartburn*'s becoming a movie," he told *Playboy.* "And I think I was also feeling some real guilt about the breakup of the marriage."

He had been irresponsible to his children, if not to Ephron, and had lost his family. The reality sunk in. "The hospital period wasn't my worst moment," he says. "It was a good moment. I decided not to sit around feeling powerless about this thing; I wanted to end this public spectacle."

The cab brakes in front of Bernstein's East Sixty-Second Street brownstone, he pays and exits. Up two flights, he skids a guitar from beneath an elaborate Chinese bed and begins strumming. In a scratchy tenor, he sings Flatt and Scrugg's classic, "Jimmy Brown the Newsboy," the Byrds' "Hickory Wind," then an old Everly Brothers tune, a mournful rocker from the fifties, "When Will I Be Loved."

"DAD, THEY'RE *BORING*," Jacob Bernstein says. "I mean, Madonna, Bruce Springsteen, Bob Dylan, Tina Turner—they're *has beens*." Twelve-year-old Jacob is lying at one end of a French daybed in Bernstein's living room, his father at the other. Jacob has a LIVE AID booklet propped on his chest. He's researching a paper for school. Bernstein, with an amused expression, asks him which artists he prefers. "Bryan Ferry, U2, Blondie," the boy says. Bernstein raises his eyebrows. "I'm getting my education in new wave from you," he says.

Jacob is a slender child with dark brown hair and a face so handsome it approaches prettiness. Both he and his brother Max are crazy for rock 'n' roll; Bernstein takes them to the Lone Star. Jacob wishes to be a journalist, and asks Bernstein whether he might alternate serious pieces with music criticism. "Sure, he says, "that's what I did." Jacob seems satisfied. Max—home with Ephron and her husband, Nicholas Pileggi—is a gifted child "for whom everything comes easy," Bernstein says, including the guitar. He and Max take lessons together each Saturday.

Bernstein's children are the heart of his emotional life. "Carl's an incredible Jewish mother," Kathleen Tynan says. And even Ephron swears that he's "consistently been a loving and devoted father."

This apartment is their second home, decorated with artifacts from Ephron's and Bernstein's past. When he moved in, three years ago, it was a wreck. The house's facade had been maintained but its interior was gutted. He rents, and rather than "put money into anything I couldn't take with me, I had this idea to sort of make the place look like a Tuscan ruin."

Window sashes are unfinished, and the haphazardly-painted walls have been accentuated in their disrepair by the artist, Chip Brawn. Bernstein's antiques, of which he owns many, are weathered country pieces: angels, a weathervane, louvered fans from a church steeple, plank tables, various pieces of folk art. The effect is of a rough-hewn or incomplete existence, one in the throes of reconstruction.

Jacob retires with a sitter while Bernstein continues his tour. He's been intrigued by decoration since childhood. "When we moved to the house in Silver Spring, I helped design the built-in furniture in my room." At the Ontario, "I gutted 3,500 square feet, and worked with a great architect." That apartment was featured in *House and Garden*. But when he moved here, he sold all real estate and quit shopping for antiques. "I don't buy much anymore, I don't feel any compulsion...I think you do that at times when you think you can fill up some holes in your life by buying things. I don't feel like that anymore."

Loyalties had become his life's focus. He'd resumed writing after showing its first sixty pages to Joan Didion, an old friend (who's since read and criticized four versions of the book). He'd handed them to her over lunch at the Jockey Club, and *Loyalties*, she remembers, "was still on that *Washington Post* flimsy paper...he didn't have a copy of it, even. I said, 'God I'm going to lose this.' It was a terrible feeling. I just had a sense he *wanted* me to lose it." But, she adds, "What was striking about those pages was how he had found a tone already. And how controlled those first pages were."

Controlling his own focus was more difficult. Renegotiations on his ABC contract were going nowhere. He wanted a guarantee of air time, and to work in New York near his kids, but executives "weren't about to give it to me." Despite his frustration, "I was scared of leaving ABC. I knew the only thing I would leave for would be to do this book."

He quit in May of 1984. But distractions were legion. Mike Nichols was directing Ephron's screenplay of *Heartburn*, and Bernstein was determined to spare his children media pain by exerting some control over his characterization (Jack Nicholson, Hollywood's premier cad, would play him—to Meryl Streep's Ephron). That task and his divorce spent a year, but he made Ephron pledge in their separation agreement that "The character of the father in the movie *Heartburn* will be portrayed at all times as a caring, loving, and conscientious father," that he might screen cuts of the film, and that their children would not be photographed or otherwise used for publicity. His actions muted the film's virulence, producing "exactly the results that I wanted...which is to say, that movie sank like a stone, it was one of the great turkeys of our time."

That done, he confronted *Loyalties* head on. It wasn't easy. "He has a very fragile armor," Kathleen Tynan says, "he's not self-protected, or protective." He'd all but quit drinking, and eventually would quit completely. "I certainly couldn't handle liquor the way I could when I was younger," he says. Booze rendered him verbose, aggressive, and occasionally violent—as a Palladium brawl with co-Liz Taylor suitor, Dennis Stein, demonstrated. But fewer late nights with the many women he'd turned to in Ephron's absence helped sharpen his writing, and opened him wider to his emotions. "It was," he admits, "a period...of great upheaval."

The press made it no easier. As he labored, a succession of bad reviews—on his marriage, ABC, *Heartburn*, its movie—were relentlessly catalogued. "Carl had a very, very rough time of it," Dick Cohen remembers. "He was an object of scorn and ridicule. It was painful to watch."

"Yes, he was in really bad shape," Kaiser agrees. "It was a really low period, very tough and very upsetting. We were scared—I was scared because there was a lot of denial, and he'd pretend that things were okay, when things were desperately not okay."

And Kathleen Tynan: "He went through a very miserable, depressed period...He was grateful to the few friends who were loyal to him. I also think he felt terribly wounded by the breakup with Nora Ephron. His public persona was not the one that he felt was the real one. And that creates depression."

But there were lighter moments. One evening at dinner, "Nora was sitting at the next table," Tynan remembers. "Carl was unable to talk about The Marriage. Instead, he talked about politics. Brilliantly. And I thought, 'God, if only Nora could be sitting next to us every time we go out to dinner, then we wouldn't have to talk about *them*, we could talk about him and politics."

Café society was not courting Bernstein, new friends turned their backs—he was being ostracized as his parents had been—and New York proved too unsettling. He fled to Washington and to his fellowship with Bob Woodward. "Bob had a lot to do with shaping him up," Kaiser says. "Bob obviously helped him block out what he had to do."

Bernstein moved into Woodward's house for several months, sleeping and writing in the third-floor "Gary Hart Memorial room," as Woodward calls it (Hart bivouacked there during his separations) and working hard on the book. Nearby, Woodward's assistants toiled in research offices dubbed The Factory. "I encouraged him to come here," Woodward says, "and get away from New York... but Carl did this book, Carl pushed *himself*. He made it and figured it out and evaluated it. And it was a struggle."

Woodward read early drafts and grilled Bernstein on his past, pushing, probing, and appraising as of old, while cranking out his own chapters of *Veil* down the hall. Woodward's energy was sustenance. "He's like a machine," Bernstein says. They traded pages, criticizing each other's work. Emotionally, Woodstein was back on deadline; Carl was home in the newsroom, snug in the cocoon of journalism.

But things were different. As a journalist, "part of my security for many years has been not to look at myself,"

Bernstein says. "I'm somebody who spent most of my life trying not to deal with feelings that are difficult, with situations that are difficult...I'd find any old way I could to push 'em away. But to do this book, you've got to look at yourself in every regard."

He managed to write it, but the emotions it excavated from him were horrifying. In facing his past he discovered that, as a forty-two-year-old father, "I was then old enough, and knew enough about life to go through feeling it. Which is what happens...boy there are days you sit at the typewriter and you scream, or you pound your desk, or you cry, and you get furious...that's what doing this kind of book is about."

The room in New York where Bernstein composed most of *Loyalties* is his second-floor study at the duplex's rear. His Apple rests on a nineteenth-century, French cheese-drying table, and a preliminary cover of *Loyalties*, wrapped round another book, lies nearby. Photos of his parents, including a 1944 *Washington Post* shot, titled VICTORY BABY OF THE WEEK, of himself in his mother's arms, decorate the table top. He swiped it from the *Post*'s library—"I ought to get something." Stacks of transcripts, documents, and 2,500 pages of FBI files on Al and Sylvia Bernstein clutter the room. An eighteenth-century Venetian podium, with angels, supports a dictionary, and tall bookcases frame windows overlooking the greenest backyards in Manhattan. Tom Wolfe lives two doors down (he's block president), David Brenner across the way, Ashford and Simpson, Don King and Bill Cosby directly out back. It is a neighborhood gorged on success. Bernstein stares out the window. "Every once in a while I'll see Cosby out there with a cigar in his mouth, counting his money."

Woodward lists "sheer financial necessity" among Bernstein's prime motivations in completing *Loyalties* (already there have been movie nibbles). But Al Bernstein's suggestion that someday he and Carl try a book together on the Loyalty issue, plus the drive to get closer to his father, seem fatter carrots.

Carl was twenty months old before he met Al Bernstein, who'd been overseas in the army. *Loyalties* is rife with filial remorse. Often his longing is expressed by the anger he felt at his father's political stance. "Sometimes I hated him for it," he writes. When he was ten he penned a note to his parents, railing at them for being "atheistic Jewish Communists." At miniature golf he almost clubbed his father, yet notes elsewhere how "oddly I felt protective toward him"...and how happy life in Chesapeake Street was, because, "For a while dad seemed to have time on his hands...it made me feel good, this chance for the two of us to be together." Later, while fleeing a HUAC subpoena, the pair spent a week in a New York hotel room: "I think it was the only time I had ever been with him that long, without my mother or sisters. It was the best time." The warmest pages of *Loyalties* show Carl and his father alone in the Sixty-Second Street apartment, pouring over transcripts and debating the book's focus. Carl describes Al Bernstein as "not a demonstrative man," but confesses that, "It is my father for whom I write, whose judgment I most respect, whose approval I still seek...."

His mother's portrait is more complex: "I missed her a lot when I was little, because I was terrified I'd lose her...she and I have never been able to reach any real kind of accord with one another. We walk around it... each taking refuge in some reservoir of hurt that makes resolution impossible." He had first abandoned the book when writing about Sylvia Bernstein in the Rosenberg chapter. She was the native Washingtonian who should have realized how "dangerous" a town it is, "more resistant to change and new ideas than any place I have ever been," Bernstein writes. He blames her, in part, for not warning his father..."certainly *she knew* that to have joined the Communist Party would be ruinous." And it is she who has most vehemently opposed the book, fearing a rehashing of the Communist Party issue. "If you center on this I think it's going to shatter my life again," she tells

Carl. "There was one little period—after Watergate—when attitudes opened up; that's gone now."

Carl, by reporting Watergate, had reduced the heat; now he was fanning the flames. "Leave it to Carl," Woodward says, "he's always stirring up trouble—that's his nature."

It was trouble for him, too. He'd tackled the most difficult of investigative tasks: to report on oneself and one's family. "Somewhere subconsciously, there was always the fear that I would stumble onto something, fall upon some parental Pumpkin Paper that would forever close me off to my parents," discovering "that my mother and father might have become ensnared in espionage...."

What he concluded from the FBI files and his reporting is that no one accused was subversive. "Yet an assumption was made that these people *were* subversive, if they were members of the Communist Party. This book says, 'none of these people were disloyal.' Whether they were members of the Communist Party or not. These people were loyal in every regard."

The true vindication of his parents comes in an interview with Clark Clifford—Harry Truman's counsel—done in 1978. The loyalty issue *"was a political problem,"* Clifford admits. "[Truman] was going to run in 1948, and that was it...My own feeling was there was not a serious loyalty problem. I felt the whole thing was being manufactured...."

"It was really a war against liberals," Al Bernstein observes. *"This order was a pivotal event in the history of this country...*I think it had a very serious effect on intellectual life...It probably took until the Kennedy administration to begin to recover; there was a whole period of a lack of intellectual pursuit, really until the Vietnam War."

The Loyalty Order and its Attorney General's list were not rescinded until 1974, in the wake of Watergate. When Carl asks his father what he thinks about having been excluded from participating in the labor movement—for

defending the accused, and for standing by his beliefs—
Al Bernstein's voice breaks, dropping to a whisper:
"Difficult," he says. "I don't like to think about it."

Carl is slouched in his living room now, one leg over
the arm of a chair, his foot bobbing. "I feel great about
this book, one, because it's coming out while my parents
are still alive, and I hope that it will be a great experience
for them...They like the quiet anonymity they've had in
their older years, and this indeed will shatter that. I've
tried to be as respectful of their privacy as I can. There's
one area where that makes them very uncomfortable, and
that's the area of the Communist party...Yet I hope and
think that maybe this will be the last great act my father
can do, by saying the things he says in this book about
his life and about this period of history. But obviously
there are going to be people who take some shots. I'm a
little used to it. My father used to be used to it, but I don't
think he's too used to it anymore."

He pauses, sipping cranberry juice. "As a family, we
share a sensitivity about the press."

So much so that neither Al Bernstein, retired from the
NCCJ, Sylvia, still working at Garfinckle's, nor Carl's
sisters—Mary, forty-one, in employee assistance at GTE,
and Laura, forty, heading a news service, Words by Wire—
will speak on the record about *Loyalties*.

His colleagues however, are full of praise. "I'm an
unabashed fan of it," Woodward says. "I find in it the
voice of the Jewish intellectual novelists—Saul Bellow,
Malamud, so forth. I see a lot of honest and worthy
introspection there, and the ingredients of the examined
life, which historically Carl has not been necessarily a
great practitioner of."

"It's a terrific book," Didion says, "it showed me
the why of certain things about him. Because of his
background, he tends to look for conspiracy. It is not
beyond his imagination, as it is beyond the imagination
of many people."

Childhood, Bernstein says, "made me very shy about

committing myself to anything." But he feels "much closer" to his parents now. "I no longer have quite the ambivalence about what they did...instead of being a source of anger, it's now a source of real pride."

Of Bernstein's emotional state, and his anxiety about reporting on his parents, Kaiser says, "God knows it's wishful, but I take the ability to finish this book as a wonderful sign...that something very good has happened. A few years ago, I would have bet a lot of money that this book was never going to be finished. And told him so."

Bernstein's done little else in recent years but toil at *Loyalties*. He's a man who defines himself by his writing, children, friends, and celebrity. Yet his companions still despair of adequately understanding him. "Carl's an enormously complex person," Kaiser notes. "There are layers and layers...Cohen and I have both said, over various crisis points over the years, that we know him extremely well and we don't know him at all...anybody who gets close to him and knows him well, has to like him and not like him, love him and be totally exasperated with him. This is not your garden-variety human being...."

Though he's less impulsive, and better about meeting deadlines and keeping appointments, Bernstein remains "a pain in the ass," Woodward says. "But there's no more caring pain in the ass, there's no more persistent pain in the ass, and there's no pain in the ass driving harder at the right values."

Spending money is one aspect of Bernstein's life that "still," he says, "I would describe at times as out of control. I'm always broke. When I earned forty-four dollars a week, I spent it all, and when I earned a few million dollars, I spent it all. And not wisely. But," he adds, "I've had a *fabulous* time. I haven't made investments, I don't own fancy things...I don't own any property. And I've been living four years without the benefit of the ABC expense account. Not to speak of the salary."

That salary was $150,000 per annum. To fill its gap, Bernstein delivers each year perhaps fifteen, five-thousand-dollar-a-pop speeches (usually about the press), lectures on *QE-2* cruises, and collects small royalties for his books. But he's published just three articles of substance in ten years: two investigative pieces for the *New Republic*, on Reagan's first term and on arming Afghanistan's rebels, and an Op-Ed piece for the *New York Times* about faulty TV reporting during the Iran-Contra hearings. Not much to help finance a New York lifestyle that includes "a fortune in rent," child support, expensive dates, dinners and late evenings out, and travel with his kids (three weeks last summer in Montana, scouting an article).

Bernstein, reclining further, insists that "I'm more relaxed than I've ever been. I really love my life. I'm... probably less arrogant, but more comfortable and secure. I have a little more humility. I think I know myself better. Also, I *love* my forties. It's just a great age. There comes a period in your life when you can no longer look outside yourself to somehow make yourself whole. Whatever feelings of inadequacy you have are no longer going to be filled by being with the right woman, living in the right house...you've got to find something within yourself. The last four years especially, that's what my life has been about. Partly as a result of doing this book, even though it's been the hardest thing I've ever done. It's put me in touch with who I really am, and there's no room for any kind of artifice...it's been deeply satisfying. I have this incredible feeling of accomplishment...I've done something that I wasn't sure I was capable of doing."

To an extent, working in the Sixty-Second Street duplex has been a foray outside the world of daily journalism for Bernstein. But he's returning to the newsroom. His next book may tackle the press (his second family) of which he's highly critical. And no doubt will address his past as "witch hunter" of bad news.

"Reporting has got to become the first priority of the press again," he says. "And there are very few institutions in which reporting *is* the first priority." His face reddens. "We have now had in the Reagan administration yet another experience like the Nixon years...but the press once again, as in Watergate, *missed the story.* Wasn't anywhere near it, and yet it was all there. Everybody in town knew what Oliver North was doing...until there was the Iran connection, nobody cared about the fact that there was this illegal foreign policy. It was a terrible failure on the part of the press."

He sits up, tugs at his belt. He has no idea what he'll learn in reporting this book. "Maybe there'll be some event that'll happen, and I'll see how the media covers it. But," he reflects, "there's a certain continuum, a line, that my work follows...*Loyalties* in a funny way really follows out of the other two books. As does the next one, about the press. The press is what I ought to be working on right now. It's the idea of taking your experience at each stage, and using it all. Into whatever that piece of work is."

The telephone sounds. Bernstein grabs it, chats a few minutes, emits a high-pitched laugh, mutters "Okay, right, okay." And rings off.

"That was Woodward," he says. "He just read the final version. Bob thinks it's...a masterpiece." He stands there, smiling. "That's a little embarrassing."

Bernstein drops into his armchair. Then exclaims, "You know, I can't *wait* to get back to reporting."

Vanity Fair, 1988

Ratfishing Manhattan

To my knowledge, I'm the only rat fisherman in New York. I became one quite by accident. On cool evenings I like nothing better than to fly cast for perch and bass in Central Park Lake. But last September, while angling off Bethesda Terrace, I made a faulty backcast and placed my fly in a pile of refuse. To my astonishment, a rat darted forward and took the fly in its mouth. I jerked my line and set the hook. The rat planted its front feet, shook its head like a dog might ragging, then shot off across the esplanade, tugging and flipping with such vigor that my reel gears screamed.

The rat's first run stripped ten yards of line and took it perilously near a hedge. This was a big Norway, two pounds of muscle and ligament, and why its teeth failed to cut the light tippet I don't know. It zigzagged right, seeking cover, then left toward the darkened arches of the Terrace arcade. Ripping at the line with its front claws, it squealed. Its second run ended by a slatted wooden trash bin. I turned it before the leader became fouled; the rat skidded on its back then regained footing. I played it gently and in minutes wrestled it to within five yards of the Bethesda Fountain. It may have been there that it saw me, for—as firemen know—a rat will charge and this one did, forcing me over the fountain's lip and into the water. The rat chose not to follow and I was able to work it from the shallows until it tipped onto its back, whiskers twitching. Only then did I break it free. I watched it retreat for the brush, trailing monofilament from its snout.

This encounter thrilled me. For weeks I cased rat feeding grounds (the shrubbery at West Ninetieth Street by the Reservoir, and the Great Lawn's expanses after a busy Sunday), and on evenings stalked the Norways. Anglers brag of thirty-to-sixty-fish days; I admit to having bagged sixteen rats of an evening, the rodents hitting every streamer I presented (Olive Matukas and White Zonkers their favorites). I've killed a few and feel badly for it. But the rat's ethic is situational. It will stalk a snagged compatriot, fight for its morsel during runs, then hover close as the angler disimpales his catch. Most people shun rats, but to watch a trophy brown race across the Great Lawn at sunset, its fur bristling with every leap against the hook, is all that sport's about.

I'm new to this endeavor, but can offer a few pointers: wear canvas shooting pants, high boots and leather gloves; use barbless hooks, a tough leader, and carry a tennis racket to deflect charges. This is catch-and-release angling; corn tongs are useful for immobilizing one's prey. Many fishermen will choose to cut their lines, surrendering flies.

Recently, I landed my 235th rat of the season. I'd been casting a pink-and-purple Double Bunny in the grass by Harlem Meer, but was surfeited, bored. It was getting dark. I glassed the lake's far shore. Three kids waved bamboo poles, and a pair of ibis waded off Duck Island. I panned my binoculars and spotted a dozen Norways, twelve-to-fifteen-inchers, tippling in Discovery Center's trash.

Enough of this genteel angling. From a still-warm

barbecue pit, I tweezed a morsel of frankfurter and worked it over the hook of my streamer.

It took five minutes to crouch walk near the working school. My first cast led it by a yard. Two rats—one husky, the other monstrous—went for the bait. I set my hook, turned the larger after twenty feet and retook a bit of line. The brute stood shivering. I felt my rod tip rise, saw a blur, then felt the rat on my boot, tearing at its laces while coughing against the hook.

"Damn," I cried. The rat skittered up my shin and vaulted to a wire basket, where it became hopelessly tangled.

I caught my breath. Tape decks thumped above 110th Street. I withdrew a thin scalpel from my vest, placed its blade against the rat's neck, stroked. It gave a shriek. Calmed now, I snipped the leader and walked to Discovery's portico. There I slung rat's-head-cum-Double Bunny across its lowest rafter.

Flatiron News, 1993

Mailer's Ghosts

Norman Mailer is tired. He steps hesitantly from the eleventh-floor elevator at Random House and rocks in a boson's gait toward his editor, Jason Epstein's office. There's something terribly vulnerable about Mailer. The man is tiny, no more than five-seven, yet massive through the neck and shoulders. His tangle of white hair has thinned and his ample gut is blanketed by a checked shirt. Black Reeboks and tattered khakis lend him more the air of an off-duty rabbi than that of New York's first-figure of letters. He hugs the wall, swaying toward Epstein's study.

"Jason's been a great help," Mailer says. "I dedicated *Harlot's Ghost* to him. He's been like a blocking back. I never felt the house was nervous about the length of the book or the time it was taking."

Harlot, Mailer's novel about the Central Intelligence Agency, took seven years to complete and is being trimmed from its two-thousand-six-hundred-and-sixty-five manuscript pages to two-thousand-four-hundred-fifty. On the final page is typed, To Be Continued.

Mailer settles at a conference table, in a window overlooking midtown. "This volume is the first half of what I'm afraid I'm going to call a meganovel," he says. "With a long book, at a given moment you feel you're making love to a three-hundred-pound woman, so that woman better be agile. I'm probably a better editor now than a writer. You can't get more talent as you get older, you're likely to end up with a little less, so you might as well work on what you can improve," he says, laughing.

He looks his sixty-eight years, yet in mirth the scarred brow and half-moons of flesh beneath his eyes contract to those of an adolescent. He squirms with fatigue. "My body never prospered when I was writing. It just puts a state of tension and stress through all your system. What's easier now is that there are less distractions. One of the hardest things about being a young writer is every day you spend writing is the day you don't meet this fabulous heroine who'll be the best heroine ever written in American fiction. I'm happily or unhappily removed from all that. Work used to be the great stone you carried on your back. Now it's just the opposite."

Mailer's labored nonstop through the eighties, publishing *Ancient Evenings* and *Tough Guys Don't Dance*, writing *Strawhead*, a play about Marilyn Monroe, directing the film of *Tough Guys*, serving two years as president of PEN…and disgorging the mammoth *Harlot*, which indulges his obsession with the CIA, an outfit he's studied "probably since the Bay of Pigs."

He sighs. "In 1973, I had that odd fiftieth birthday party where I wanted to start a—I cringe when I think of the name now—a People's CIA." There he introduced The Fifth Estate, a group slated to monitor the CIA and FBI. "That failed utterly as far as getting anything going." A month later, Watergate broke. "Then in 1976, I wrote something about the CIA called 'A Harlot High and Low.' That stayed in my mind, like 'God, there's got to be a novel there somewhere.'"

That essay's germ was conspiracy. But amid speculation

about secret Agency funds, a bugging of the Federal Reserve, and Howard Hunt in Dealey Plaza, he struck an odder note: "The human brain is divided: into a right lobe and a left lobe; a bold side and a cautious one; a moralist and a sinner; a radical and conservative...a hard worker and a sloth. Consider the overlays of personality which accompany these shifts of identity when [an agent's] cover story is added—" In the introduction to 1982's *Pieces and Pontifications*, Mailer described himself as "a divided man—not schizophrenic—divided. His personality is bicameral and built on two points of reference." This notion was born in 1970's *Of a Fire on the Moon*, nurtured in 1973's *Marilyn*, matured by 1978's *Genius and Lust*, and has been toyed with in every book since. Duality of character is at the core of *Harlot's Ghost*. Jason Epstein whispered, "He's obsessed by that... he has an idea that we're *all* two people."

In *Harlot*, Mailer's mouthpiece is Kittredge, a darkly beautiful ingénue. She's "this Radcliffe girl," he says, "with a very overheated, but essentially innocent background. Her father is a Shakespearean professor at the highest level. She's had a particularly sheltered life, but she is brilliant. She comes up with this extraordinary thesis that Allen Dulles adores," the basis of her book, *The Dual Soul*.

Kittredge feels we have "two psyches," she explains, going "through life like Siamese twins inside one person." These are Alpha and Omega, a male and female psyche each with its own superego, ego and id. "Artists, and extraordinary men and women have dramatically different Alpha and Omega," she says. "So do the feebleminded, the addictive, and the psychotic." Her assumption, she boasts, "could prove the first reliable psychological theory to explain how spies are able to live with the tension of their incredible life situations."

Psychology has been fundamental to Mailer's interests. He composed a novel while at Harvard titled *A Transit to Narcissus*, set in a mental hospital—he worked there one week—containing the "most terrible themes of my own life," he later wrote: "the nearness of violence to creation, and the whiff of murder just beyond every embrace of love." He spent the fifties studying Wilhelm Reich, experimenting with orgone energy, peyote, mescaline, marijuana and "too much sex"...and promised an epic novel, reconciling Marx with Freud, that would "make a revolution in the consciousness of our time." He wrote in 1959, "I thought often of becoming a psychoanalyst." He was committed to Bellevue, in 1960, for seventeen days' observation after stabbing his second wife, Adele...an event so key to his life that, Gay Talese predicts, "it will be in his obituary."

Mailer's work focuses on two grand themes, he acknowledges, "establishment and identity." Raised lower-middleclass Jewish, he's long considered himself an outsider. The CIA's leadership represents the apex of WASP culture to him, and the WASP mentality is one "I've been trying to figure out all my life." In "A Harlot High" he wrote, "It could be said that the Agency was the militant arm of the Establishment." *Harlot's Ghost* broadens that focus: Hugh Montague, a counter-intelligence officer, calls the CIA "the mind of America."

Mailer chugs at a seltzer. "In this book, it's much more a question of identity...of the choices in identity and the idea of that age-old adolescent question, 'who is the real me?' In intelligence work you get into that probably at the deepest levels society offers."

He interviewed Agency sources for *Harlot*—a novel blending fact with fiction, that charts the Agency from its OSS roots through the Bay of Pigs—but says, "I could have written the book without sources. It would have suffered a bit, but not terribly."

Why fiction rather than nonfiction, for which he's won a Pulitzer (two, if *The Executioner's Song* counts as journalism) and a National Book Award? "I write fiction because it's the only way I can ever make nonfiction believable to myself. Nonfiction always has these fabulous stories to tell, and I never can put people in them. So you write fiction in order to make nonfiction believable." He glances across the rooftops. "Here you have these extraordinarily respectable people in the CIA, many of them good Harvard men of the sort I knew reasonably well when I was there. Now fifteen, twenty years later they're out trying to murder Castro. Well how do you get to that point, what's the reasoning? I thought, 'That's worth writing about.'"

Why should he trust his take on spies? "Because I could have been one." He pauses. "If I'd had a totally different background and came from another kind of family, and had a different set of politics when I was a young man, I could have been in the CIA. And I probably would have been pretty good at it."

He leans back, stretching. "Somewhere along the way I began to think, 'In the spy and the actor there are profound similarities...and what does that mean to us, that pulls us to step out of our own identity?'"

KLIEG LIGHTS bathe a crowd straining the velvet ropes before Manhattan's Hard Rock Cafe, as notables dart beneath the antique-Cadillac canopy. Robert Duval's film, *Convicts*, has been previewed, and a benefit for the Actor's Studio is underway. Mailer stands center-floor, poking his drink at Paul Newman, then Harvey Keitel. Robert DeNiro, Burt Young, Ron Silver, and Wallace Shawn pass by. Mailer introduces a young screenwriter to Newman—a gray Hud, scowling in tight Levi's and cowboy boots. "We actually had a *conversation*," Mailer shouts. He's in slacks and blue blazer, his chest straining its fabric, his thick neck pinched by a tie. He looks enormous. *Entertainment Tonight* plays its lights on the group and Mailer swells. He seems ten years younger and half a foot taller.

His sixth wife, Norris ("the last," friends predict), is a tall, auburn-haired knockout in a purple dress and gold bag, who's onstage introducing Marilyn Sokol of *Guilt*

Without Sex. Sokol will sing a number, as will Paul Hipp of *Buddy* and Keith Carradine of *The Will Rogers Follies*. Norris is co-chairing this benefit. She's a portrait painter, model, and actress who's worked in films and TV soaps. She's written two Actor's Studio plays and has starred in others.

"Norris could have been a musical comedienne," Mailer insists, "if she'd had a different life." He met her at a friend's house in Arkansas in 1975; was so struck with her beauty, he fled the room. "She's half my age and twice my height," he likes to quip. Raised a Freewill Baptist, she never swears and drinks abstemiously. "She has a sense of self that's enormous," a relative notes. Norris has been married to Mailer since 1980; has a thirteen-year-old son, John Buffalo, by him.

"She's the best thing that's happened to Norman," everyone agrees.

Mailer snorts. "If there's anything a husband can't bear, it's that all he has he owes to his wife." He smiles. "There's something about those pious guys who go around saying, 'I got just such a wonderful wife, everything turned out alright for me.' You want to hit them with a blivit—that's two pounds of shit in a one pound bag."

John Buffalo's starred in an Actor's Studio play, and is out on auditions. "I don't know if I really approve of that," Norris says. Of Mailer's nine children, five work as actors or producers; four of his wives have been actresses. He himself has directed four movies, acting in three, plus Milos Forman's *Ragtime*. He's been associated with the Actor's Studio since 1957, and serves on its board.

But his fascination with theatricality began in childhood. Robert Lucid, Mailer's archivist and authorized biographer, says, "His parents had him writing and reading virtually from the moment he opened his eyes. But the movies are an unmistakable influence."

Mailer's earliest story, at six, was about cowboys: "One was an outlaw with his band. They were riding over a hill, and the outlaw was *boasting* about being an outlaw." His first novel, *The Martian Invasion,* was thirty-five thousand words and written the summer he was ten. "People on earth," Lucid says, "discover the planet is going down the tubes. They go to Mars and begin from a colonial point of view. By and large the Martians are bad guys, in the sense that they're grotesque and they do all kinds of very, very frightening things."

"I'd been listening to Buck Rogers on radio all winter," Mailer recalls. "So that summer I wrote about my hero, Bob Porter. And there was a Dr. Huer—the origin of Hugh Montague in *Harlot's Ghost.* I don't remember if there was a devil, but there certainly were villains; there were dark presences in it."

In 1978, Tuli Kupferberg published a few pages in *First Glance: Childhood Creations of the Famous.* There Captain Bob Porter and Private Ben Stein are captured by Martians. "The captives were placed in a prison for several days in which they were brutally treated by their captors," Mailer wrote. "Bob had a hard time restraining his temper."

Mailer's home life, in 1933, was "rough," his sister says. Barbara Wasserman remembers the Depression as "very hard...there were times when my father didn't have a job." He was a South African accountant and closet gambler whose debts Norman later would pay. Their mother, Fanny, supported the family by working in a small fuel-oil business. Barney Mailer "was charming and feckless," Barbara says. "He never did anything terrible to us, but he was not as dominating a figure as my mother. In a certain sense he lived in his own world; he had a secret life he would indulge himself in whenever he had the chance."

Barney owned theatrical style, speaking in a British accent. "It seemed very glamorous," Barbara remembers. "He was a guy," Norman adds, "who'd go out looking for a job during the Depression wearing spats and a cane. He was a *sly* guy...a very odd, quirky fellow. I was never as close to him as I was to my mother, but I did get awful fond of him because he had a lot of class."

Lucid, a friend of thirty years who knew both parents, says: "They had a fairly stormy relationship, but Norman unquestionably was treated as the apple of everyone's eye. Nevertheless the childhood reveals a fairly rough terrain." Barbara recalls Norman as "very intense; our older cousin used to call him 'Desperate Ambrose.'"

Each summer the Mailers retreated from Brooklyn to Long Branch, New Jersey, on the shore where Norman was born. There Fanny worked in the tourist business. "It was an established thing for Norman to write during the summers," Lucid says. "It developed almost as soon as he could handle a pencil." His other talent was constructing model airplanes; flight obsessed him, as proved evident with *The Martian Invasion*. Yet he was terrified of heights. "In a kind of Alexander Portnoy way," Lucid says, "Norman was treated as just the most fabulous kid who ever lived," but was given "this tremendous sense of mission" within the family, "which was nearly messianic."

A monster promises Bob Porter in *The Martian Invasion*: "You shall die a nice death...Suffocation is nice isn't it. A slow long drawn out death." Mailer condensed the sentiment by 1959's *Advertisements for Myself* to, "The shits are killing us."

In his vocabulary, Alpha and Omega were formed by the contradictory natures of his parents: one "feckless" and charming, the other hardworking and conscientious. "We have...two complete personalities," a fictionalized Marilyn says in 1980's *Of Women and Their Elegance*. "We are made from two people, aren't we?"

"Remember," Kittredge says in *Harlot*, "Alpha and Omega originate from separate creatures. One is descended from the sperm cell, Alpha; Omega from the ovum."

"I have a great fear with this book," Mailer confesses. "What if Alpha and Omega succeed and it becomes a new talking point? I've got to *deal* with that crap for the rest of my life."

Right now he's indulging his Alpha. Or is it Omega? Having retreated to Hard Rock's balcony, he sips Miller Lite with a group of writers. Jokes are traded, workout strategies limned (he no longer boxes, but pumps weights), tales spun of jockish pals. "Jose Torres," Mailer barks, "is writing fiction. He's having trouble, he says, because he can't tell the truth." Chuckles. "In the ring, fighters always try to trick you."

A reporter challenges Mailer to a bout of thumb wrestling. "I'm the all-time champ," Mailer says, brightening. He extends his hand, which is startling in its softness. The goal is to pin one's opponent's thumb, holding it three full seconds. Fingertips grip as thumbs wiggle like little boys' penises. Mailer beams. Ten minutes pass; the reporter grows weary and succumbs. Mailer's gracious in victory, orders another Lite. A beefy poet approaches and someone blurts, "He wants to head butt with you."

Mailer's somber. "Is he a writer?"

"Yes."

"I never head butt with writers." He taps his forehead. "All their strength is here."

HE'S ON HIS BROOKLYN HEIGHTS terrace, chatting with Alexandra Schlesinger while Dominique Nabokov photographs him against the Manhattan skyline. "I think it would be wonderful if I could keep writing at a reasonably good level until I'm eighty," he says. "I may well be *alive* at eighty, but I may not be strong enough to write a novel. So no more quick, dopey books."

The Arthur Schlesingers are friends of the Mailers— as are Willie Smith's family, the Buckleys, Pat Kennedy Lawford, Mort Zuckerman, Jan Cushing, and other East Side luminaries. Alexandra's arranged this photo session, she says, "just for me." Tugs honk and ferries clear their stacks as one explores the apartment. It's decidedly bohemian: a fourth-floor walkup, in an 1838 brownstone high above the river. Here Mailer announced his campaign for 1969's mayoralty, promising "a hip coalition of the right and the left." Here he welcomed killer Jack Abbott after easing his release from prison; here he's wooed five wives, and has entertained characters as varied as Abbie Hoffman and Jacqueline Onassis.

Mailer bought this house in 1961, but as wives left, exacting alimony, and the IRS nagged, he sold all but its top floor. "The servants' quarters," he says. A pug named Huey—for Hubert Humphrey—yaps at Alexandra's and Dominique's exit.

"Huey's very depressed," Mailer explains, patting the dog. *"See what you get for falling in love with John Buffalo? He hasn't walked him in two days."*

This afternoon Mailer's neither large nor small... medium. Wearing a white-collared, blue oxford and khakis, he sits at a rosewood table in a window facing the harbor. Nearby is a desk stacked with material on Picasso ("my next interpretive biography"); books line the walls, fill cases, clutter furniture and obstruct traffic. There's a multi-volume Talmud, opposite a miniature pool table and various paintings by Norris. One is of her and her mother on the steps of their Arkansas house: it's hauntingly gothic, and hangs above Mailer's seven-foot-high Lego sculpture of a "vertical city of the future." John Buffalo's electric piano rests near a Wurlitzer jukebox, racked with hits from the sixties.

It's Bob Dylan's fiftieth birthday. "I didn't know that," Mailer allows. What happens to the aging hipster?

He strokes his chin. "The idea from 'The White Negro' [his 1957 exegesis of hip] is that with each moment of existence we're growing into more or less...this is the vision of the hipster. But there are very few aging hipsters, as such. To be a hipster you have to be considerably oriented toward sex. So as you get older, you don't need to lose that much sex before you have a different point of view. At the moment the possibility of being the best lover in the area is gone, when you no longer qualify as a real hard-rock stud, then you're no longer a hipster."

One no longer evaluates one's character by the orgasm?

"That you can still do, but maybe you don't do it on drugs anymore."

Norris is forty-two. "Yes." She may want to go out, party..."Look," he interrupts, "If I were someone else sitting here, you wouldn't *dream* of asking me these questions." He grunts. "You're looking at the remnants of a legend! I'm blessed, because Norris loves to go out, but she can do without it. We're well balanced. Don't forget, we were born on the same day." A minute apart, on January 31. "We're Aquarians," he reminds, "and we have to be near water."

By water was where he learned to write, and the interior of this apartment, with its plank ceiling and nautical rigging, its compact galley and cabins aft, is fitted like a ship. "Norman's a workaholic," Norris says, "we've never gone on any trip that wasn't a working trip." They shuttle between two waterfront offices—in Brooklyn Heights and Provincetown. *The Naked and the Dead* was begun in P-town. "But most of it I wrote in Brooklyn Heights," Mailer says. "I tend to circle back to a place where I've been able to do reasonable writing. If I have twenty-five books, I don't think there are more than six or seven that weren't written in part up in Provincetown."

P-town is the setting for 1984's *Tough Guys Don't Dance* and its 1987 film—but more tellingly for sections of that "big novel" he's promised since *Advertisements*. There he pledged "to attempt an entrance into the mysteries of murder, suicide, incest, orgy, orgasm, and Time," hoping to become "the first philosopher of hip."

The fifties were a period of dislocation for Mailer. After the enormous success of *Naked*, the tepid reception of 1951's *Barbary Shore* and a rejection by seven publishers of *The Deer Park* (for obscenity) before its 1954 appearance to mixed reviews, he grew depressed. He seemed paralyzed by the prospect of failure. He'd entered Harvard at sixteen, won *Story* magazine's college-fiction contest at eighteen, graduated at twenty, survived combat in the Philippines by twenty-one, and published *Naked* (his fourth novel) at twenty-five. "I'd been frightened in the womb by my mother's dream of having a little Einstein in her belly," he explains.

The McCarthy era was unfolding; he came under surveillance by the FBI for his leftish politics. And he found the literary tribute he'd won in 1948 withdrawn. This was staggering. "Norman always complained," Barbara says, "that our mother loved us so much she didn't teach us how to cope with people who didn't." He wrote in *Advertisements*: "Defeat has left my nature divided...and anger has brought me to the edge of the brutal."

Advertisements proved an ideal vehicle for this rage. He found his distinctly combative voice, and acknowledged his character to be split: "I contain within myself the bitter exhaustions of an old man, and the cocky arguments of a bright boy." *Advertisements*' cover included photographs of the author in five separate guises, from scholar to goateed hipster. Defeat—or success—had cleaved him.

"Most of the urge I used to have for experience was that I felt I had been *deprived*," he says, "by becoming successful too early. Which left me in such a dislocation of my own identity that it took me the next fifteen or twenty years to rebuild an identity."

The fifties saw him through incarnations as Hollywood scenarist, autobiographer, playwright, poet, furious novelist, co-founder of the *Village Voice* and its columnist "General Marijuana"...plus bouts with Benzedrine and Seconal addiction, too much booze, divorce, remarriage, political reporting and a fling as mayoral candidate.

On November 19, 1960 the Mailers threw a party at their West Side apartment to announce his first bid for mayor—on the Existentialist ticket. It was Camelot in Washington (Mailer's "Superman Comes to the Supermarket" helped elect JFK) and he fantasized something comparable for New York. They invited a "natural constituency" of street people, junkies, prostitutes, athletes, artists, actors, writers, "the power structure" and celebs. Few power-people showed; instead, mostly cops and Times Square hustlers. "The hostility was all-pervasive," one guest told biographer, Peter Manso. Mailer lapsed into different accents—Southern, Irish, British—to a degree that, his friend Doc Humes said, "It didn't seem to be Norman." He fist-fought guests, batted George Plimpton across the face with a rolled newspaper, divided his entourage into those for or against him, and, near dawn, stabbed Adele in the upper abdomen and back, almost killing her.

The party that began as Camelot, finished as Altamont.

In a sense, Mailer'd already lived the sixties. His experiments with sex, magic, psychedelics, radical politics, psychology and hipsterism would define that decade. And despite his genius, they'd nudge him close to madness. Today he characterizes his stabbing of Adele as "a species of derangement." A doctor who examined him that bloody morning in 1960, wrote: "It is my opinion that Mr. Norman Mailer is having an acute paranoid breakdown with delusional thinking and is both homicidal and suicidal."

He entered Bellevue but was released after two weeks. Adele refused to press charges. Later she remembered, "Norman began to develop these mannerisms, the accents, which he had never used before with me. He became a different person. Something was happening that was very, very, very wrong."

A shifting of accents, and referring to oneself in the third person (which Mailer did both in conversation and in print) are symptomatic of dissociation...the extreme of which is a division of selves into what Kittredge calls Alpha and Omega, but what psychiatry calls multiple personality disorder.

DSM-III-R, psychiatry's Bible, defines MPD as, "A. The existence within the individual of two or more distinct personalities or personality states (each with its own relatively enduring pattern of perceiving, relating to and thinking about the environment and one's self)" and, "B. Each of these personality states at some time, and recurrently, takes full control of the individual's behavior." Those, coupled with amnesia between states, are MPD's diagnostic criteria.

Mailer argues that "I don't consider Alpha and Omega multiple personality. Kittredge is saying this is the *normal condition*. Multiple personality would be a form of psychosis, as far as I'm concerned."

Not according to Dr. Frank W. Putnam, author of *Diagnosis and Treatment of Multiple Personality Disorder* and a specialist in MPD at the National Institute of Mental Health: "The evidence is that *everybody's* multiple, at some level. We all come into the world with that potential. But," Dr. Putnam adds, "with halfway-reasonable parenting, we learn to smooth the transitions and develop an integrated self...multiples seem to teeter continuously on the brink of disaster."

Mailer did that. By *Armies of the Night* he wrote of "a slumbering Beast" who'd exasperate the bookish Mailer by hooting onstage in rapidly cycling accents, hopping in odd gaits, and shouting invectives. The Beast frequented New York's toughest dives, challenging patrons to head butting, arm wrestling, staring matches or fist fights; it appeared drunk on television, enjoyed being arrested, brawled at parties, fucked inconsolably, insulted Mailer's friends, spent lavishly on his doomed movies, slowed his serious literary production, and sabotaged a second bid for mayor with besotted public performances. When the Beast slumbered, Mailer wept.

MPD is invariably a response to trauma, usually childhood. The mind splits into alternate selves, so that no single personality must endure all. In Mailer's case—his suffering from "Alpha and Omega"—one can only speculate what trauma may have occurred, for as Lucid asserts, "He's not his own best source on this...not a deeply introspective player." One looks to the prose: In "Maybe Next Year," a story written at Harvard, a boy walks the railroad to flee his parents' bickering. Which floods his mind: "don't compare the child to me," his father screams, "the goddamn child is splitting us up the middle." The boy himself divides: "The railroad tracks made a funny kind of mirror. I could see myself in them, one of me on each side..." In later work, Mailer's heroes are amnesiac, orphaned, or uncertain of their past. Molestation, buggery and incest are common. *Harlot's* protagonist, Harry Hubbard, a half-Jewish writer and CIA agent, is sexually-abused by an assistant chaplain at the elite prep-school he attends. "What a bend it put into the shape of my psyche," Hubbard exclaims. He beds Kittredge, his third cousin and wife of his godfather, Hugh Montague. Eventually he marries her, she preferring the sensitivity of Hubbard to Montague's coarse priapism. Nicole and Gary in *Executioner's Song*, Menhettet in *Ancient Evenings*, Monroe in *Marilyn*, Deborah in *An American Dream*, Denise in "The Time of Her Time"... the victims either rise above or stay locked in equivalents to "the one personality [Mailer] found insupportable," he wrote in 1968: "the nice Jewish boy" with "the softness of a man early accustomed to mother love."

He admits to having been over-mothered: "You're talking about Jewish mothers!" he roars. "'*Oh, oh, watch out, you'll get hurt!*' I mean, once I was boxing in Vermont (I was forty-eight) with Buzz Farbar, who was a good street fighter. We were banging away at each other and my mother, who was watching, was just horrified. Buzz was very funny about it afterwards, he said, 'There he is breaking his thumb on my head, and his mother is saying, 'Don't hurt Norman!'"

There's little doubt Mailer's mother invested more in him than in his father, who by the tough standard of immigrant-Jewish wives, was a failure. "We used to go to ball games occasionally," Mailer says of Barney. "He had a lot on his mind all the time, because things weren't going well. And he was a man who *wanted* to be very successful and wasn't." He halts. "But I don't like to talk about my parents—I want to write about them some day." Harry Hubbard writes of *his* father: "I came near to hating him, because he was disappointed in me and I didn't hear from him enough. My mother was a different matter."

Lucid says, "Norman began to win, in certain odd ways, very early." Mailer harrumphs. "People have this idea I was *dominated* by my mother, but it's just not true. It's a matter of who loves whom. When you have a mother who adores her children, and lives for them, then she can't be a match for them. My sister and I got more from her than we gave back. Which means that we dominated her."

Nevertheless that "species of derangement" with Adele was directed at a woman, feminists would remind. And the bloodletting focused him. "A decade's anger made me do it," he said. "After that I felt better." He'd written in 1957's "White Negro" that the hipster/psychopath "murders—if he has the courage—in order to purge his violence, for if he cannot empty his hatred he cannot love," and would write in 1991's "How the Wimp Won the War," that "The country needs a purge, a fling, some sacrifice of the blood of others, some colossal event, a triumph."

Asked whether he'd gone a little nuts by the time of Adele's stabbing, Barbara states: "I'd rather not say. But my *mother* used to say that in one point in her life, she was very very upset. Her parents were dying, and she realized my father was a gambler; she went to her doctor and told him, 'I think I'm going to have a nervous breakdown.' He said, 'Fanny, there's nothing I can do for you. You're going to have to pull yourself together.' My mother said, 'And so, I pulled myself together.' In a certain sense, Norman just pulled himself together."

It wasn't easy; among other things, he was deeply narcissistic. "Narcissism is a mixture of having a considerable fear of the world, with a powerful desire to dominate," he says. "That's how I came to these notions, or let's say my dear Kittredge came to these notions, of Alpha and Omega. What narcissists always feel is this detachment from others and an enormous absorption in their self. This whole idea that narcissists *love* themselves is absolutely ridiculous. There's nothing more onerous and shameful and humiliating than to be unduly preoccupied with oneself. It's the worst way to learn the world. But it's the only way you've got. And you can put it to use, and I did. But I'm very happy to have gotten out of it."

How did he cure his narcissism? "Boxing." He chuckles. "No, you get out of it by encountering the real world. You know, I hardly think about myself anymore...in that sense, I don't feel near to myself as I speak. I feel like I'm talking about someone else."

The sixties and seventies became *his* era, with forays into "existential filmmaking," political commentary, criticism of the women's movement, brilliant social analyses (in the third person) of every national event, and the novels *An American Dream*—in which the hero murders his wife, then buggers her "Nazi" maid—and *Why Are We in Vietnam*, where he, like Sam Peckinpah, mined his proclivity for violence with stunning honesty. He was unapologetically self-promoting. "The way to save yourself and reach more readers is to advertise yourself," he bragged. He became America's Writer, the literary champ, molding opinion and prickling sensibilities, much as Hemingway had prickled his.

"What I admire about Mailer," novelist Thomas McGuane says, "is that he's made these startlingly reckless changes in direction. He's reached into his skull and taken handfuls of color, and flung them on every goddamned thing around." Robert Stone feels "Mailer produced far and away the best example of the New Journalism in *The Executioner's Song*. It's one of the great books since the War." Joan Didion calls it, "an absolutely astonishing book." Larry McMurtry concurs, adding "There were two books that stuck in my mind as a young writer, remarkable for their freshness: one is *On the Road* and the other is *Advertisements for Myself*." Camille Paglia says of *The Prisoner of Sex*, "Mailer's picture of the sexes is totally similar to mine. We're very pugnacious, we like to punch people...he *created* that style, that public discourse that is totally realistic and very knowledgeable about the way war and politics actually work. All of contemporary culture is being refracted through his consciousness, which is a very complex consciousness." Gay Talese notes, "He's a fascinating, many-personed Mailer, a great man. Everything he does is big."

The eighties saw the death of his mother (Barney died in 1972), election to the American Academy of Arts and Letters, and publication of *Ancient Evenings*, his longest book before *Harlot*. It's part of a trilogy he admits now will never be completed. Though set in eleventh-and-twelfth-century BC Egypt, Barbara says *Evenings* is "his most autobiographical novel—he's *all* those characters." It maps the growth of protagonist Menhettet (of Manhattan?) through four lives and three incarnations. Barbara feels Mailer's "had other lives...I don't completely believe in reincarnation, but if I did, it would partly be because of Norman." Norris agrees. "I always tell him he was Beethoven in another life. He looks a little like Beethoven, he's a little deaf like Beethoven, and he has absolutely no musical talent. I say, 'You used that up in your life as Beethoven.'"

If *Harlot* is an evisceration of WASP culture, where Hugh Montague is prepared to "die for Christ" in the Agency's war against Communism, *Evenings* explores the pre-Christian mindset, where compassion is absent, magic reigns, and the "seven spirits of the self" survive death. "I was enormously preoccupied with death," Mailer reflects, "and the Egyptian notion that when you died your true adventures began. I've believed for a long time that a lot of people's irrational behavior could be understood only as that they wished to die before their souls died within them. They move not toward suicide, but toward self-destructiveness; practically destroying one's life came out of this inner instinct that if one stays alive too long, one would be dead within."

Executioner, written between bouts with *Evenings*,

works similar themes. Both works prefigure a synthesis of good and troublesome selves. "To the degree Alpha and Omega can live with one another," Mailer says, "then extraordinary things can happen...because they accomplish so much more."

Dr. Putnam writes: "A number of older MPD patients reach some form of reconciliation among their alter personalities," yet these multiploids "often had turbulent adult histories filled with personal suffering and anguish." Asked whether Mailer might qualify as multiploid, Putnam says: "I wouldn't touch that with a ten-foot pole."

"THIS IS A GOOD PARTY!" Mailer scans the Rainbow Room and Grill, crammed with 2,500 American Bookseller Association conventioneers, plus assorted authors. It's a petting zoo for salesfolk, with three orchestras tinkling against the sunset, platters of shrimp, salmon, and filet mignon circulating to lubricate purchase orders, and champagne at every table. *Harlot* is Random House's major fall book. It's author looks huge. Double-breasted in the twilight, he chats with Norris, Jean Stein, Jason Epstein, and other literati. A fan approaches: "I'm the world's least-known writer," he says. Mailer offers the young man his hand. "You couldn't be doing that bad if you're at Random House's party!" The fellow mentions his *Christopher Columbus, Half-a-Millenium Funny Book*, as one steers Norris toward the dance floor.

What of Alpha and Omega? "That's something I just take for granted," she says, "that we all have two complete personalities. I certainly do. There's the good old girl from Arkansas—still the little old hometown girl—and there's the New York woman. Norman might have a couple of Alphas and Omegas; he has a lot of different personalities. There's the dad, the guy who hangs out with the kids, there's the writer..."Does she see him change? "Sure. It's always very exciting when he's speaking in front of audiences—then at home we just hang out, watch old *Twilight Zone* tapes and talk."

His best friend, Richard Stratton, is a muscular forty-six-year-old novelist who says of Mailer: "There's this tremendously intelligent and artistic writer who's embattled with a man who's an outlaw. The switch happens fairly fast, and there's a certain point where you just know you're either in for the night, or you're going to go home and hide your head. You can't reason with him at that point. It's not a question of, 'Look Norman, don't start a fight with the biggest guy at the party,' because if that guy insults him, that's who he's going to start the fight with. He's an amazing character to be with when that side takes over." Another friend says, "Norman was always a terribly sweet man, very affectionate, anticipating your feelings. Then at the same moment he'd go berserk and start tearing the house apart. But he's becoming more or less one *nice* person, rather than one nice and one awful one."

Mailer stops en route to the buffet. What of this Beast?

"I don't have to struggle against that anymore," he says. "The self-destructive side is much less active now." He bristles. "But I never *saw* it as self-destructive. That was the inquiring side, the side that was looking for new experience. Usually I fucked up. So people said, 'Oh, he's so self-destructive!' I never felt that way. My feeling would be, 'No, no, they don't understand what I'm getting at in this. I'm prepared—not always, but very often—to pay the price.' If people wanted to laugh at me, or they thought I was bizarre, if they thought I was unbalanced, alright, that was the price I was paying."

How about with Adele?

Mailer's voice thickens. "That was a large price. Too big a price for too many people, including Adele and myself." Was that a conscious act, to stab her for experience? "No, no, no. That was self-destructive. And destructive to a lot of other people. It didn't do my girls any good, didn't do Adele any good."

Traces of the Beast were glimpsed, during the 1980s, in his defense of Jack Abbott (who murdered on parole) that, "Culture is worth a little risk." Then in his support of Stratton and Bernard Farbar at their 1984 drug trial. "Rick just got out of prison," Mailer says, "for trying to smuggle seven tons of hash out of Lebanon." He frowns. "But Buzz committed suicide last year."

Buzz Farbar was Mailer's great chum of the sixties, running his film company, acting in the films, generating book projects and boxing in their Saturday-morning clash, The Raging Jews. Farbar and Stratton were convicted for conspiracy to import and distribute hashish. They were sentenced to six and ten years, respectively. Then denied parole.

"There was a tremendous amount of pressure on me to implicate Norman," Stratton says. "They had this theory that he was involved, which was bullshit. They said, 'We'll let you go if you give us Mailer, Hunter Thompson, and a few of these other famous people we know are involved in drugs.' I told them that was nonsense, and I refused to cooperate with them in any way."

Mailer and Stratton owned a farm (from which marijuana was seized) in Maine, and Mailer had paid Farbar money, "probably related to gambling," Stratton guesses. "Buzz was working for a bookie, and for me as a money courier to Europe and Lebanon." The DEA had Stratton under surveillance; when he returned to New York from Lebanon, the first or second person he'd call would be Mailer. "They thought I was reporting to him. Then Buzz threw a party and introduced Norman as 'the Godfather,' to some Arabs with whom I was in the drug business."

Farbar was arrested, and wore a wire against Mailer "to prove Norman's innocence"—a transgression Mailer forgave. "Norman knew what I was doing," Stratton admits, so Farbar's ploy was risky. Mailer failed to incriminate himself. He testified as a character witness at Farbar's and Stratton's trial, and threw a coming-out party at Farbar's release. A group of nine writers, including William Styron, Peter Matthiessen, George Plimpton and Gay Talese had written to *The New York Review of Books* in support of Farbar's parole, saying, he "will continue to suffer because of the government's continued hope that somehow, through the enormous pressure being brought to bear on him, they will be able to 'get' Mailer." Asked whether he thinks Mailer was involved in the smuggling, Stephen Abrams, the Assistant United States Attorney who prosecuted the case, says, "My opinion's not relevant. We didn't indict Mr. Mailer." But, he adds, Farbar told a conspirator, who was secretly wired, that "Mailer had lost his investment in the shipment."

Stratton speculates that "Norman's been a target of the government for a long time. In the late sixties, his New York apartment was broken into and personal property in his bedroom was rifled. Nothing was taken, but there was a small amount of marijuana in a baggie—maybe half an ounce, a personal stash—that they left right in the middle of his bed as sort of a message. And he was constantly being hassled at customs. I think they saw him as a real threat. They'd have loved to discredit him by saying, 'The guy's a hop-head and involved with criminals.'"

These friends were drawn to Mailer by their love of existentialism—and to crime by their addiction to "adventure," Farbar said, or "the adrenaline high" of a Rimbaud-type artist's life "on the edge," Stratton says. "There was that mutual respect and admiration of men who saw in each other what they themselves possessed. Norman's books were the major influence on my young life."

Mailer visited his pals in lockup, appeared on TV in support of Farbar's parole, and wrote Stratton forty-odd pages of single-spaced letters. He critiqued Stratton's fiction (his novel, *Smack Goddess*, was published in 1990), sent him books, and "was incredibly supportive," assuring Stratton he would "yet prove to others" he had "the true makings of a hero," wondering if "this long, slow endless imprisonment that has been put upon you is some cosmic avatar where you're being hardened for a mission...the mark of a great country would be to recognize that its prison population consists not only of victims and monsters but heroes who crashed."

He seemed to be writing of Bob Porter in *The Martian Invasion*. Or his own caged selves.

A sixties-style combo shouts "Proud Mary." Mailer stands in the far corner, sparring verbally with a reporter. "I don't think I've had pot in three years," he says. "I'd smoke it if there were good pot around. But I wouldn't smoke it if I were working. It would disrupt the next week's work."

Is work all that matters?

"Kazan once said, 'Work is a blessing.' I loved him at the moment he said it, because I realized I had something I could tack over the desk." Mailer stiffens. "As you get older, you begin to realize that you're not going to get it all done, and that becomes a passion, to get as much of it as you can somehow take care of. When I was younger I used to think, 'If I'm not a great writer, the world's going to falter.'" He shrugs. "It may come apart, but even if I'd been twice the writer I am, I don't know that it would have made a difference. I hope not. 'Cause if it would have made a difference, then I've got a great deal on my conscience."

The band's packing up; guests are queued before the Rainbow Room's elevators. A last question: Will Mailer direct another film?

"If one comes walking in the door that I want to do. Nothing gives me more pleasure and excitement. What I'd *like* to do are larger movies with bigger budgets. I'd like to see how much I could do with a movie now, rather than see how little I could shoot it for."

What about *Wild 90*, his first film (shot for almost nothing) in which he and Buzz Farbar played Mafiosi? Mailer beams. "That's the one that needs subtitles." He cackles. "You can't hear a word in it. You have speeches where…" He cocks his head. "I play somebody called the Prince. He's particularly inarticulate, so at a given moment he'll say"—Mailer's face contorts, he shudders, sprays saliva—"'WE-ULLL TELL DA FUZZ, AND WE'RE GONNA UNNNHHH'"—he lunges, rolls his eyes, trembles—"'UNHHH UH-UNNNNH??? UNNNHHH!'"

Then all is calm. "You could have fun with subtitles," Mailer says distractedly. He sips his drink. "You could say, 'The Prince is somewhat displeased.'"

Vanity Fair, 1991

Acknowledgments

Thanks to Ken McCullough, William C. Woods, Terry Winch, Sandy Rock, and Scott Wright for their friendship and proofreading skills; to S. Jack Odell for a philosophical overview; to Dick Victory and Jack Limpert then at *Washingtonian*; to Tina Brown then at *Vanity Fair* and *The New Yorker*; to Terry McDonell then at *Rolling Stone*, and Jann Wenner at *Rolling Stone*; to Adam Moss then at *Esquire*; to Peter Biskind, Tom Wiener, and Susan Campbell then at *American Film*; to Michael Stephens then at *Flatiron*; to John Rasmus then at *Outside*, to Richard Goldstein then at *The Village Voice*, and to editors of the *Washington Post* where other of these pieces were published. Thanks to my agent, Ellen Levine, at Trident Media, and to Allen Jones of Bangtail Press for his editorial guidance and publishing savvy. Thanks to Belinda Winslow for urging me to collect these pieces. Thanks especially to Lynette Zwerneman, whose friendship and encouragement were invaluable, and whose strength is a beacon.